The Embattled Self

The Embattled Self

French Soldiers' Testimony
of the Great War

LEONARD V. SMITH

Cornell University Press

Ithaca and London

First published 2007 by Cornell University Press
First printing, Cornell Paperbacks, 2014

Library of Congress Cataloging-in-Publication Data

Smith, Leonard V., 1957–
   The embattled self : French soldiers' testimony of the Great War / Leonard V. Smith.
      p. cm.
   Includes bibliographical references and index.
   ISBN-13: 978-0-8014-4523-1 (cloth : alk. paper)
   ISBN-13: 978-0-8014-7956-4 (paper : alk. paper)
   1. World War, 1914–1918—Personal narratives, French. 2. World War, 1914–
1918—Literature and the war. I. Title.
   D640.A2S55 2007
   940.4092'244—dc22   2006102978

Cloth printing   10 9 8 7 6 5 4 3 2 1
Paperback printing   10 9 8 7 6 5 4 3 2 1

To Ann Sherif

Contents

Preface

Unexpected things can influence an academic career for a protracted period of time. In a lecture course during graduate school, I heard mention of a book published in 1929 entitled *Témoins,* by an obscure professor of French at Williams College named Jean Norton Cru, himself a French veteran of the war of 1914–18. In a study of some three hundred testimonies of the Great War published in French, Norton Cru had showed in considerable detail how literary staples taken as "true," such as mountains of corpses and rivers of blood, were physically impossible, even if every soldier on the battlefield had been killed. Intrigued, I took the book out of the library and read it more closely. I came across a remarkable quote, stating that if all French soldiers had obeyed orders to the letter, the entire French army would have been massacred by August 1915. While today this strikes me as somewhat obvious, Norton Cru's observation had a profound influence on my dissertation and my first book.

But that was not the end of my encounter with Norton Cru, who subsequently was rediscovered and became a figure of some historiographical controversy in France. As I became interested in published testimony as a research topic, I read more and more deeply into his lengthy book. *Témoins* and its shorter version *Du Témoignage* (1930) are monuments to the notion that "experience" in the trenches of the Great War is empirically knowable. Norton Cru believed it could be determined with certainty in most any situation what did and did not happen in the trenches. But the more testimonies I read, the more convinced I became that this in fact was not the case—certainly not now, and probably not then. Therein lay the problem that bedeviled this project for many years. Given the impossibility of

Norton Cru's task, how could I think analytically about experience as represented in the written word? Given that the culture wars burned brightly over much of the gestation period of this project, how could I avoid being tarred with the brush of relativism by arguing that one war story was as good as another and that there was no truth of experience to tell?

This project became a book about how experience becomes understood as such through narrative. I argue that any combatant's testimony is testimony to *something,* but that something is often not an empirically verifiable reality. Rather, these texts are about a struggle for coherence. They seek to create a narrative of experience and a narrator capable of telling the story and conveying its meaning to the public sphere through the written and published word. But while I renounced Norton Cru's task, his influence is still present on every page of this book. Theorists have often maintained that much of the reading of a text is done before the reader picks it up. In other words, readers absorb new texts largely in terms of already existing ways of understanding. I have tried not to read soldiers' testimonies the way Norton Cru did. But in many cases, the texts he praised most highly are still by far the most sophisticated and revealing, even (and perhaps most especially) if read differently.

I have made no effort to have the last word on French soldiers' testimonies of the Great War, let alone on testimony more generally. Scholars familiar with the subject are likely to find inclusions and exclusions of which they will disapprove. I have tried to provide ways of thinking about these texts as a body of documentary evidence. I will be delighted if I can simply contribute to debates on questions of testimony, and can encourage research that will modify the conclusions here.

This is not a long book, but it took a long time to write. In bringing it to completion, I incurred many debts that I am happy to acknowledge. Work on this project began thanks to a Mellon Fellowship at the National Humanities Center, a National Endowment for the Humanities Fellowship for College Teachers, and a Research Status Appointment and Andrew Delaney Fellowship from Oberlin College. Thanks to a Rockefeller Foundation Fellowship from the Institute on Violence, Culture, and Survival at the Virginia Foundation for the Humanities, this book began to assume its present form. A visiting appointment at the Université de Paris VII-Jussieu, UFR-Sciences de Textes et de Documents, and two visiting appointments at the École des Hautes Études en Sciences Sociales in Paris, helped further direct my thinking. Other grants included a John N. Stern Fellowship at the Newberry Library and a Powers Grant from Oberlin College. I am deeply grateful for all of this support. It has also been my great privilege to have been invited to present sections of this project in many different venues—

Yale University, Fort Hays State University, the University of Michigan, Trinity College (Dublin), the New York Area French Studies Seminar, Case Western Reserve University, the International Society for First World War Studies at the University of Oxford, the University of California at Berkeley, the Stanford Humanities Center French Culture Workshop, the Université de Caen, the University of Florida, the Université de Paris X-Nanterre, and the Wisconsin French History Group. I benefited enormously from all the input I received.

No less important has been the support of colleagues and friends. I am most grateful for the community I have been privileged to find at the Historial de la Grande Guerre in Péronne, France. Stéphane Audoin-Rouzeau, Annette Becker, and Christophe Prochasson have exemplified the best in a new generation of historians in France not only comfortable in reading English but keenly interested in the work of foreign scholars. John Horne has employed his boundless generosity and superb critical mind toward keeping this project on track. At the National Humanities Center, Luise White and Chris Baswell taught me that intellectual rigor and silliness could be two sides of the same coin. At Cornell University Press, John Ackerman has guided me through the latter stages of this project with a truly remarkable level of concern and professionalism. John LeRoy and Ange Romeo-Hall did a marvelous job copyediting the manuscript. Clayton Koppes, Nicholas Offenstadt, Dan Sherman, Carine Trevisan, and Jay Winter have all contributed to the completion of this work in a variety of ways.

But the greatest thing that happened to me over the course of writing this book was the chance to form a family with Ann Sherif and Ian Wilson. More profoundly than I can express, they have broadened my horizons and made me see what really matters in life. Ann is my joy, and I am proud to dedicate this book to her.

L. V. S.

Cleveland Heights, Ohio
August 2006

The Embattled Self

Introduction

EXPERIENCE, NARRATIVE, AND NARRATOR
IN THE GREAT WAR

This book turns a historical truism into a historical problem: we can understand the Great War of 1914–18 only as a tragedy and the soldier who fought it only as a victim. Historians have always been taught to uncover the problems they investigate by turning to the original sources. Here, these comprise a vast and poorly understood body of historical documentation—French soldiers' published testimonies of the Great War. The increasing importance of visual media notwithstanding, published testimony remained the most important means through which experience in the trenches entered the public sphere. Testimony took many forms, such as diaries, letters, reflections written during the war or thereafter, short stories, and novels. They do not tell a single story of experience, nor should we expect them to. The truism of tragedy and victimization in the Great War certainly enables us to interpret testimony clearly, but at the cost of closing off our understanding of the creativity with which soldiers grappled with their predicament. This truism has its own history, which is in part the subject here.

No one more thoroughly disrupts a conventional understanding of experience in the trenches of the Great War than Blaise Cendrars, today perhaps best known as an avant-garde poet. A rising star on the Parisian literary scene before 1914, the Swiss-born Cendrars joined the French Foreign Legion at the outbreak of the war. His military career proved short. Cendrars lost an arm in the allied offensive in the Champagne in September 1915 and spent the rest of the war in Paris, where his literary career resumed. It is easy to date his writings before and after 1915, because after his amputation he had to learn to write with his left hand.[1] If Cendrars kept

---

1. Jay Bochner, *Blaise Cendrars: Discovery and Re-creation* (Toronto: University of Toronto Press, 1978), 58.

too close to his radical artistic roots ever to become a tremendous commercial success, his prestige remained considerable until his death in 1961. He counted among his friends and acquaintances Guillaume Apollinaire, Fernand Léger, Igor Stravinsky, Abel Gance, Al Capone, and many others.[2] Cendrars never had prominent public political attachments—Right or Left, militarist or pacifist. He wrote of horrible things, but usually in a detached and sometimes humorous language well suited to today's aesthetic sensibilities. He wrote for the rest of his life about his experience at the front, and how that experience made him who he was physically, emotionally, and artistically. His work regularly transgressed genres and, above all, lines of demarcation between fiction and nonfiction. Readers of Tim O'Brien or Kurt Vonnegut might find themselves on familiar ground.

Cendrars slipped in and out of seemingly self-contradictory roles of perpetrator, victim, and witness. He became a perpetrator in one of his early postwar publications, *J'ai tué* (I Have Killed), one of the very few descriptions of killing an enemy soldier in hand-to-hand combat.[3] *J'ai tué* is a short book (twenty-one small printed pages), clearly influenced by evolving practices of cinematography. As if holding a camera, Cendrars moved from the wide-angle shot of national mobilization to the close-up of himself cutting the throat of a German soldier. He described the thousand trains that carried men and material to the front, and the clean, efficient ambiance of the supreme headquarters. The only thing disrupting the cool and vaguely forbidding calm of the scene was the obscene, misogynist song of the soldiers marching by:

> Catherine has the feet of a pig
> Ankles badly turned
> Crooked knees
> A mouldy crack
> Putrid breasts[4]

Cendrars's literary camera then shifted to the battlefield by recording the bombardment that killed in obscurity, the unearthly light given off by phosphorescent flares, the horrible wait in the trenches. Once the men received the order to go "over the top," the assault proceeded mechanically: "You go forward raising the left shoulder, shoulder blade bent toward your face, the whole body deboned, to try to make a shield out of yourself. Your

2. See the informative, if adoring, biography by Miriam Cendrars, *Blaise Cendrars* (Paris: Éditions Ballard, 1993).

3. *J'ai tué* (Paris: Éditions Georges Crès, 1919).

4. Ibid., 7. Unless otherwise noted, all translations are my own.

temples were on fire, and you felt anguish throughout your body. You were completely tensed up. But you march forward all the same, well aligned, and with calm."[5]

The attack continued, while some men died with cries on their lips straight from official propaganda: "Long live France!" or "This is for my wife!" Generally, the witness reported, the quiet ones led, followed by some hysterics, who managed somehow to encourage the others. As the French organized the conquered trench, Cendrars reflected on the debris that came from all over the world to create this brutal and chaotic scene—minerals from Chile, jam from Australia, shovels from America, workers from China, even chocolate from Batavia: "We turned inside out the entrails of the world, and the morals. We exploited virgin regions and we imposed an unavoidable destiny on inoffensive beings."[6] Beyond the immediate pandemonium of the battle, production of the means to make more war continued everywhere.

Without even beginning a new paragraph, Cendrars abruptly transformed himself into a perpetrator. He faced a German, both of them armed only with knives and their fists. Somehow, the partners in combat had managed to survive the instruments of anonymous, blind, industrial warfare—mines, artillery, gas, rifle and machine-gun fire. He seemed positively to luxuriate at last in facing a flesh-and-blood enemy, so like himself:

> I am going to face this man. My mirror image. An ape. Eye for an eye, tooth for a tooth. Now, it is up to us. A punch, a stab with a knife. Without mercy. I leap upon my opponent. I deliver him a terrible blow. His head is nearly cut off. I killed the Boche. I was more aggressive and quicker than he. More direct. I struck first. I had the sense of reality, me, the poet. I acted. I killed. Like the one who wanted to live.[7]

Typically in Cendrars's writing, it is impossible to tell whether the incident in *J'ai tué* actually happened. Also typically, empirical reality appears not to have been Cendrars's central preoccupation. The "truth" lay in the identity of the character created by the story.

Readers of Cendrars need to pay close attention to every word, in his prose as in his poetry. The amputee nowhere sought to evoke pity—certainly not for himself, and not much for the enemy he killed. He told an ironic story. The great productive capacities of the world came together to effect destruction and mass killing. Yet his own act of killing took place be-

5. Ibid., 13–14.
6. Ibid., 18–19.
7. Ibid., 20–21.

tween completely commensurable individuals in a brief but passionate encounter, with a knife not much more sophisticated than those of prehistory.
Nowhere did he seem to reject the social or cultural forces that brought him
face-to-face with the enemy, or with the prospect of his own death. Combat, particularly personal combat, had an autonomous, material logic. Indeed, he seemed relieved to have been freed, at least for the lethal moment,
from the anonymous, industrial war that killed by the thousands men who
never saw each other. Yet violence remained curiously detached from morality. It had its own rules.

Later, Cendrars wrote more as a witness to and victim of violence. But
he seemed never to resent the war that had mutilated him and nearly destroyed his adopted country. Like many well-known writers of the Great
War, Cendrars traveled the world after 1918 and wrote extensively of his
journeys. At the outbreak of World War II, he rejoined the French army, in
which he served as a translator for the British army. After the defeat of
1940, he retired to his home in the Unoccupied Zone in Aix-en-Provence,
where he wrote nothing at all between June 1940 and August 1943. Thereafter, however, he began to write prolifically and published four autobiographical books in as many years, some of his best-known prose.[8] All of
these books treated Cendrars's experience in the Great War, *La Main
coupée* (The Severed Hand) exclusively. His need to narrate his experience
in the Great War, it seemed, had become inextricable from his own restored
creativity as a writer. In a letter to a friend with which he began *L'Homme
foudroyé* (The Astonished Man), he wrote: "Because to write is to burn
alive, but also to be reborn from the ashes."[9] Narration in this later period
did not just recount violence but became a violent and creative enterprise
in itself.

In *L'Homme foudroyé* Cendrars told a story in which individual identity
seemed annihilated through the destruction of the physical body. One chapter near the beginning of the book comprised mostly a description of a quiet
sector and of a certain Sergeant Van Lees. The sergeant had somehow kept
a listening post far in advance of the French front lines supplied with a remarkable amount of wine. In part simply to alleviate the boredom of the
sector and in part to perform Legionnaire bravado, Van Lees organized any
number of drunken debauches in his small corner of No Man's Land. But
in the text, Cendrars abruptly shifted chronology and place to describe the

8. *L'Homme foudroyé* (1945), *La Main coupée* (1946), *Bourlinguer* (1948), and *Le Lotissement du ciel* (1949).
9. *L'Homme foudroyé*, in *Oeuvres complètes de Blaise Cendrars,* 6 vols. (Paris: Denöel,
1960–61), 5:49.

death of Van Lees. To Cendrars, it was "the most appalling death it has been my lot to witness on a battlefield."

> as we were moving up to the assault, he was blown up by a shell and I saw, with my own eyes, I saw, this handsome legionary sucked up into the air, violated, crumpled, blasted in mid-air by an invisible ghoul in a yellow cloud, and his blood-stained trousers fall to the ground *empty* while the frightful scream of pain emitted by the murdered man rang out louder than the explosion of the shell itself, and I heard it ringing still for a long moment after the volatized body had ceased to exist.
>
> Apart from the empty trousers, I recovered nothing else of Van Lees; there was therefore no corpse to bury.
>
> Let this little ex-voto from the astonished man serve as his funeral oration![10]

Cendrars had clearly departed from the gritty realism, or at least the literal plausibility, of *J'ai tué*. As stated, the account of the death seems physically improbable. Why would the pants of the deceased survive if the explosion vaporized his body? How could a human scream possibly be heard longer than the explosion of so powerful a shell? Given that Van Lees presumably had been killed instantly, how could he have screamed at all? And even if he had, how could Cendrars have heard him over the explosion? But here, the representation of an empirically verifiable event seems not to have been Cendrars's point. What mattered instead was the capriciousness of violence, which could annihilate any physical trace of anyone at the front, at any time. There remained no trace of Van Lees's body to bury, and thus no physical locus of death. Only human utterances survived, the fleeting scream and the written words of Cendrars himself. Violence intruded into the chapter as abruptly as it took away the life of Van Lees. The author renounced further explanation. His little ex-voto would have to do.

Violence also abruptly intruded into a chapter of *Le Lotissement du ciel* (The Parceling of Heaven), a book principally about one of Cendrars's trips to Brazil. Something suddenly made him recall his amputation, an experience recounted in one of the most complex and troubling passages in all of his work. Here he wrote as victim. At one level, he wrote of a phenomenon common among amputees, of feeling precise sensations and pains where the missing limb used to be. But he wrote in fantastic, dreamlike language that spoke to the many ways the violence of the war had permanently marked his being. Cendrars recalled his recovery in a hospital outside Paris, where

10. *The Astonished Man*, trans. Nina Rootes (London: Peter Owen, 1970), 18–19.

I was being cared for in 1916 and was taken by so many nightmarish sensations after my amputation. The soul wandered, as though it wanted to follow, situate, identify, localize the survival of a severed hand that made itself painfully felt, not at the end of the stump, nor in the radial axis nor in the center of consciousness, but as a soul that will have, somewhere beyond the body, a hand, hands that multiply and develop and open like a fan, the vertebral column of the fingers more or less effaced, the ultrasensitive nerves that end up imprinting on the soul the image of the dancing Siva, who was turning under a circular saw, so as to amputate in succession all of his arms, that one is Siva himself, the man made divine. It is appalling. Hence the smile.[11]

As with his description of the death of Van Lees, Cendrars meditated on the relationship among spirit, matter, and identity. Here Cendrars's metaphysical being, separated not just from the amputated arm but from his entire physical body, looked for the missing hand that was at once everywhere and nowhere. This identity lurked for a certain time in a nether region between life and death. The ubiquitous hands ended up imprinting on him the famous image of the Hindu god Siva, who dances in a ring of fire. Conventionally, the five arms of Siva represent seemingly contradictory aspects of being—creation, evolution, destruction, incarnation, illusion, salvation, and many others.[12] Here, the ring of fire became a scythe enacting again and again the amputation. Yet the repetition of the violence that mutilated Cendrars proved creative as well as destructive. Indeed, through reenacting the amputation, the wandering, wounded spirit *became* the god. Powerful, destructive, creative, and inscrutable, violence reproduced the familiar, enigmatic, and harrowing smile of Siva.

Where is the real Cendrars here, and which story conveys his real experience? Certainly, these stories provide no shortage of identities. He is a hypermasculine warrior, an oddly bemused witness to an atrocious death, and a quasi mystic, who stands in awe of the violence that mutilated him yet drove his creativity. All of these stories have violence at their center—violence that shapes identity, and no doubt the reverse. They all resist closure and seem to raise more questions about experience in the trenches than they answer. *J'ai tué* simply stops with the death of the German enemy. There is no conclusion apart from the brutal, straightforward moral of "kill or be killed," with which the author seems content. The death of Van Lees concludes more ambiguously than it might seem. If the meaning of the story lies beyond empirical reality, what is it? The author leaves the reader with

---

11. *Le Lotissement du ciel,* in *Oeuvres complètes,* 6:386.

12. See Ananda K. Coomaraswamy, "The Dance of Shiva," in *The Dance of Shiva: Fourteen Indian Essays* (New York: Noonday, 1957), 66.

a cry, a bloody pair of pants, and a notice that simply telling the story is sufficient to constitute a funeral oration. In the story of the hallucination, identity itself inhabits a liminal region between the living and dead parts of the body. The inscription of Siva blesses and curses the author. Above all, it shows that the terrifying and ambiguous effects of his amputation are permanent.

Conventional wisdom would have us shoehorn these various stories into a single, overall narrative structure, and Cendrars into a single identity. Accordingly, the stories must add up to tragedy, in which Cendrars must, one way or another, play the role of tragic victim. The essential experience of the Great War is known in advance, because we understand the true nature of that conflict so clearly. Yet Cendrars's stories themselves, in their riddles and their contradictions, suggest that conventional wisdom is not enough to understand his experience. In his relative celebrity and his undisguised presentation of his writing as "literature," Cendrars is to some degree an unusual figure in this book. But his stories are complex and rich enough to encapsulate most of the issues examined here. Like countless other more obscure and less "literary" accounts, his stories ask whether the nature of experience in the trenches should be taken as a given at all. Therein hangs the central problem investigated in this book—not what was the essential nature of experience of the Great War, but how did experience become experience? I argue that it did so through narrative, and that authors created and were created by the testimonial text.

Identity, Narrative, and the Metanarrative of Tragedy

Whatever else they may have done, the "culture wars" of the late 1980s and 1990s reminded historians of the ways that narratives serve to structure as well as to describe the reality of the past. At the same time, historical narratives contain within them overt or covert statements about the selfhood of the individuals whose lives they recount. In this sense, historical narrative tells us something about what makes individuals function, and how individuals in turn shape history. As Jerrold Siegel's massive study indicates, few issues have so preoccupied Western intellectuals as the question of what constitutes individual identity.[13] My focus here is much more narrow, in that I consider only testimonial literature, and only a specific historical period. My analysis is based on a premise not in itself especially new, or by now especially controversial. Simply put, narratives and narrators

13. Jerrold Siegel, *The Idea of the Self: Thought and Experience in Western Europe since the Seventeenth Century* (Cambridge: Cambridge University Press, 2005).

create each other. Firsthand testimonies share a common goal of constructing "the embattled self," an identity as well as a text. At the heart of that identity lay the experience of the war of the trenches.

The problem of identity and experience in the Great War has long been considered solved, its solution even self-evident. A particular narrative tradition from Great War literature proved to have resonance far beyond the world of letters. The war of 1914–18 became construed as a tragedy, and the hero in it, the soldier of the trenches, a tragic victim. A figure of great virtue (sincerity, honesty, and above all bravery) but also of great flaws (notably a youthful innocence bordering on gullibility), he is swept away by forces of fate well beyond his control. The victim is annihilated whether or not he survives in body. This destruction is foreordained, in this case through his elders who hold the reins of power. Should he survive, the shattered veteran can simply testify to his victimization, for the possible benefit of civilian society and above all posterity. In a sense, a literary turn in the study of the Great War took place back in the 1930s, with a general acceptance as "true" of a model drawn from Great War literature. From this model of the war as tragedy, and the soldier as victim, emerged a metanarrative, an overarching explanation that transcended academic disciplines.[14] Historians, literary critics, sociologists, psychologists, political scientists, and economists could all agree on the basic narrative structure of the Great War and its meaning. Indeed, to many it ceased to be recognizable as a narrative explanation at all. The Great War as tragedy became self-evident.

Historians operating within a metanarrative of tragedy found themselves spared a knotty methodological problem—the need to distinguish between fictional and nonfictional sources representing experience in the trenches. For example, the specific events portrayed in a novel might not be literally true or even plausible as written. Jean Norton Cru proved many years ago the physical impossibility of "mountains of corpses" and "rivers of blood."[15] But within a metanarrative of tragedy, testimonies in all genres produced their own truth that transcended empirical evidence—of the soldier as victim. Historians could thus feel comfortable with, or even ignore, the confused boundary between fiction and nonfiction in soldiers' testimonies. No one restated the metanarrative of the Great War as tragedy more convincingly, or showed the symbiotic relationship between the literature and the history of the Great War, than Paul Fussell, whose *The Great*

14. I explain this argument further in "Narrative and Identity at the Front: Theory and the Poor Bloody Infantry," in *The Great War and the Twentieth Century*, ed. Jay Winter, Geoffrey Parker, and Mary Habeck (Yale University Press, 2000), 132–65.

15. Jean Norton Cru, *Témoins: essai d'analyse et de critique des souvenirs de combattants édités en français de 1915 à 1928* (1929; repr., Nancy: Presses Universitaires de Nancy, 1993).

War and Modern Memory (1975) remains the foundational work on the subject.[16]

The metanarrative of tragedy gave the soldier of the trenches two seemingly contradictory but actually complementary identities: the simple victim and the brute. Both could be considered victims in that both experienced the annihilation of the rational, morally accountable identity produced by modernity in the nineteenth century. One had his volition itself more or less removed by experience in the trenches. The other had his will perverted, so that he came to desire and identify with the violence that shaped him. Both forecast a dire future for the civilization that produced them. The violence of the Great War served as the instrument of fate, the destroyer of individuals and societies.

The simple victim found his archetype in Paul Baümer, the protagonist in what even today remains the most widely read testimony of the Great War, Erich Marie Remarque's *All Quiet on the Western Front* (1928). Seduced by his teacher into joining the army at nineteen years of age, Paul saw his very soul destroyed by the violence of the war. His comrades all died horrendous deaths one by one, each death conveyed in gruesome detail. Indeed, by 1928 readers were expected to take it as a given that the more ghastly the details, the more true the testimony. Experience at the front destroyed Paul morally long before it destroyed him physically. Remarque writes of his actual death as an afterthought, on a day in October 1918 described in official dispatches as "all quiet on the Western Front."

Paul Baümer's brutish counterpart was Ernst Jünger, the stormtrooper who came to love violence through internalizing the twisted ethos of the war itself. As Jünger wrote in *War as an Inner Experience* (1922), "The war, father of all things, is also our father. It has hammered, cast and tempered us into what we are."[17] Fighting as described by Jünger became a highly sexualized encounter with physicality and domination. In *Fire and Blood* (1925) he wrote:

> But now we will rip away this veil instead of gingerly lifting its corner. We approach as conquerors, armed with all the means of power. We will force open the closed door and enter by force into the forbidden land. And for us who have, for so long, been forced to accumulate in desolate fields of shell holes, the idea of this thrust into the depths holds a compelling fascination.[18]

16. I explore the long-term influence of this book in "Paul Fussell's *The Great War and Modern Memory*: Twenty-five Years Later," *History and Theory* 40 (2001): 241–60.

17. Quoted in Eric Leed, *No Man's Land: Combat and Identity in World War I* (Cambridge: Cambridge University Press, 1979), 153.

18. Quoted ibid., 158–59.

This binary of victim and brute connected the microcosm and the macro-cosm of tragic experience in the Great War. It also connected the two great European wars of the twentieth century. The victims of 1914–18 emerged from the war too debilitated to resist the fascist evil that produced the even more horrible war that began in 1939. Paradoxically, the duo of victim and brute seemed to close down rather than invite further investigation by historians. For given the self-evidently traumatic history of Europe in the first half of the twentieth century, who could doubt that this agony originated in the violence of the trenches? There seemed little left to say. Average readers could simply consume *All Quiet on the Western Front*. The exceptionally curious could add as much Jünger as they could tolerate, preferably followed by a few pages of Adolph Hitler's *Mein Kampf*. Both simple victim and brute are stable, indeed static identities, and both certainly make sense as far as they go. But like any identity produced through narration, they achieve stability through inclusion and exclusion. What they leave out is precisely what is of interest here.

The metanarrative of the Great War as tragedy even provided common ground in the culture wars between two broad categories of scholars referred to by Joyce Appleby, Margaret Jacobs, and Lynn Hunt as "modernists" and "postmodernists."[19] "Modernist" narratives, they contended, assert progress toward some positive teleology of history, and a rational, morally responsible individual underpinning that teleology. "Postmodernist" narratives, on the other hand, reject progress and even teleologies, in favor of indeterminate games of power that depend on an individual constructed through the tensions and hierarchies of discourse. For modernists, the Great War became the great calamity that tragically stole the promise of nineteenth-century positivism, at least until 1945. The victimization of the individual soldier became the microcosm of European civilization itself, as war gave way to embittered peace, depression, fascism, renewed war, and Holocaust. Postmodernists could read the Great War as that time when the grim power games of Western civilization simply revealed themselves for what they were. Categories such as "nation," "honor," and "duty" quite literally deconstructed in the carnage of the Western Front. A metanarrative of tragedy made for strange epistemological bedfellows.

My first book began to question this metanarrative and drew from practices of French social history. In this book I told the story of one French army infantry division from 1914 to 1918, and I argued that a struggle over authority relations took place within the French army over the course of

19. Joyce Appleby, Margaret Jacobs, and Lynn Hunt, *Telling the Truth about History* (New York: W. W. Norton, 1994).

the entire war.[20] This implicit struggle became explicit with the French army mutinies of 1917. Borrowing the idea of proportionality from Just War theory, I concluded that soldiers would cease to behave violently when they considered that doing so was disproportionate to the sacrifices expected of them. In other words, they ceased to fight aggressively when they saw no point in it. They imposed an outcome in the field that the command structure was obliged to accept as adequate. Violence in the trenches was governed, in short, by a cost-benefit analysis. My analysis relied—in the opinion of some, excessively—on a rational self that was able to calculate and act on his calculations.

Beneath the narrative structure of *Between Mutiny and Obedience* lay a preoccupation with the struggles of ordinary soldiers to impose some form of empowering order on the chaos around them. As I interpreted them, soldiers had opposed, not unsuccessfully, the forces of authority that underpinned a metanarrative of tragedy. This characteristic of the book plainly irritated its first reviewer, John Keegan.[21] I later suggested that the book could be thought of as a response to the call of Carolyn Bynum, Lynn Hunt, and others for history in the "comic mode," meaning history that demonstrates an awareness of the contrivances of narrative itself.[22] While today I stand by the main conclusions of *Between Mutiny and Obedience* as far as they go, the present book is about what lay beyond rational calculus in understanding experience in the trenches. Even while completing my first book, I became intrigued by a related question. If my thesis was correct, how did we come to understand the experience and the identity of the soldier of the Great War so differently?

Because of its studied confession that historical narrative by definition is at some level contrived, history in the "comic mode" does not rely on any one version of identity, or on any fixed identity at all. Rather, stories are as diverse and changeable as the individuals who tell them. A given individual, such as Blaise Cendrars, can also tell any number of seemingly contradictory stories. At the very least, the writings by Cendrars point to the limits of a metanarrative of tragedy, and to the possibilities of rethinking experience in the trenches itself based on the writings of individual soldiers.

20. *Between Mutiny and Obedience: The Case of the French Fifth Infantry Division during World War I* (Princeton: Princeton University Press, 1994).

21. "An Army downs tools, mutiny in the First World War: theory and the poor bloody infantry," *Times Literary Supplement,* 13 May 1994.

22. See Smith, "Narrative and Identity," 145–61. See also Carolyn Walker Bynum, "In Praise of Fragments: History in the Comic Mode," in *Fragmentation and Redemption: Essays on Gender and the Human Body in Medieval Religion* (New York: Zone Books, 1991), 11–26; and Lynn Hunt, "Introduction: History, Culture, and Text," in *The New Cultural History,* ed. Lynn Hunt (Berkeley: University of California Press, 1989), 1–22.

Certainly, Cendrars fits uneasily into the binary of hero and victim. But neither is his imagination adequately captured in terms of a cost-benefit analysis of the utility of his consent to the war. The experience of violence helped make Cendrars a shifting figure of victim, perpetrator, and witness. The violence he lived was certainly never "overcome," in the sense of being comfortably resolved. But neither do terms familiar to discussions of combatants of the Great War, such as "brutalization" or "trauma," seem sufficient to interpret the meanings of his stories or the identities that emerge from them. Any narrative form both includes and excludes. What is excluded if we consider the Great War as a tragedy and the soldier as a victim? What do the war and the soldier look like if we put whatever is excluded back in?

Témoignage, or Emplotting the Witness

At a theoretical level, the question of experience has been a fraught one in scholarly circles for some time. Long gone are the days when "experience" was simply "what happened," which people explained in stories that scholars either accepted or rejected according to objective standards of truth or falsehood. Particularly at the hands of post–World War II French intellectuals, as Martin Jay put it, "*l'expérience vécu*' [lived experience] was stigmatized as an ideologically suspect, discursively constructed, and woefully outmoded concept."[23] In her now-classic investigation of the question, Joan Scott concluded: "it is not individuals who have experience, but subjects who are constituted through experience."[24] Perhaps the most heated disputes have revolved around whether or not "experience" has any independent standing apart from the identity it creates. Jay himself has waxed artistic on the matter, turning to song as a metaphor in a survey of debates about experience that focused on why such debates have been so deeply felt.[25] Dominick LaCapra, observing an "experiential turn" in historical writing, became interested in connecting theories of experience to psychoanalysis and particularly to trauma.[26] Yet these inquiries have paid more attention to the epistemological status of experience than the means through which it came to be construed as such.

23. Martin Jay, "Roland Barthes and the Tricks of Experience," *Yale Journal of Criticism* 14 (2001): 469.

24. Joan W. Scott, "The Evidence of Experience," *Critical Inquiry* 17 (Summer 1991): 779.

25. Martin Jay, *Songs of Experience: Modern American and European Variations on a Universal Theme* (Berkeley: University of California Press, 2005).

26. Dominick LaCapra, *History in Transit: Experience, Identity, Critical Theory* (Ithaca: Cornell University Press, 2004), 3.

In this book, I reflect on how experience became structured through narrative practices. "Experience" then entered the public sphere through the published word. Such an approach, I argue, makes it possible to think differently about experience in the trenches. This is not, as I thought for a long time, a book about memory of the Great War. Rather, it is a book about the sources of memory, and how they became so. As John Horne has reminded us, experience and memory are not easily disentangled.[27] "Experience" is never a matter exclusively of recording a "now." Intrinsically, experience looks both forward and back. "Having had an experience" can only occur in anticipation of a future in which the past experience will have some kind of significance. In terms of simple cognition, experience can achieve some sort of coherence only through recollection. But Janet Watson's rather severe distinction between "experience" as something construed during the war and "memory" as something construed afterward seems more analytically convenient than accurate.[28] Narration produced identities (and the reverse) through essentially the same means before the armistice and after. This book explores means of transition between "what happened" on the battlefield and "experience" as rendered in published texts. These texts and their consumption then became part of a whole set of cultural practices encoded as memory.

For all the difficulties in the way he uses it, Jean Norton Cru's term *témoignage* (testimony) still seems best to describe the documentary base for this book. The author of a témoignage is a *témoin* or "witness."[29] Témoignage has both empirical and moral components. The témoin reports verifiable events, as a witness might report the facts of a car accident. But there has to be some sort of moral component, which explains why the témoignage was being recorded in the first place. The témoin did not recount the events of the Great War, even as he himself lived them, simply for the sake of doing so. So great a story had to have a moral. This tension, between the empirical and the moral, drives much of the analysis of this book. I consider published testimony across genres, from trench newspapers to collections of letters to memories and reflections to novels. As the case of Cendrars shows, it remains uncomfortably difficult to draw clear boundaries between fiction and nonfiction. Hence the importance of the term *testimony.* All of the texts considered here, independent of genre, claimed

27. John Horne, "Entre expérience et mémoire: les soldats français de la Grande Guerre," *Annales HSS* 60 (2005): 904–5.

28. Janet Watson, *Fighting Different Wars: Experience, Memory, and the First World War in Britain* (Cambridge: Cambridge University Press, 2004), 4–5.

29. I explore *témoignage* and the *témoin* as concepts in "Jean Norton Cru, lecteur des livres de guerre," *Annales du Midi,* no. 232 (2000): 517–28.

some form of truthfulness and testified to *something*. This book is about figuring out what that something is.

The study of témoignage and of the témoins who write them has generally been haunted by the question of "authenticity," or of empirical veracity. Most commonly, historians have applied what Renaud Dulong called a "juridical model" (*modèle judiciare*) approach to firsthand testimony.[30] That is to say, the historian treats the text the way a lawyer handles the deposition of a witness. Authenticity itself then constitutes the justification of the account, and the moral of the story. The establishment of objective knowledge is its own justification. This sort of approach to testimony of the Great War has been the subject of considerable interest and controversy, from the days of Norton Cru to our own.[31] It is never my intention to denigrate a juridical approach as such. By no means do historians need to read all accounts as in some equivalent sense true—the dreaded reproach of "relativism" so often leveled at history influenced by even the mildest formulations of contemporary cultural theory. But as I hope these pages will show, Norton Cru showed the limits of such an approach many decades ago.

Tim O'Brien, perhaps the greatest American veteran-writer of the Vietnam War, finally gave up the quest for juridical truth—or at least he claimed to. "In war," he contended, "you lose your sense of the definite, hence your sense of truth itself, and therefore it's safe to say that in a true war story nothing is ever absolutely true."[32] Narrative practice has its own requirements, which undermine the stated purpose of conveying truth in a juridical sense: "In any war story, but especially a true one, it's difficult to separate what happened from what seemed to happen. What seems to happen becomes its own happening and has to be told that way."[33] This book assumes that in the end, the search for juridical truth in Great War testimony breaks down—not because of deception or a lack of sincerity on the part of the witness, but because true testimony meant so many different things to different people.

According to his 1964 autobiographical book *Les Mots,* the nine-year-old Jean-Paul Sartre found himself in October 1914 in Arcachon, far from

30. Renaud Dulong, *Le témoin oculaire: les conditions sociales de l'attestation personnelle* (Paris: Éditions de l'École des Hautes Etudes en Sciences sociales, 1998).

31. I have my say in the remarkably durable debate over Norton Cru in France in "Jean Norton Cru et la subjectivité de l'objectivité," in *Histoire culturelle de la grande guerre,* ed. Jean Jacques Becker (Paris: Armand Colin, 2005), 89–100.

32. Tim O'Brien, "How to Tell a True War Story," in *The Things They Carried* (New York: Broadway Books, 1990), 82.

33. Ibid., 71. Of course, O'Brien bases his claim of non-truth on the evidence of experience.

the front in southwestern France. He became consumed with a desire to write about the war. His mother dutifully purchased a number of notebooks for him, each suitably emblazoned with a helmeted Joan of Arc on the cover:

> Under the protection of the Maid of Orléans, I began the story of the soldier Perrin. He captured the kaiser, brought him tied up to our lines, then, before the assembled regiment, provoked him into single combat, struck him down, and forced him, knife at the throat, to sign a humiliating peace, giving us Alsace and Lorraine.[34]

Yet no sooner did he complete the story than he became aware of its difficulties. The kaiser, handicapped from birth by his withered arm, and alone and surrounded by hostile French soldiers, did not make much of an opponent for the magnificent specimen who was Perrin. Moreover, young Sartre's story prognosticated a speedy and victorious peace, whereas the newspapers and grim-faced adults around him foresaw a protracted, deadly, and uncertain struggle. He looked again at his text, this time red-faced: "Was it me, *me* who conspired in these puerile fantasies?" His malaise subsided only when he buried his notebook in the sand at the beach. Literature had its secrets, which would unveil themselves to him as he grew up. "In the meantime," he concluded, "my young age required me to maintain an extreme reserve. I did not write anything more."

Though assuredly not a soldier, the young Sartre was nevertheless a kind of witness to the Great War. He needed to tell a story—ostensibly not about his own experience, but about the war itself through a fantasy of experience. He did so using narrative, the emplotment of events in time. His story made use of the tools at hand, as he admitted—children's literature of derring-do, typically against some sort of colonial enemy in Africa or the western United States. The moral of the story involved a repetition of an assumption, that of a quick and total French victory, held by many adults at the mobilization. The result, the young Sartre concluded, was a problematic narrative, ill suited to describing the actual state of the war at the time it was written.

Yet this is not where the usefulness of Sartre's story as testimony ends; rather, it is where it begins. For in his modest tale, the young Sartre had created both a narrative and a narrator, a figure with specific characteristics capable of telling the story. And inadvertently, that story proved very much of his own experience—or the lack thereof. The story itself revealed that the writer was a nine-year-old child, bright beyond his years perhaps, but

---

34. Jean Paul Sartre, *Les Mots* (1964; repr., Paris: Gallimard, 2004), 173–75.

a child nonetheless. The young Sartre understood this virtually from the moment he finished the text. This revelation embarrassed him and produced a malaise that required him literally to bury a text that in fact had revealed all too clearly who the narrator was. The historian's interest in the story lies not in the rather silly events portrayed in it, but in thinking about why Sartre (as a child and then again as an adult) wrote it down the way he did.

Soldiers who wrote about their experience in the trenches did essentially the same thing as the young Sartre in his story of Perrin and the kaiser. Soldiers emplotted both a narrative and a narrator, using the tools at hand.[35] The experience narrated, and the narrator it created, proved so extraordinary that the specific terms describing them made a special claim to truth—such as *témoignage de guerre* and *témoin de guerre*. If the text entered the public domain by publication, the witness could become a war author. Michel Foucault once described the author as "the ideological figure by which one marks the manner in which we fear the proliferation of meaning."[36] Foucault posited the author less as a person than as a social necessity. The author demarcates and is demarcated by the thinkable in a given society. In the Great War, the linchpin of authorship was firsthand experience in the war of the trenches, and the text the meeting place between that experience and the rest of society. To narrate that experience was to represent a coherent identity that has had that experience and that can properly discern its meaning.

Yet no experience seemed more volatile and fragile, or more fraught with ideological significance, than the experience of fighting the Great War. No identity seemed more problematic than that of the combatant. Anxiety as to the instability of experience infused combatants' earliest writings. The first issue of a trench newspaper called on soldiers to set down their experience as soon as possible:

> These stories that you repeat in the dugouts, at rest, in the billets, when time is dragging on, you must save them from forgetfulness. The memory of men is short, fragile like a vase. Fix it in writing. Trace from this moment the details of battles, gather together these innumerable incidents, bitter or pleasant, which constitute the great drama.[37]

35. I expand on what follows in "Le Récit du témoin: formes et pratiques d'écriture dans les témoignages de la Grande Guerre," in *Vrai et Faux dans la Grande Guerre,* ed. Christophe Prochasson and Anne Rasmussen (Paris: La Découverte, 2004), 277–301.

36. Michel Foucault, "What Is an Author?" in *The Foucault Reader,* ed. Paul Rabinow (New York: Pantheon Books, 1984), 119. This phrase appears to have been added by Foucault himself for the first English publication. It does not appear in the original French version: "Qu'est-ce qu'un auteur," *Bulletin de la Société de Philosophie* 64 (1969): 75–106.

37. *81ème Poil . . . et Plume,* May 1916.

The anxiety here is perhaps not so much that experience would actually disappear immediately into "forgetfulness," but that it would become instrumentalized by the social imagination surrounding the soldier, and later the veteran. Putting experience into writing would fix it in words, and stabilize both the experience and the identity of the author who had had it.

But just how to employ language in order to fix identity and experience? One could argue that the most "realistic" record of experience would be a protracted succession of "nows." Yet such a record would prove confusing and directionless, with no indication of just why it exists. Paul Ricoeur has argued that experience makes sense through narrative, through the emplotment of events in time. Following Martin Heidegger, he concluded that experience unfolds according to "a common conception of time conceived as a continuation of 'nows,' succeeding one another in an abstract line steered in a single direction."[38] That direction is not simply reported but actually created through temporal structures. These structures fit together as narrative through language. As Ricoeur put it: "I take temporality as the structure of existence—let us say the form of life—that reaches language through narrativity, and narrativity for the structure of language—let us say the play of language—that has for its ultimate referent temporality. The relationship is thus reciprocal."[39]

For Ricoeur, narrative figures as prominently as it does in literature and in history because time itself exists as a lived human experience largely through narrative.[40] The most common narrative structure is a plot, which situates events as they unfold. "The plot," says Ricoeur, "is that which gives the notion of an event its historical distinctness. To be historical, an event must be more than a singular occurrence. It defines itself by its contribution to the unfolding of a plot."[41]

The challenge of narrative, then, is emplotting the events of experience in a way so as to bring them under a structure of time, with a distinct relationship to past, present, and future. As Hayden White put it, "the narrative represents the aspects of time in which endings can be seen as linked to beginnings to form a continuity within a difference."[42] In forming this continuity, the person who tries to fix firsthand experience in writing "em-

38. Paul Ricoeur, "La Fonction narrative et l'expérience humaine du temps," *Archivio de filosofia* 80 (1980): 343–67.

39. Ibid., 343.

40. On this point, see Hayden White, "Ricoeur's Philosophy of History," in *The Content of the Form: Narrative Discourse and Historical Representation* (Baltimore: Johns Hopkins University Press, 1987), 169–84.

41. Ricoeur, "La Fonction narrative," 349.

42. Hayden White, "The Question of Narrative in Contemporary Historical Theory," in *Content of the Form*, 52.

plots the witness," by definition creating a figure of sufficient authority to impose some sort of order on the story.

The Great War was arguably the last war in Europe through which experience in battle entered the public sphere primarily through published testimony rather than through visual media. However defined, published testimony in France comprises a substantial body of work. Indeed, the corpus is still expanding, as unpublished testimonies continue to find their way into print. Even with the application of very strict (and perhaps capricious) criteria, Norton Cru still considered some three hundred volumes appropriate for study. Maurice Rieuneau has posited that at least a thousand published French writers took part in the Great War.[43] I have made no attempt here to study this body of work "scientifically," in the sense of obtaining a "representative" sample or of making quantitative statements that pertain to all texts. I chose specific texts simply because they seemed to have something to contribute to the issues at hand of narrative and narrative strategies. Some, particularly novels of the 1930s, are very well known in France and beyond. Others appeared only in small editions and remain obscure.

Nearly all of the texts examined here were published either during the war or in the interwar period. Generally, texts reached the public sphere through publication because they responded to or sought to create some broader cultural need—such as wartime mobilization, postwar demobilization, or the expression of interwar disgust with the conflict. But the transmission of the experience in the trenches into the public sphere has been an ongoing process, thanks particularly to the renewed interest in the Great War at the end of the twentieth century. Recent publications of previously unpublished primary texts have tended to respond to present-day cultural requirements, and have brought out aspects of identity and experience less prominent in older publications. Occasionally, I refer to recent publications as illustrative of specific points of analysis.

Karen Halttunen has observed that, for better or worse, historians remain "resolutely committed, for the most part, to the narrative form, and unconvinced that any other representational practice would prove any less problematic, fictive, and ideologically loaded."[44] In this tradition, I have set up the chapters of this book to tell a kind of story. I show how witnesses tried and largely failed to invent a definitive narrative and narrator, until the narrative became a tragedy and the narrator a victim. But narrators at-

---

43. See Maurice Rieneau, *Guerre et révolution dans le roman français: 1919–1939* (Paris: Klinksieck, 1974), chap. 1.

44. Karen Halttunen, "Cultural History and the Challenge of Narrativity," in *Beyond the Cultural Turn*, ed. Victoria E. Bonnell and Lynn Hunt (Berkeley: University of California Press, 1999), 177–78.

tempted a variety of different approaches along the way, and I hope through bringing these approaches to the forefront to show the richness and complexity of the sources. "Experience" in the Great War cannot be understood without confronting the contradictions, the passions, the doubts, and the uncertainties of témoignage as a whole. While testimony does not tell a single story, I argue that it is possible to think about it coherently and analytically.

The organization of this book corresponds to a series of tools at hand, taken up by writers to contain experience within language, and to create narrators and narratives. Chapter 1 considers attempts to understand the initiation to combat as a rite of passage. Yet rites of passage, by definition, have determined outcomes. Initiates know in advance what they will become through their initiation. Not so for the combatant, given the physical and existential perils of this new kind of war. Chapter 2 explores how narrators sought to master specific experiences of death, mutilation, and killing. But such extreme forms of experience resisted constraint within narrative and created a fascinating textual world of peculiarities, inconsistencies, and ambiguities.

The last two chapters take up questions of form and content. Chapter 3 examines consent as an ideological system rooted in internalized absolutes inherent in republican citizenship. Republican ideology bound soldiers individually and totally to one another and to the national community. Soldiers could not disengage from the war without in some sense disengaging from themselves. Consent had a particular genre: nonfictional testimony, much of which was published during the war or within a year of the armistice. Chapter 4 examines the search for closure through the novel, the genre which became the predominant form of testimony by the 1930s. This change in form took place alongside a change in content, as consent morphed first into rejection and then into trauma. The novel of the 1930s articulated and helped establish the metanarrative as tragedy, and the soldier as tragic victim. Through the novel, permanent injury became the end and the moral of the story of experience in the trenches of the Great War.

1

Rites of Passage and the Initiation to Combat

In his first major statement on the Great War, Sigmund Freud lamented how the experience of less than one year of war had overwhelmed the existing means of understanding experience itself:

> Swept as we are into the vortex of this war-time, our information one-sided, ourselves too near to focus on the mighty transformations which have already taken place or are beginning to take place, and without a glimmering of the inchoate future, we are incapable of apprehending the significance of the thronging impressions, and know not what value to attach to the judgments we form.[1]

Time had gone out of joint, or at least narrative time, which could connect in a linear form past, present, and future. Freud sought to articulate a passage from one world to another. At the heart of his anxiety lay profound uncertainty about that next world and the rules, if any, according to which it would be governed. Perhaps more appropriately than he knew, Freud did not distinguish between civilians and soldiers. But certainly the brutality of the transition from peace to war would be most pronounced among those initiated into fighting it. The chaos of warfare created precisely the situation Freud described—fragmented information, alongside immense physical and emotional peril. I have previously noted that experience "as it happens," in the sense of a succession of nows is intrinsically incompatible with narrative. The initiation to combat would seem to prove this incompatibility obvious.

---

1. Sigmund Freud, "Thoughts for the Times on War and Death" [1915], in *Civilization, War and Death,* trans. E. Colburn Mayne, ed. John Rickman (London: Hogarth, 1939), 1.

Yet because experience abhors a vacuum, the succession of nows requires the imposition of some sort of linear, narrative order. Anthropologists have long maintained that societies invoke rites to structure specific pivotal personal and collective experiences. A rite imposes a kind of performed narrative on a major transition. "We *undergo* passages," wrote Ronald L. Grimes, "but we *enact* rites."[2] René Girard observed that rites often revolve around violence. Rites both make violence comprehensible and regulate it within ceremonial boundaries.[3] They mark and act out a predictable transformation if carried out correctly, whether the rite involves violence or not. A boy becomes a man, two people become married, a person is prepared to die, a common person becomes a warrior—all through rites of passage. The initiate may not fully understand the transformation being performed during the rite. But societies around initiates do, which explains the social functions of rites.

Rites of passage are commonly thought of in terms of a three-stage narrative structure, as outlined in 1908 by Arnold van Gennep.[4] Preliminal rites separate the initiate from the societies of which they had been a part, and from their previous identities. Liminal rites are both the most important, as well as the most uncertain and unstable. In a sense, they *are* the transition between the old identity and the new, as the initiate encounters the sacred in some direct and often brutal way. Clearly, liminality provides a way to read Freud's sense of the present in 1915. But rites of passage, by definition, must have closure. Postliminal rites occur for just this reason, to certify the new identities of the initiates and to reincorporate them into the societies whence they came.

Soldiers in 1914 who survived their initiation to combat looked for a structure through which to understand it. They found a set of narratological tools for doing so through rites of passage. There was nothing especially new in 1914 about this. The term *baptême de feu* had become as common in French as the English "baptism of fire." Moreover, rites of passage offered an immediate way to explain experience in 1914 according to the most basic narrative structure of beginning, middle, and end (or situation, crisis, and resolution). This is not where the significance of adopting

2. Ronald L. Grimes, *Deeply into the Bone: Re-inventing Rites of Passage* (Berkeley: University of California Press, 2000), 5.

3. René Girard, *Violence and the Sacred,* trans. Patrick Gregory (Baltimore: Johns Hopkins University Press, 1977), chap. 11. Girard posited a transcultural need for sacrificial victims. Barbara Ehrenreich, on the other hand, explained war itself as a rite, a continuing attempt to allay primordial anxieties of human beings as prey. See Ehrenreich, *Blood Rites: Origins and History of the Passions of War* (New York: Henry Holt, 1997).

4. Arnold van Gennep, *The Rites of Passage,* trans. Monika B. Vizedom and Gabrielle L. Caffee (Chicago: University of Chicago Press, 1960, 21.

rites of passage as a guide to narration ends, however, but where it begins.

"Ritual, like art, is a child of imagination," wrote Grimes, "but the ritual imagination requires an invention, a constantly renewed structure, on the basis of which a bodily and communal enactment is possible."[5] He, like most contemporary anthropologists, is skeptical of considering the three-part division of rites of passage as timeless and transcultural.[6] But as Grimes would agree, the importance of such rites goes beyond taxonomy. I will argue that rites of passage provided a toolbox for understanding experience. Soldiers in 1914 used the rites of passage to put together experience in a seemingly endless variety of ways. What interests me is both the prevalence (stated or unstated) of rites of passage and the insufficiency of that structure. However testimonies invoked rites of passage, they failed to produce a stable narrative or narrator. Thought of as an organizing principle of narrative, a fully enacted rite of passage has to produce closure. Stories of the initiation to combat in 1914 did not do so. In his pioneering book on combat experience in the Great War, Eric Leed argued that testimony become forever "stuck" in the middle or liminal stage.[7] While I use rites of passage in a different way and come to some different conclusions, it is certainly clear that structuring experience in 1914 according to rites of passage raised more questions than it answered. Indeed, doing so set the stage for issues that would bedevil telling the story of experience in the Great War for decades to come.

Rites of Separation: The Mobilization

In the first phase of the classic rite of passage, initiates are ritually separated from the collectivity. Generally, anthropologists have conceived this separation as some form of symbolic death. The former identity is killed or eradicated, in preparation for the liminal stage creating the new one. For example, Victor Turner described in great detail circumcision rites among the Ndembu people of Africa.[8] The novices, typically eight to ten years old, are kept separate from the rest of the tribe for a certain time and allowed to eat only specific, ritually prepared foods. Through an elaborate series of ceremonies, which play out any number of power relationships within the

5. Grimes, *Deeply into the Bone*, 4.
6. Ibid., 107.
7. Eric Leed, *No Man's Land: Combat and Identity in World War I* (Cambridge: Cambridge University Press, 1980), esp. 12–33.
8. Victor Turner, *The Forest of Symbols: Aspects of Ndembu Ritual* (Ithaca: Cornell University Press, 1967), chap. 7.

village and within families, the novices are "killed" as children and prepared for rebirth as very young men. They are forever set apart, not just
from women, but from other males deemed unworthy of circumcision. The
key aspects of rites of separation here are the tearing asunder of the former
identities and the establishment of absolute commensurability among the
initiates.

It does not take a great leap of imagination to consider European military rituals of conscription and mobilization as rites of separation. It is easy
to forget in the highly demilitarized Europe of today how prominently military identity figured in the public sphere before 1914. In republican France,
citizenship and military service were much more closely linked than in
Britain or the United States. To be a soldier, as Richard Challener put it,
was to carry "both the badge and the moral consequence of citizenship."[9]
Nothing did more than conscription to make democracy in France a conspicuously male enterprise. Likewise, citizenship in France made rituals of
conscription and mobilization ipso facto rites of male passage.

Departure, whether for the barracks or the front, articulated the citizen-
soldier's relationship to the political community and his civic equality with
his fellow conscripts. With equality went commensurability, each conscript
becoming politically identical to every other. Indeed, at some level the soldier in uniform would surrender his individuality, notably his individual
agency, to the collectivity of his comrades. The armies of the Republic became a representation of the sovereign people. Each individual would thus
become subsumed into an incarnation of Jean-Jacques Rousseau's General
Will, in which the whole would be much greater than the sum of its parts.
Rites of separation thus had profound political significance. As we will see,
they provided the ideological infrastructure for wartime consent.

Down to the definitive abolition of conscription in 2001, few drafted into
the French army in peace or war ever admitted to enjoying it. But a carni-
valesque spirit often infused rituals marking the departure of young conscripts, particularly in the provinces. For decades before and after the Great
War, *le départ* was a major spectacle in hundreds of towns and villages
throughout France. Young recruits would parade noisily down the main
street, often accompanied by music and cheered on by their civilian compatriots. These pre-soldiers would wave tricolor flags and wear distinctive
hats, often decorated with tricolor ribbons. But the initiates still wore civilian clothes and marched in disorganized groups, both celebrating and
marking the end of their lives as preadult, "passive" citizens. The initiation

9. R. D. Challener, *The French Theory of the Nation in Arms, 1866–1939* (New York:
Columbia University Press, 1955), 4.

to the world of Mars also meant initiation to the world of Venus. The draft-board determination of *Bon pour le service* (fit for service) became the cliché *Bon pour les jeunes filles* (fit for young girls). A conscripts' song pop-ular around 1900 sought to channel the sorrow families felt at the depar-ture of their young men:

> It is not for us that you must weep
> Fathers and mothers of families
> It is not for us that you must weep
> It is for the love of your daughters.[10]

Of course, conscription rituals were also rehearsals for mobilization, the massive gathering of active and reserve citizen-soldiers in the event of war. The young man had to know his cues well, should he be asked to make the transition from soldier to warrior.

Thanks to the work of Jean-Jacques Becker and others, we now under-stand that Europeans in August 1914 did not embrace war in a unanimous spasm of atavistic fury.[11] Beyond media and literary circles, grave ap-prehension and cold resolution were far more prevalent than nationalist euphoria. It was this apprehension that gave written testimony of the mo-bilization an inherent incertitude. In the separation rites of August 1914, the French, like the other peoples of Europe, relied heavily on tradition. Some aspects of the general mobilization looked like the departure of con-scripts. In larger cities cavalry and dragoons, still the most socially presti-gious branches of the service, accompanied large parades in sartorial splendor. Hundreds and sometimes thousands of soldiers marched off to patriotic music, cheered by disproportionately female crowds. Infantrymen wore bright red pants similar to those worn by their fathers and grandfa-thers in 1870. Often derided by military historians for making French sol-diers such fine targets, such attire spoke to the end of an era in which soldiers had to be rendered beautiful in distinct and separate ways in order to make war.

By definition, a rite of passage is supposed to produce a predictable out-come in the transformed initiate. Of course, such certainty was not possi-

10. Quoted in Michel Bozon, *Les Conscrits* (Paris: Berger Levrault, 1981), 70. On con-scription in France before the Great War, see also Odile Roynette, *"Bons pour le service"*: *l'expérience de la caserne en France à la fin du XIXe siècle* (Paris: Belin, 2000).

11. Jean-Jacques Becker, *1914: comment les français sont entrés dans la guerre* (Paris: Presses de la fondation nationale des sciences politiques, 1977). For Germany, see Jeffrey Ver-hey, *The Spirit of 1914: Militarism, Myth and Mobilization in Germany* (Cambridge: Cam-bridge University Press, 2000).

ble in the mobilization of August 1914. There had been no general European war since the defeat of Napoleon in 1815, and no major war involving France since 1871. Few in France or elsewhere really understood the long-term implications of industrialized warfare. No rite could speak with much certainty as to what such a war would ask of the soldier who fought it. Surrounded by familiar symbols, the rites of separation at the mobilization in August 1914 marked the transition to the unknown but assuredly deadly. The one certainty was the submission of the individual to the whole. Particularly after 1918, acceptance of this submission would later become construed as the fatal moment, the prelude to victimization. Assent would lead inexorably to consent later on.

The first best-selling novel of the war documented the mobilization as rites of separation. René Benjamin's *Gaspard,* published in November 1915, was a naive and propagandistic work surpassed well before 1918. But in its unconvincing certainty, it illustrated the uncertainty of the story of the mobilization. The basic features of the mobilization in the novel, in fact, were essentially the same as those in far more thoughtful accounts. Gaspard was a brash, working-class Parisian, who made his living before August 1914 selling snails in Les Halles. No slave to middle-class morality, he proudly lived with a woman not his wife. Yet Gaspard emerged in the first few pages of the book as almost a high priest of the mobilization, who always knew just what to do and say. His modest class origins and expansive manner helped him mediate between the stereotypically strong, simple, rustic Normans and the sophisticated if somewhat soft Parisians in his regiment.

Gaspard intuitively understood that soldiers marching into the unknown must look the part. With an abrasive charm perhaps more appealing to readers at the time than today, he made a theatrical exit from the train, announcing loudly: "Oh, look at this regiment! As soon as Frenchmen become soldiers, they become slovenly."[12] He more or less personally took charge of finding missing pieces of uniform and equipment for the men. His own officers duly deferred to him as their natural-born leader. The haphazard supply situation meant that Gaspard was only partly successful. Yet, when "the regiment, half-constituted, half-equipped, half-awake, marched at the sound of the drum," the sun redoubled its energy, bathing the departing soldiers in confidence and courage. Nature itself blessed the beginning of their transformation. By the time they departed, the fact of the soldiers' commensurability transcended the specifics of their attire. A uniform is so called for a reason: "That which makes a departing regiment

12. René Benjamin, *Les Soldats de la guerre: Gaspard* (Paris: Arthème Fayard, 1915), 12.

strangely beautiful, it is first of all the uniform, this first mark of discipline which so strikes the eye."[13]

Témoignage in nonfictional genres also took note of the uniforms as the accoutrement of transition. While walking along the Marne River waiting for his unit to depart, Eugène Emmanuel Lemercier, a painter in civilian life, wrote to his mother on August 16: "I had the chance to glimpse the countryside, despite the invasion of red and blue. What's more, these brave people in red and blue gave the very best moral impression."[14] The mobilized soldiers complemented the beauty of the land they were about to defend, and vice versa. Captain Pierre de Mazenod of the 44th Artillery Regiment found soldiers with military tunics and civilian pants, or military uniforms and civilian hats. "But all took this gracefully in stride," he assured readers, "and the man so walking past, half dressed like a civilian and half like a soldier, was set for first-rate success as he walked past, by a group of regular army soldiers."[15] Experience itself would complete the homogenization of the initiates.

Uniforms marked the separation of soldiers from the civilian collectivity and their submersion in the collectivity of initiates, whatever the point of view of the témoin on the war. Léon Werth's *Clavel soldat* (1919) was an early and bitter antiwar novel. It began in August 1914 with Clavel vacationing with friends in the Pyrenees. When war seemed likely, Robert Sauvant, a reserve officer, asked his wife vaguely, "Do you remember where you put my uniform?"[16] The soldier was expected to keep his uniform after his time of active duty, as a permanent and practical reminder of the link between citizenship and military service. Lucette Sauvant, of course, remembered exactly where the uniform was. Caring for it was her separate-and-unequal civic duty, her counterpart to male military service. She preserved the uniform in mothballs, "for the same reason she celebrated Easter. In any event she believed solely in moderation, whether in mothballs or in the Church."[17] But all concerned understood what keeping the uniform and knowing its location meant.

Nothing mattered more in the rites of separation than establishing boundaries of gender between those on their way to fight and those in

13. Ibid., 27, 31.

14. Eugène Emmanuel Lemercier, *Lettres d'un soldat* (Paris: Librairie Chapelot, 1916), 4–5. See the biographical sketch in Jean Norton Cru, *Témoins: essai d'analyse et de critique des souvenirs de combattants édités en français de 1915 à 1928* (1929; repr., Nancy: Presses Universitaires de Nancy, 1993), 530–31.

15. Pierre de Mazenod, *Dans les Champs de Meuse: souvenirs d'un commandant de batterie (1914)* (Paris: Plon, 1921).

16. Léon Werth, *Clavel soldat* (1919; repr., Paris: Éditions Viviane Hamy, 1993), 7.

17. Ibid., 7–8.

whose name they ostensibly were fighting. As his artillery unit departed, Paul Lintier was especially struck by the persistence of women with children at the train station:

> The women, a crowd of women with children in their arms or hanging on to their skirts, waited there under the bright sun. They kept standing for hours on end, watching the parade of military cars, decorated in greenery, and covered with simple crayon drawings.[18]

Women wore their own uniforms. As Benjamin observed, "The women had their light-colored blouses, their new shoes, their hats decorated with flowers."[19] To Lintier, the idyllic radiance of the flowers rivaled the radiance of the women themselves: "Their faces, lit up by the sun, by the emotion of the hour, their brilliant eyes, their hair full of light finished in the center with flowers"[20] At one point, the women actually barred the route to cavalrymen accompanying the artillery, so as to give them time to decorate their departing heroes.

Jean Galtier-Boissière, observing the demarcation of gender boundaries within families, felt a bit of regret that he could experience the performance of the appropriate roles only vicariously. He had already been on active duty when the war broke out, and thus "the war appeared like a scheduled exercise, after the training marches, the maneuvers, and the camp in Châlons."[21] His regiment was departing from the Paris area, where his parents lived. But he told them not to come to the train station, "fearing it would be too emotional for them," though "now, in the middle of all the kisses and hugs, and all the adieux, I felt alone and a bit of an orphan."[22] As he observed the scene, all played their parts. Mothers wept, fathers "fought against emotion, spoke about 1870, slipped one more coin in the hand of their boys." The initiates themselves completed the scene: "Dissimulating their emotions, the soldiers joked around with the boastful air of young people who are getting away."[23]

Of course, what made the mobilization of August 1914 different from conscription rituals was an actual war against an actual enemy. The Germans here represented the unknown. Perhaps to portray absolute confi-

---

18. Paul Lintier, *Avec une batterie de 75, Ma Pièce: souvenirs d'un cannonnier, 1914* (Paris: Plon-Nourrie, 1916), 18.

19. Benjamin, *Gaspard*, 34.

20. Lintier, *Ma Pièce*, 19.

21. Jean Galtier-Boissière, *En rase campagne, 1914: un hiver à Souchez, 1915–1916* (Paris: Berger-Levrault, 1917), 5.

22. Ibid., 7.

23. Ibid.

dence in the efficacy of the rite of passage that few actually felt at the time, testimony across genres acknowledged the German, scorned him, and dismissed him. To the now-uniformed Gaspard, the Germans were a malevolent if somewhat ill-defined nuisance. The French, now miraculously united, would dispatch an enemy not really worthy of them.

> Ah, the Alboches, they want war? Very well, we'll make them see war up close! And what's more, we will do so well heeled, well turned out, well armed! So lets go, fill up these train wagons! Ah, the pigs!![24]

The prospect of death, like the enemy, was acknowledged and summarily dismissed. A diligent sergeant-major asked each soldier for his family address in case of death. Without a trace of irony or doubt, Gaspard responded:

> Oh that, that's disgusting. No, that's not good manners . . . It's fine with me to get myself killed, I just don't want anybody to talk to me about it . . . If I don't come back, I'll stick it to them by giving false information, 'cause that . . . Ah, that, I think it's gross![25]

More sophisticated versions of the story of the mobilization tended to refrain from mentioning the possibility of death at all. But they conceptualized the war in equally straightforward terms. The Germans, in the end, would have to answer for the rites of passage the Frenchmen would have to undergo as warriors for a just cause. Jules Émile Henches was a career artillery officer in his early forties when the war broke out.[26] He prefigured the notion that the real war was against war itself in a letter to his wife on August 2, 1914 (the day after the declaration of the general mobilization): "I curse war. I can find only in my horror sufficient hatred to do my best." But for the moment, the enemy was the invader: "I think that Germany must be humiliated. The easiest means to do so is by force of arms."[27] Even the venomous Léon Werth had André Clavel imagine the Germans in a similar way at the time of the mobilization. His former comrades on the Left across the Rhine had betrayed him by surrendering to war, although he had done no differently himself: "There was no doubt that the German gov-

24. Benjamin, *Gaspard*, 17. "Alboche" was the precursor to the more commonly used "Boche."

25. Ibid., 26. Suspension points in quotations from the French are reproduced in this book as three spaced periods: " . . . "; my own omissions are indicated by brackets around ellipses: "[. . .]."

26. See the biographical sketch in Norton Cru, *Témoins*, 519–20.

27. Jules Émile Henches, *À l'école de guerre: lettres d'un artilleur* (Paris: Hachette, 1918), 2.

ernment had wanted war, and that the German Socialists had gone along with it. Clavel was going to do battle against the German government and the German Socialists . . . He was going to defend France, land of the Revolution, France who was going to impose peace on the world."[28] Later, Clavel would bitterly regret this crucial, initial act of assent.

The culmination of the mobilization of August 1914 as a rite of separation comprised two elements: the actual physical departure, typically by train, and the performed submersion of the individuated identity of the soldier into the collectivity. Together, these two components ratified each individual's acceptance of his duty as man, citizen, and soldier. For the time being, he existed primarily through the collectivity, the vanguard of the nation in arms. Read in this sense, the departure in Benjamin's propagandistic novel testified to the mobilization as a powerful cultural construct.

> Are they carried away? Are they gathering momentum? They don't know, they don't belong to themselves anymore. They no longer think "I," they have become "us," and the heart swells, as their energy seizes them. Those who have not served, who have not marched through a city, pack strapped on, don't know one of the strongest sensations a man can have, to be nothing but a tiny cog in a social machine, very dependent. But it is a servitude that gives pride, because it celebrates in each one a value to the nation. A man under arms, marching step by step, finds in himself a force and a mission. It is no longer about his personal value, he has become a symbol; his uniform is in the colors of his country, and he feels what a great thing it is that a regiment is departing.[29]

Nonfictional *témoins* wrote about this submersion of the individual self in very similar terms. The individual merged with his unit and, through the collectivity of soldiers, with the nation itself. Pierre de Mazenod described his artillery unit at the moment of departure as a microcosm of the nation: "It was born of the activity of everybody, it would continue to perfect itself in action, to instruct itself under fire. But already, it was a force to reckon with. It departed full of faith in victory, passionate, proud of contributing to the grand task ahead, resolved to strike with all its might."[30] Christian Mallet, a cavalryman who eventually would volunteer to join the infantry, wrote that "the most humble faces became transfigured, and I understood at that moment, for the first time, the grandeur of France."[31] The singing of the national anthem confirmed that in some sense they had be-

28. Werth, *Clavel soldat*, 28.
29. Benjamin, *Gaspard*, 32.
30. De Mazenod, *Dans les Champs de Meuse*, 20.
31. Christian Mallet, *Étapes et combats: souvenirs d'un cavalier devenu fantassin, 1914–1915* (Paris: Plon, 1916), 10.

come France, and France had become them. Light infantryman Henri Libermann wrote of soldiers and civilians alike weeping as they simultaneously united and separated: "The 'Marseillaise' arose with trembling, bursting out their chests, in the same cry of hope [. . .]. It was not only the song of some brave isolated soldiers, it was the call of the invaded country calling on her children to defend her menaced frontiers."[32] Galtier-Boissière described a similar scene. The collectivity could not guarantee that any given initiate would survive the passage to war. But the immortal community of France, embodied in the collectivity of its citizen-soldiers, would live on victorious:

> Unworried about tomorrow, proud of the confidence of the civilians, delighted at the idea of seeing the country and of winning battles, ready to make any sacrifice for France. Without anybody ordering it, we started singing as loudly as we could the only song that could accompany this triumphal march:
>
> > Allons, enfants de la Patrie,
> > Le jour de gloire est arrivé![33]

The disillusioned Werth understood all too well by 1919 the importance of the effacement of individual identity at the climax of the mobilization. The war and the invaded nation had created their own ways of thinking about the self and the collectivity that even the most committed internationalist could not long withstand in the heady days of August 1914. For Werth, this was precisely what made the war a tragedy. From the moment soldiers accepted mobilization, they submitted to a destiny of victimization that they would not understand until it was too late. As Clavel's train left the station, "his companions were calm and resolved. They had been attacked . . . They would defend themselves. No one doubted this. The idea of aggression, right, wrong, in any event indeterminable, was born like the legend of Garros shooting down a zeppelin. You might say that war spontaneously creates the ideas it requires."[34]

Rites of Liminality: The Sacra of the Battlefield

Kande Salifou Kamara was a Susu noble born in what was then the French colony of Guinea. Against his parents' wishes, he volunteered for

---

32. Henri Libermann, *Ce qu'a vu un officier de chasseurs à pied* (Paris: Plon, 1916), 4; ellipses added.

33. Galtier-Boissière, *En rase campagne*, 11.

34. Werth, *Clavel soldat*, 28–29. Werth alluded to the legend (not true, in the event) that the famed French aviator Roland Garros had shot down a German zeppelin at the beginning of the war.

the French colonial army and served on the Western Front in the Great War. Interviewed as an old man in 1976, Kamara seemed a bit vague on dates or even the specific unit to which he had belonged. But he remembered very clearly the moral of the story of his initiation to combat:

> To be a soldier in those days was like being circumcised. [When you went into the] secret bushes, there were many things you never knew about before that they would tell you; and after you left the circumcision bush you'd be aware of a lot of things [that you never understood before]. And that's the same parallel as warfare, as being a soldier.[35]

Kamara told of his experience in terms of what anthropologists would call liminality, the central phase of the rites of passage. In the liminal stage, the initiate undergoes the actual transformation. The knowledge obtained in this stage is not incremental but transformative. The initiate becomes a fundamentally different person. As Victor Turner put it, liminality alters "the inmost nature of the neophyte, impressing him, as a seal impresses wax, with the characteristics of his new state. It is not a mere acquisition of knowledge, but a change in being."[36] In the liminal phase itself, the initiate is "betwixt and between," neither the old identity nor the new.

Liminal rites impart knowledge typically through physical objects known as *sacra*—such as knives, relics, masks, or effigies. In ritual use these objects inscribe the knowledge that turns princes into kings, girls into women, boys into men. The *sacra* often inflict pain, in the case of circumcision the physical inscription of manhood on the penis. Inscriptions of femininity in some cultures can prove even more invasive, and can involve infibulation.[37] Through such practices, people achieve adulthood by absorbing the knowledge conveyed by instruments of pain. Adults are people who have experienced pain, and whose lives after the ritual testify to the meaning of that pain.

In the metropolitan French army, only Jewish soldiers would typically have been circumcised. But many testimonies recounted the actual exposure to fire for the first time as though it were a confrontation with the

35. Quoted in Joe Harris Lunn, "Kande Kamara Speaks: An Oral History of the West African Experience in France, 1914–1918," in *Africa and the First World War*, ed. Melvin E. Page (London: Macmillan, 1987), 39–40. Additions in brackets by Lunn.

36. Victor Turner, "Betwixt and Between: The Liminal Period in Rites of Passage," in *Forest of Symbols*, 103.

37. See, for example, Corrine A. Katz, *Affecting Performance: Meaning, Movement, and Experience in Okiek Woman's Initiation* (Washington: Smithsonian Institution Press, 1994); and T. O. Beidelman, *The Cool Knife: Imagery of Gender, Sexuality, and Moral Education in Karuru Initiation Ritual* (Washington: Smithsonian Institution Press, 1997). I am indebted to Luise White for encouraging me to think of the centrality of pain in rites of passage.

sacra. In peacetime the connection between war and pain could be conveniently pushed to the sidelines. The rituals of mobilization carefully avoided the physical perils to follow. But once exposed to battle, soldiers instantly and dramatically confronted a seemingly endless barrage of shells and bullets destroying human flesh. Going into battle meant facing death, the outer boundary of experience for living people, and the point beyond which earthly experience could not go. Like Kamara, soldiers from metropolitan France represented their initiation to combat as a liminal experience, as part of a narrative structure of rites of passage. But how to find the words to explain and structure liminality?

Combat represents an extreme case of the impossibility of incompatibility between recording experience in what we might call "real time" and narration. But as close an approximation as is likely to survive of a "real time" account came from Marc Bloch, later a famous medieval historian and World War II Resistance martyr. A sergeant in the 272e Régiment d'Infanterie in 1914, Bloch kept a diary from the first to the last days of the war.[38] The beginning of the diary recorded a succession of nows. With equal emphasis and equal lack of explanation, Bloch noted data as diverse as the assassination of Socialist leader Jean Jaurès (August 1), the contents of his own pockets (August 2), and a description of a corporal as a "neurasthenic man of the world, not much of a warrior" (August 23).

Internal evidence suggests that his account of his initiation to battle was written between the night of September 9 and the early morning of September 11, 1914, before his unit was relieved. The longest entry in the entire diary is cited here in its entirety. It recounted the events of September 9–10:

> [September] 9 at 10 o'clock at night. we had hardly lain down when the alert sounded; long night march; we passed the Marne and we made long detours; pelting rain with cold; we arrived at the farm of Grand Perthes toward 5 o'clock in the morning; we got into position (formation against artillery) under rain that stopped after about an hour; and toward 6 o'clock march forward; it is a terrible day we advance ridge to ridge, by clumps of woods first, under a rain of percussion and time-fuse shells, and of shrapnel (50 machine guns!) we did not fire and with so little efficiency up to the last ditch toward 5 o'clock; losses; the leader and Sergeant Levasseur killed, the colonel, the major of the 5th battalion, Captain De Connyack and the one with 17 wounded, Captain Wirth killed; the next day we will count 89 wounded, killed or missing in the company; noise, artillery, the signal rocket; case shot like a swarm of wasps—episodes I leave and find again the section, Corpo-

38. Marc Bloch, "Le Carnet de guerre 1914," in *Écrits de guerre, 1914–1918,* ed. Étienne Bloch (Paris: Armand Colin, 1997), 41–68.

ral Scalbre; I am lightly wounded and in dressing the wound Oriol caught a bullet in the leg, the section panics and the horses hauling the machine guns; the trench with Samuel and the adjutant; the colonel and the last rush, lost! no contrary a bit less bad; the next morning I will find a hole like a point in my canteen, a tear on my greatcoat on the right at the shoulder, a bullet hole in my greatcoat between the two legs; nighttime, the German machine guns (finally!) are reduced to silence by our own we turn around in the forward direction last slope of the night; the wounded, the smell, sleeping on the ground, sardines; relieved toward morning, visit of the field ambulances![39]

As a very general rendering of events, what happened in Bloch's account seems clear enough despite the lack of complete sentences. The passage moved from the general to the specific, and returned to the general at the end. His unit advanced under heavy and deadly fire. What exactly happened in the middle of the account is less clear. There was some sort of panic in his section, though Bloch does not indicate that it had serious military consequences. His regiment suffered many casualties, several of whom Bloch knew well enough to name. The entry ended in some sort of "present" time. Bloch noted his discovery of his near miss with death, various sensory perceptions of the battlefield, and their departure from the battlefield. Clearly, this was an exceptional collection of nows.

But what Bloch's account of liminality clearly is *not* is a narrative. The text lacks the combination of details into a story in which, as Hayden White put it, "endings can be linked to beginnings to form a continuity within a difference."[40] Experience stands somewhat incoherently on its own here, as no sense is conveyed of why the story is being told. The story certainly has no moral, in the sense of basic conclusions drawn from its outcome. Yet it is hard to imagine how Bloch could have provided a more "accurate" description of his initiation to combat as a lived experience. Bloch lived this day from each "now" to the next in the liminal space between life and death, quite literally surrounded by the *sacra* of modern warfare. He had no way of knowing minute to minute if he would be a victim of violence, a perpetrator, or a witness. In the liminal state proper, he could only record the dangers and casualties. This was an initiation with no hint of outcome. Experience written in this way seldom enters the public sphere through publication. Indeed, it is likely that Bloch's diary would never have been published had he not later become famous for other reasons, precisely because it is not recognizable as narrative. Bloch's diary is also unusual in that

39. Ibid., 43. Punctuation preserved from the original.

40. Hayden White, "The Question of Narrative in Contemporary Historical Theory," in *The Content of the Form: Narrative Discourse and Historical Representation* (Baltimore: Johns Hopkins University Press, 1987), 52.

he later wrote a second, more narrative version of the same episode that I will examine in the next section.

If we think of rites of passage as a narrative form, the liminal phase is the dramatic high point of the story, as the phase where the actual transformation of the initiate takes place. There is a reason why Bloch's entry for September 9–10 is the longest in the entire diary.[41] But rites of liminality operate very differently from rites of separation in the formation of the initiate's frame of reference. The hallmark or rites of separation is the establishment of unity and commensurability among members of the collectivity. I have argued that their individuality itself is to some extent temporarily effaced. Liminality, on the other hand, happens to individuals. Just as individuals are circumcised one by one, soldiers on the battlefield are killed, mutilated, or spared individually, often arbitrarily. Experience, in short, fragments in the liminal stage.

Heroic conceptions of what war ought to be about did not necessarily vanish as témoins approached the battlefield, or even arrived at it. Wild, optimistic rumors circulated long after there was good reason to believe otherwise. Jacques Brunel de Pérard, a young soldier in the artillery, reported in his journal entry for September 2 that "word is going around that the Russians, 50 kilometers from Berlin, have just given Germany an ultimatum, giving it four days to submit."[42] In fact, the tsar's forces had already suffered the grave defeats at Tannenberg and Masurian Lakes. No one could accuse Galtier-Boissière of an unreflective love of militarism. But he wrote the day before he entered combat: "We feel that we must soon deserve all the bravos and all the kisses that were lavished upon us, on credit, all the way from Paris to the border."[43] He did not really even fully comprehend that combat involved danger until the next day. It took a foretaste of battle, when a cavalryman on patrol riding near him was killed: "We knew that in any battle some men were going to get killed. But we were in such a joyful and unworried state that, in the face of this sudden unhappiness, we became suddenly subdued, like when a tragic and unforeseen accident comes to sadden an enjoyable party."[44]

Some carried conspicuously male elation into fire itself. Lieutenant Mar-

41. For additional explanation of Bloch's war writings, see my essay "Le Récit du témoin: formes et pratiques d'écriture dans les témoignages sur la Grande Guerre," in *Vrai et faux dans la Grande Guerre*, ed. Christophe Prochasson and Anne Rasmussen (Paris: La Découverte, 2004), esp. 287–88, 296–300.

42. Jacques Brunel de Pérard, *Carnet de route (4 août–25 septembre 1914)* (Paris: Georges Crès, 1915), 67–68.

43. Galtier-Boissière, *En rase campagne*, 33.

44. Ibid., 41.

cel Dupont was a career officer in the cavalry. By September 4, a good two
weeks after the disastrous beginning of the fighting along the frontiers and
two days before the French counteroffensive along the Marne River, he had
good reason to know the limitations of cavalry in modern warfare. Yet he
wrote with less than subtle word choice of the impending French attack:
"The charge! This is the indescribable thing that is the cavalier's reason
for being, the sublime act that penetrates, that rips open, that crushes in a
furious dash, at a frantic gallop, saber erect, the mouth howling, eyes
mad! . . . Let us then finally be able to join battle with them [the German
cavalry] and measure the length of our sabers to that of their lances!"[45]
Even Pierre Drieu la Rochelle, the consummate failed initiate, as we will
see, got carried away at first in the fighting at Charleroi in Belgium:

> I felt at that moment the unity of life. The same gesture—to eat and to love,
> to act and to think, to live and to die. Life, it was a single stream.[46]

Military sociologists have long known that on the battlefield most combatants quickly lose much sense, not just of the overall strategic situation,
but also of most anything that happens beyond the small group of men they
can actually hear and see.[47] The witness, thus, understands much less about
the battle in a conventional sense than those not present. Perhaps the most
famous formulation of the problem came from Stendhal's novel *La Char-
treuse de Parme* (1839). The young hero Fabrice del Dongo finds himself
on the battlefield of Waterloo in 1815. He is totally baffled as to just what
he is witnessing, and only after the fact does he have even the vaguest idea
that he had been present at one of the turning points of European history.
As Jean Norton Cru described the paradox attributed to Stendhal, the individual soldier on the battlefield "is the only one not to know, not to understand the battle. The commanders, on the contrary, the civilians, all
those who are neither actors nor witnesses, see the event with lucidity."[48]
Conventional military history has sought to finesse this problem by focus-
ing on the macro picture of how a given battle was won or lost and why.
The outcome of the battle provides its narrative structure. Here, however,
the paradox attributed to Stendhal *is* the story. The confrontation with the

45. Marcel Dupont, *En campagne (1914–1915): impressions d'un officier de légère* (Paris: Plon, 1916), 67–68.
46. Pierre Drieu la Rochelle, "La Comédie de Charleroi," in *La Comédie de Charleroi* (Paris: Gallimard, 1934), 59
47. For a survey of these findings, see Richard Holmes, *Acts of War: The Behavior of Men in Battle* (New York: The Free Press, 1986), 136–75.
48. Norton Cru, *Témoins*, 16.

sacra in the liminal stage of the rite of passage shatters the uniformity so carefully nurtured in military training and the mobilization. The focus of the witness shifts dramatically to the level of the individual.

Intoxicated by their own enthusiasm, Drieu and the group of men around him advanced on the enemy position, at first without opposition. "Surprised to be standing, to be men, they start running, timidly yet rashly."[49] Then the Germans opened fire: "What a thrashing of bullets. It is so easy to tear apart a centimeter of flesh with a ton of steel."[50] The initiates fell into a ditch, which ended their fighting ingloriously, but which probably saved their lives. The men had no sense of what had happened elsewhere. Galtier-Boissière's unit suddenly came under artillery fire: "The explosions, the bullets sailing through the air, a big case from a spent shell came buzzing by and planted itself next to my knee. Instinctively, as though to parry a blow, I went to protect my face with my arm."[51] His lieutenant responded according to regulations and ordered the men to form a kind of shell with their haversacks in front of them. This dubious move, in fact, made them rather a more concentrated target for enemy fire. In desperation, the lieutenant ordered them to advance by section to a wall some fifty meters away, toward a farm where they could take cover. "Pell-mell," Galtier-Boissière wrote, "the men climb over the obstacle, tumbling one over the other, the small ones pleading for help. As soon as they get there, the men curl up next to the wall, pale, panting, their eyes bugging out of their sockets."[52]

The radically narrowed vision of the battlefield, and the resulting disintegration of the broader military picture, led to the dramatic reassertion of individual identity. The message of comfort at the mobilization, that the collectivity would survive whatever happened to a given individual, became meaningless, at least for the moment. Soldiers on the battlefield remained commensurate in that any individual was about as likely to suffer harm as any other. Indeed, the indiscriminate nature of artillery, machine gun, and rifle fire did much to undermine time-honored distinctions between heroes and cowards.

Infantry Second Lieutenant Guy Hallé published a series of highly stylized and poignant vignettes in October 1917. One vignette described the death of a particular soldier in September 1914 during the French counteroffensives following the Battle of the Marne. Hallé and the this soldier had been part of a small band of skirmishers advancing through a wooded

49. Drieu la Rochelle, "La Comédie de Charleroi," 61.
50. Ibid., 63.
51. Galtier-Boissière, *En rase campagne,* 41.
52. Ibid., 44.

area, their unprotected heads down.[53] Hallé saw the victim fall when a bullet hit him in the stomach. Particularly at the beginning of the war, with medical services inadequate and in disarray, such a wound almost always meant death. "At first," Hallé recounted, "he did not seem to suffer. He seemed light-headed, so light-headed that it did not occur to him right away what had happened. Then, pain came over him, in one blow, its claws grabbing so deeply into his flesh that his whole body shuddered."[54] The "battle," in the meantime, had subsided or drifted elsewhere.

By nightfall, the mortally wounded soldier had regained some form of consciousness and for hours cried out, "Mama, Mama, Mama!" With no field hospitals in the vicinity and with orders to get such sleep as they could, Hallé and those around him simply lay down among the wounded. As he put it, "conquered by the horrible weariness of the day of battle, it broke our hearts to hear these dying men suffering."[55] Toward morning, the voice of Hallé's comrade weakened because of the loss of blood, which had gathered in a pool around him. He could only mutter, "Give forty, give forty," perhaps a reference to some sort of bequest. By dawn, he had died.

The "moral" of the story seemed to be not about closure but about identifying a terrifying mixture of sameness and difference between Hallé and the deceased in the encounter with the *sacra* in battle. The two were entirely commensurate at the moment the bullet struck. As Hallé told the story, there was no reason whatsoever why that bullet should have gone into the stomach of the deceased and not his own. The moral of the story revolved around the wholly arbitrary nature of death in the state of liminality.

Artilleryman Paul Lintier recounted a step-by-step annihilation of the identity produced by the mobilization, and an encounter with the *sacra* suffused with fragmentation and pollution. The battle came to him in one of the earliest encounters between the French and the Germans in Belgium. On August 22, 1914, his battery spent the entire day just trying to get into a position to join the fight. His specific gun did not fire a single shell. Eventually, the battle welled up around them, forcing them to retreat. Lintier's vision narrowed as he became preoccupied with his own survival. When the first shell exploded nearby, he began to understand the gravity of his situation. But he did not yet admit fear: "I feel an anxiety rise up in me, as though the flow of my blood were slowing up. . . . I can forgive myself for being anxious; a baptism of fire is always emotional."[56] Even as it became

53. French infantry did not have helmets until the summer of 1915.

54. Guy Hallé, *Là-bas avec ceux qui souffrent* (Paris: Librairie Garnier Frères, 1917), 10.

55. Ibid., 11.

56. Lintier, *Ma Pièce*, 73.

clear that his battery had come within range of the German machine guns, he tried to reflect calmly, "clearly the time has come to sacrifice my life." In the abstract, he could envisage his death—notably his twenty-one-year-old body, bloodied and splayed out across the battlefield. Yet also in the abstract, he saw his likely fate as consistent with the identity produced at the mobilization: "My destiny must be sacrificed to the accomplishment of higher destinies. It is the life of my country, of everything I love, and of everything I miss at this instant. If I am to be dead to myself, I consent; it is done! I would have thought it harder than this."[57] As if to affirm that, for the moment, he was still the same person he was when his train left for the front, he began unconsciously to sing an inane song popular in the barracks during the last days before the war broke out. It seemed all too appropriate to his present predicament:

> Tra-la-la, that's hardly gonna work!
> Tra-la-la, that's not gonna work!

A shell flying directly overhead introduced him to the *sacra* of the battlefield. He waited what seemed like an eternity for the shell to explode: "One, two, three seconds; hours. I stretch my back, and I tremble. I feel throbbing within me the instinctive need to escape. The beast rears itself up facing death!" The shells continued to fall, combined with machine-gun fire. "I'm sweating," he confessed. "I'm afraid . . . I'm afraid. But I know that I will not run away, that I will let myself get killed where I stand."[58] But as his personal situation continued to deteriorate, the smartly attired soldier who departed to defend his native land from the invader realized that he had entered a distinct and exceedingly fragile realm of existence: "it seems like I am awakening into a stupor, full of horrible nightmares. I'm not afraid anymore."[59] Diving into a ditch in the confusion of the battle, he noticed a terrible smell. A comrade had somehow dug in, then soiled himself. The terrified man, jealously guarding his unenviable situation, told him: "Don't even think about it, buddy! I'm the one in the s[hit], but I wouldn't give you my place for twenty francs." Staying put or leaving swiftly became a moot point, as French infantry begin to stream past them. Lintier had no formal orders to follow at this point. But clearly he had to either join the retreat or fall into German hands. His initiation to combat concluded ingloriously: "The battle is lost. I do not know why or how. I saw nothing."[60] In Lintier's liminal experience, he ceased to be afraid precisely when his situation be-

57. Ibid., 76.
58. Ibid., 77.
59. Ibid., 80.
60. Ibid., 81.

came most perilous, not because of the identity prepared for him at the mobilization, but because he had entered some different world where rules of courage and fear no longer applied in the same way.

It sometimes happened that the liminal experience involved panic and the disintegration of formal authority. Maurice Genevoix became one of the truly gifted narrators of the Great War, the author of an epic compilation of books covering the first six months of the war. *Ceux de 14* all but eradicates the line between fictional and nonfictional testimony and presents its own narratological issues, which I will explore further in chapter 3.[61] Genevoix, mobilized as a reserve second lieutenant, told a story of liminality on the battlefield that explored Stendhal's paradox in spare but vivid language. The date was September 6, 1914, the first day of the French counteroffensive that began the Battle of the Marne. The particular attack in which Genevoix participated appeared at first to go well. The men advanced as ordered, "with the same ease as they showed on the field during maneuvers. And bit by bit, an excitement rises in me that carries me away. I feel in all these men the living sense that only a gesture from me moves them forward, into the bullets flying toward their chests, their faces, their living flesh."[62] He heard bullets hitting the ground all around him. He raised his hat, signaling his men to advance, and to empty their rifles firing the enemy as they do so. But not all of them moved forward:

> A cry is stifled to my left; I had the time to see the man, knocked down on his back, throwing his legs forward; a second, his whole body stiffens; then a relaxation, and it is only an inert thing, of dead flesh that the sun will help decompose tomorrow.[63]

Genevoix's men continued to advance, if only because staying in the same place proved more dangerous than trying to move forward. The men continued to fall, "some just thrown as one piece on the ground without a word, the others, as a reflex, covering their wounds with their hands. They say: 'That's it!' or 'I'm finished.' Often just one word, very French. Nearly all of them, even if wounded lightly, get pale and change their facial expression."

The attack began to break down in an adjoining section when its leader was killed.

> A shell just exploded in the section of men of Saint-Maixent. As for him, I saw clearly the shell explode right in front of him. His hat flew off, a tail of

61. Maurice Genevoix, *Ceux de 14* (1950; repr., Paris: Flammarion, 1983).
62. Ibid., 31.
63. Ibid.

his greatcoat, an arm. A mass without form on the ground, white and red, a nearly nude body, crushed. The men, without a leader, scatter.[64]

Other sections likewise disintegrated, though notably not that of Genevoix. However, his men ran the risk of becoming isolated and surrounded. A captain commanding a company finally appeared, saying that his superiors have ordered a fighting retreat, which happened in a disordered manner with units mixed in together. Only at nightfall could they regroup. The confused survivors did not seem aware of having participated in arguably the greatest French military victory of the twentieth century.

On the face of it, the German enemy ought to have provided a frame of reference in the chaos of the liminal state. It was after all, the enemy who had forced the soldier to undergo the rite of passage in the first place. Moreover, a given soldier's chances of actually encountering the enemy in open field in August and September 1914 were much higher than in the war of the trenches later on. As John Horne and Alan Kramer have shown, it did not take long for stories of German atrocities in Belgium to reach the French at the front or behind the lines.[65] Yet as would prove the case throughout the war, hatred toward the enemy in the abstract and in the aggregate was one thing, hatred of a fellow human in another uniform a short distance away was another. A highly racialized image of the enemy was more likely to be the result of cultural mobilization than the precondition for it in the first battles of the war. Moreover, German soldiers inhabited precisely the same liminal space at precisely the same moment as the French. Contradictory images of the enemy appeared in accounts of first contact.

The *sacra* of liminality involved the prospect of not just one's own death but that of the enemy. As would prove true later in the war, the more indirect the témoin's involvement in killing, or the more atypical the killing itself, the more he seemed to enjoy it. Germans had crept up on the sleeping cavalry unit of Christian Mallet. As the astonished French frantically tried to mount their horses and escape, he wrote, "I saw that there was still one German left alone, caught between the fire from his regiment and our galloping horses. Turning my head to look, I laughed with joy, seeing a comrade run him through with his lance while passing by."[66] Whatever

---

64. Ibid., 33.

65. Word of the German army executing two Belgian boys for alerting the gendarmes of approaching cavalry was published in France as early as August 7. John Horne and Alan Kramer, *German Atrocities, 1914: A History of Denial* (New Haven: Yale University Press, 2001), 175.

66. Mallet, *Étapes et combats*, 66.

vengeful or sadistic (if vicarious) pleasure Mallet enjoyed at that moment, medieval-style combat proved a rare way indeed to die in the Great War.

Artillerymen, as a group responsible for much more killing than infantry, were among the most reticent in writing. Captain de Mazenod took a specific, somewhat detached joy in firing directly on a line of German infantry on August 14, a day of disastrous fighting for the French. Such opportunities for artillerymen actually to see the enemy were not much more common than the chance to stab an enemy soldier with a lance.

> And when the fire had finished, when the smoke had dissipated, I saw scattered across the ground black, immobile spots. Two or three among the spared got out of those human ruins, and dragged themselves over to the ridge.
> It was the most beautiful moment of my life.[67]

It did not prove difficult to enjoy the killing of an enemy who looked like struggling black spots. In contrast, artilleryman Henches wrote to his wife of sentiments that approached remorse: "Our fire must be terrible, if it is conducted well, and I surprised myself by thinking about what we must have been doing, because often we fire without knowing the results, because of the distance."[68] His further thoughts on September 15 seem to apply equally to both sides: "The effect of these shells is dreadful. The books of [H. G.] Wells themselves cannot convey the idea of what we see and what we have experienced."[69]

Medical personnel at the front comprised a unique group of témoins, as they were essentially noncombatant combatants. They incurred considerable physical risk because of their proximity to the fighting, and were often themselves in the front lines. In addition they constantly saw death and mutilation at close range. The tension between their duties as care providers and as participants in the conflict particularly complicated their image of the enemy upon initial contact. Abbé Félix Klein was chaplain to the Ambulance américaine, a medical unit funded with private money from the United States. His was a very early *témoignage de guerre,* published in early 1915. Klein told a story of a French soldier with a perforated lung who had been taken prisoner. He had been stripped before the Germans abandoned him, "and it was out of pure meanness, because they didn't even take anything."[70] Yet Klein also praised the professionalism of German military

67. Mazenod, *Dans les Champs de Meuse,* 72.
68. Henches, *À l'école de guerre,* 6.
69. Ibid., 9.
70. Abbé Félix Klein, *La Guerre vu d'une ambulance* (Paris: Armand Colin, 1915), 82.

doctors, who gave coffee, bread, and soup to wounded French soldiers. When the German retreated, wounded prisoners were left behind rather than killed (as might have been expected). Lucien Laby was a young medical student mobilized in the French army who at various points wanted to become a combatant. In the confused retreat of August 25, he and a friend removed their medical armbands and became indistinguishable from combat soldiers. "It's more chic this way," he observed with considerable nonchalance under the circumstances. "I hope to knock over a few Boches. We won't tell anybody about this, though, because these little amateur expeditions would be suppressed."[71] Yet later in the same diary entry he wrote of treating a gravely wounded German with some compassion:

> A German officer was not moveable, with half of his cerebellum outside his skull. I made him a shelter with his tent sheet, to provide him with shade—and I continued on—a German offered me his coin purse if I would kill him; he was atrociously mutilated, broiled; I put him in my car.[72]

No consistent image of the enemy, in short, emerged from these first encounters.

The liminal phase, that of actual contact with the enemy, fragmented the initiates' experience and dramatically contrasted with the rites of separation. The mobilization had revolved around creating absolute commensurability among the initiates and the submersion of their individual identities. Liminality brought individuality back to center stage, suddenly and brutally. Some initiates would die, some would be mutilated, and some would live—all as individuals. Therein hangs the problem of using rites of passage to create a coherent narrative of the initiation to combat. Kande Kamara may not have known precisely what would happen at the circumcision bush, but he knew that he would arrive at the bush as a boy, suffer pain there, and leave it as a man. The entire structure of the rite and its moral was known in advance. Not so for the *témoins* of 1914. Rites of passage as a narrative form worked insofar as they served to mark a fundamentally transformative experience. But how to piece together a narrative and a narrator with the beginning and the middle of the story so at odds with each other, with the middle so self-contradictory and unknowable, and with no discernible end?

71. Lucien Laby, *Les Carnets de l'aspirant Laby, médicin dans les tranchées: 28 juillet 1914–14 juillet 1919*, ed. Sophie Delaporte (Paris: Bayard, 2001), 41.
72. Ibid., 42.

Rites of Reincorporation

In the classic conceptualization of rites of passage, the initiate ultimately leaves the liminal state and is reintroduced to the community with an altered and superior status. As Victor Turner put it, "The ritual subject, individual or corporate, is in a stable state once more and, by virtue of this, has rights and obligations of a clearly defined and 'structural' type, and is expected to behave in accordance with certain customary norms and ethical standards."[73] Such a conclusion, of course, assumes that the roles played before, during, and after the ritual process are all properly understood in advance.

The outcome of Kande Kamara's experience in the Great War as a rite of passage proved considerably less certain than that of his circumcision. Joe Harris Lunn, the historian who brought Kamara's oral testimony into print, seemed sure of the meaning of that experience. To Lunn, Kamara exemplified the colonial victim of the Great War. In a futile quest for equality with his colonial masters, Kamara had been duped into fighting the white man's war. Upon his return to Africa, he soon found that had less status than when he left. Factious village politics and suspicion of the French colonial authorities excluded him from the succession as chief, and led to a plot on Kamara's life. He ended up having to flee village and family, and became an itinerant trader wandering through West Africa. The transformed veteran never successfully reintegrated into the African society from which he had come. Lunn provided a clear moral for his subject's story: "Kamara paid the penalty for a youthful idealism which failed to distinguish between the world as it was and as he believed it to be."[74] The same, certainly, has often been said of white soldiers of the Great War.

But Kamara's own testimony as cited by Lunn does not always support Lunn's moral. Kamara, in fact, pointed to the mutual transformation of black and white soldiers because of the war.

> At the beginning [of the war], the white people were always in the front line . . . But when we got to understand them . . . and when they started trusting us . . . that changed. At the very end [of the war] we were all mixed, because by then everyone knew that mind and their heart [*sic*] and no one was afraid of color except for innocents.[75]

Indeed, one could argue that Kamara considered the comparison between circumcision and combat quite appropriate to his experience in the Great

73. Turner, "Betwixt and Between," 94.
74. Lunn, "Kande Kamara Speaks," 48.
75. Ibid., 44.

War writ large. He entered the war as some form of minor in the eyes of the colonizer, and left it an adult. Before the war, Kamara maintained, "the white man considered us animals—beasts." But near the end of a long and difficult life, he testified to a remarkable confidence in the long-term effects for men such as himself of having fought for France in the Great War:

> If we hadn't fought, if we—the black people—hadn't fought in western wars, and had been taken overseas, and demonstrated some ability of human dignity, we wouldn't have been regarded today as anything.[76]

From this point of view, colonial soldiers had been reincorporated into the broader world as less unequal in some sense. Which interpretation, however, represents the "real" Kamara? It is not my purpose here to decide one way or another. Rather, my point is that if *témoins* used rites of passage as a narrative structure through which to understand the initiation to combat, reincorporation was not an event but a process. If the combatants had been transformed, so too had been the war and the society around them.

Eric Leed, whose work on liminality in 1914 provided the starting point for my analysis, remained acutely aware of the narratological difficulties of using rites of passage as a formal structure. "Clearly war is *not* a ritual event," he wrote, "but an historical event. Rituals of initiation do not kill initiands, however much the symbols of death might be used to characterize their anomalous situation, and however much they might be marked and mutilated in ritual operations."[77] In Leed's analysis, it became necessary to foreshorten the rites of passage and essentially to suspend it in the liminal stage. He concluded that soldiers of the Great War were never successfully reincorporated into postwar societies, or indeed into their own identities. "No Man's Land" was to be their permanent home, socially and psychologically. "The veteran," he wrote, "was a man fixed in passage who had acquired a particular 'homelessness.'"[78] In this permanent alienation lay the contribution of veterans of the Great War to the general condition of "modernity."

But stopping the rites of passage in the liminal stage obscures the inventiveness of testimony of the Great War and foreshortens considerably the history of that testimony. What Leed considered a permanent state of liminality, I will reinterpret in chapter 4 as trauma, a formal construct that was created during the interwar years and culminated in the war novel of the 1930s. Leed's argument, while pioneering in itself, perpetuated the meta-

76. Ibid., 48.
77. Leed, *No Man's Land*, 32.
78. Ibid., 33.

narrative of the Great War as tragedy, a designation that I am trying to interrogate.

The term "reincorporation," of course, raises the question, reincorporation into what? As Freud noted, the war that began in August 1914 seemed day by day to be transforming being itself. The initiated combatant needed to be reincorporated into a war culture taking shape around him. Reincorporation in the sense I use it here involved establishing, in Hayden White's phrase, a "continuity within a difference." The combatant needed to establish that he was still "himself" in a transformed state, and that he had become a figure able to convey his exceptional experience to the public sphere. Paradoxically, the *témoin* as a cultural figure had an interest in preserving something unknowable about the front. If one could fully understand the initiation to combat by reading about it, then that experience would no longer be the exclusive realm of combatants themselves, precisely what set them apart forever from their compatriots and gave them a special authority to speak on the war. Reincorporation, then, was about establishing a proper relationship among experience as created in the text, the author as the mediator of that experience, and the reader learning about both vicariously, through the written word. What is most interesting about attempts to employ reincorporation as the conclusion of the rite of passage is the variety of strategies employed, and the partial nature of all of them. The most complete are the most problematic.

Certainly, the issues of narrator and narrative intrigued and perplexed Marc Bloch, who wrote a second version of his liminal experience. After his evacuation from the front in January 1915 for typhoid fever, Bloch began to rewrite his diary into more of a narrative. He never identified the public he envisaged for his text—whether himself, his friends and family, a future academic audience, or a more general public. He began modestly:

> I intend to use this respite to fix my recollections before their still fresh and vibrant colors fade. I shall not record everything; oblivion must have its share. Yet I do not want to abandon the five astonishing months through which I have just lived to the vagaries of my memory, which has tended in the past to make an injudicious selection, burdening itself with dull details while allowing entire scenes, any part of which would be precious, to disappear. The choice it has exercised so poorly I intend this time to control myself.[79]

Immediacy was of the essence, as was the need to fix in words the meaning of his experience at the front. Memory, the unconscious gatekeeper of nar-

---

79. Marc Bloch, *Memoirs of War, 1914–15,* ed. and trans. Carole Fink (Ithaca: Cornell University Press, 1980), 77.

rative detail, would always prove inherently unreliable. Marc Bloch as witness and Marc Bloch as narrator had to create each other.

The second version of his initiation to combat, now precisely dated September 10, 1914, began with a kind of thesis—the exceptional nature of the experience itself. What he witnessed that day had changed him forever. But ever the honest scholar, he admitted both the detail and the inherent disorder of his memories of the episode, then but four months old.

> It is likely that as long as I live, at least if I do not become senile in my last days, I shall never forget the 10th of September, 1914. Even so, my recollections of that day are not altogether precise. Above all they are poorly articulated, a discontinuous series of images, vivid in themselves but badly arranged like a reel of movie film that showed here and there large gaps and the unintended reversal of certain scenes. [80]

True to the original source of his diary entry, the future famous historian followed the basic chronology—the advance of his unit under heavy fire and heavy casualties. He presented what he remembered as a coherent list of images and events, some more and some less connected within the overall structure. This version comprises some five printed pages, as compared with one long paragraph in the diary entry.[81]

But this version of Bloch's emplotment of his initiation to combat established White's "continuity within a difference." Bloch created a warrior who told a war story, with a conclusion that explained why it was set down in the first place. The apparently random remembered details of the day all cohered around a kind of moral. The events of that day were exceptional and unforgettable because he had witnessed and experienced great danger and had survived.

> Despite so many painful sights, it does not seem to me that I was sad on that morning of September 11. Needless to say, I did not feel like laughing. I was serious, but my solemnity was without melancholy, as befitted a satisfied soul; and I believe that my comrades felt the same. I recall their faces, grave yet content. Content with what? Well, first content to be alive. It was not without a secret pleasure that I contemplated the large gash in my canteen, the three holes in my coat made by bullets that had not injured me, and my painful arm, which, on inspection, was still intact. On days after great carnage, except for particularly painful personal grief, life appears sweet. Let those who will condemn this self-centered pleasure. Such feelings are all the

80. Ibid., 89.
81. Ibid., 89–94.

more solidly rooted in individuals who are ordinarily only half aware of their existence.[82]

The moral of the story revolved around a subtle but fierce joy Bloch took in having lived. He had won, for now, the bet the combat soldiers placed with the *sacra* of the battlefield. His experience set him apart from those who had not been initiated to combat, and authorized him to scoff at those who would question either his story or its moral. The story itself connected the reincorporated soldier to the evolving war culture.

In time, Bloch himself would express doubts about his ability to narrate his own experience at the front. "But as for formulating written confessions and judgments," he wrote in a letter to the sociologist Georges Davy in September 1917, "truly, I am hardly capable of it. I would have too much to say, and all of it too mixed up and sometimes too self-contradictory. And besides, I don't have enough distance."[83] Bloch would never finish his "souvenirs," which would be published only many years after his death. Eventually, he would feel more comfortable emplotting human experience in the *longue durée* of the Annales school of historians.[84] But few who wrote about their experience in the Great War offered historians a better opportunity to look over their shoulders.

Like Bloch, other *témoins* identified considerable contradictions in reporting a coherent story of their initiation to combat. Cavalrymen had a particular challenge, given how thoroughly the first battles of the Great War had proved the limitations of the armed horseman. Hussard René de Planhol reflected on his unit, as they lay exhausted and sleeping in open field after their first contact with the Germans:

> They had not previously imagined [the "real" nature of combat], amid the furious fanfares, the bloody euphoria, and the idea of the Boches who scattered and ran away. Bold and puerile vision! War, if truth be told, was immobility under a storm of fire, firing on an enemy very good at concealing himself, marches and counter-marches of which one knows nothing. What's more, war is retreat, suddenly, and for what? . . . War consists of not fighting.[85]

At the end of his day, cavalryman Marcel Dupont wrote that what he had just lived through "is the inverse of battle, the moment when you feel the

82. Ibid., 94.

83. Marc Bloch to Georges Davy, 16 September 1917, in *Écrits de guerre,* 117.

84. See Smith, "Le Récit du témoin," 295–300.

85. René de Planhol, *Étapes et batailles d'un hussard, août–septembre 1914* (Paris: Attinger Frères, 1915), 31; ellipses added.

weariness of the spirit and the body, and the infinite sorrow of thinking about those who are no longer there."[86]

Surviving the initiation proper was an event, reincorporation a much longer transformative struggle. Galtier-Boissière wrote:

> All of us, we believed in the story of the Alboches who would surrender for a *tartine* [a slice of bread with butter]. Persuaded of the crushing superiority of our artillery and our aircraft, we imagined the war naively as something of a military parade, a rapid succession of easy and brilliant victories. The thunderclap that followed, in showing us the terrifying disproportion between the engines of death and the tiny soldiers, whose nervous systems were not up to such a shock, abruptly made us understand that the struggle then beginning would be a terrible ordeal.[87]

In his diary entry for September 6, 1914, infantryman Paul Tuffrau wrote an early version of the common image of combat as industrialized killing:

> And from time to time, beneath the regular sound—the methodical work of killing machines—someone, among all these men lying down and immobile, would cry "Ah!" trailing off and prolonged, the moaning of someone exhausted, pushed over the limit, which seemed to say, "This will never finish, never, never!"[88]

The first response to surviving the initiation to combat could simply be some form of collapse. Infantryman Emmanuel Lemercier wrote to his mother on September 21: "When these torments were finally over, I had such a nervous release that I cried without knowing why."[89] The puzzling thing is that Lemercier seemed genuinely puzzled.

"Every war constitutes an irony of situation," Paul Fussell famously put it, "because its means are so melodramatically disproportionate to its presumed ends."[90] Yet irony surely does not tell us everything we need to know about the initiation to combat. Something, behaviorally and textually, has to follow the identification of irony. Every soldier under fire in 1914 must have noted irony in Fussell's sense, and yet the survivors continued to fight the war for more than four more years. Some sort of narrative structure and some sort of narrator had to fill in the experiential

86. Dupont, *En campagne,* 78.

87. Galtier-Boissière, *En rase campagne,* 45–46.

88. Paul Tuffrau, *1914–1918, quatre années sur le front: carnet d'un combattant* (Paris: Imago, 1998), 46.

89. Lemercier, *Lettres d'un soldat,* 16–17.

90. Paul Fussell, *The Great War and Modern Memory* (New York: Oxford University Press, 1975), 7.

vacuum created by irony. The French warrior of the trenches would eventually become known as the *poilu,* or "hairy one," referring to his unkempt hair and beard. Like Samson from the Hebrew Bible, his hair signified his strength. Témoins fashioned pieces of what would become the poilu out of old and new elements.

Some created a narrative of reincorporation into the mobilizing war culture in familiar and heroic terms. Readers today need not take such interpretations at face value, but neither should they disregard them out of hand. Light infantryman Henri Libermann told a highly gendered tale of shame and triumph. During the retreat between the Battle of the Frontiers and the Battle of the Marne, he saw an old woman alongside the road: "Like a fury of legend, she practically foamed at the mouth, and her invective turned heads and lowered faces." "The border is not that way," she shrieked at them, "it's over there! Cowards!"[91] Yet this tongue-lashing, not just the female chastising the male but the past chastising the present, helped energize the retreating soldiers. It would make them even more determined to erase the defeat of 1870 and show themselves the true sons and heirs of the soldiers of the Year II of the French Revolution, who likewise had stunned Europe with their unbeatable combination of ferocity and righteousness. They continued their march through a village on the way to battle:

> Everywhere calm, smiling, sure of their strength, the French advanced with an irresistible élan, sweeping away before them the surprised, vanquished enemy:
>
> > Victory in song shows us the way!
> > Liberty guides our steps!
>
> The noble words of the warrior hymn thrilled the French soldier to the marrow, reawakening in him revolutionary enthusiasm which, a century before, had swept our victorious legions along to the frontiers.[92]

Other accounts affirmed conventional notions of courage in more nuanced and complex terms. Maurice Genevoix's semifictional account had the reserve second lieutenant surveying his men on September 12, 1914, during the pursuit of the retreating Germans following the Battle of the Marne. His soldiers had dirty faces and were sprouting beards. Mud and rain rendered particularly pathetic their efforts to mend uniforms torn at the elbows and knees. "Most of them," he added, "looked infinitely exhausted and miserable."[93] Yet from precisely this inversion of the image of

91. Libermann, *Ce qu'a vu un officier de chasseurs à pied,* 31.
92. Ibid., 191.
93. Genevoix, *Ceux de 14,* 60.

the beautiful soldier going off to war came his reborn and reinvented strength.

> Nevertheless, they were the ones who had just fought with superhuman energy, who had shown themselves stronger than the German bullets and bayonets. They were the victors! And I would like to have spoken to each one of the warm affection that drew me to all of them, soldiers who now deserved the admiration and respect of the world, to have sacrificed themselves without boasting about it, without even understanding the grandeur of their heroism.[94]

Through the rite of passage initiating the soldier to combat, the enthusiastic, red-trousered neophyte who departed the train station at the mobilization had emerged from the liminal state a warrior. Flesh, for the moment, *had* triumphed over machinery. The French soldier had beaten back the invader in the greatest feat of French arms since Napoleon. And however long the struggle, those who would become poilus could not lose, "because there lived in them a force of the soul that would not weaken, that on the contrary the certitude of victory would strengthen, and that would always triumph over the weariness of the body."[95]

There were ways to pronounce the initiation to combat definitive. One kind of account proved particularly amenable to heroic convention—the writings of the dead. By definition, the dead had completed their rites of passage. Henceforth, they could be reincorporated into the emerging war culture as semidivine exemplars, unsullied by the bloody, dirty, vermin-infested, and above all stalemated war of the trenches. Charles Péguy, for example, could live on in testimony written even before the war. Art could transcend earthly experience itself, as in Péguy's most famous poem, "Heureux sont" ("Blessed are Those," 1913):

> Blessed are those who died for carnal earth
> Provided it was in a just war.
> Blessed are those who died for a plot of ground.
> Blessed are those who died a solemn death.[96]

A martyred Péguy, killed during his liminal experience, could be more easily incorporated than a living one into the national war effort. "This dead man is a guide," wrote the right-wing politician and author Maurice Bar-

---

94. Ibid.
95. Ibid., 61.
96. From Charles Péguy, "Eve," in *The Lost Voices of World War I,* ed. Tim Cross, trans. Ann Green and Julian Green (Iowa City: University of Iowa Press, 1988), 269.

rès on September 17, twelve days after Péguy's death: "This dead man will continue to serve, this dead man more than anybody is alive today."[97]

More obscure figures could likewise find a legitimacy as témoins in death that could have proved more problematic in life. Jacques Brunel de Pérard was twenty-one years old when he died early in the morning of September 27, 1914. A student in his second year at the École de droit and the École des sciences politiques, he did not have time to make his mark in the literary world. But the survivors who brought his journal into print could praise the unfulfilled genius of the deceased. The anonymous author of the preface was sure that "his literary and political futures were showing themselves of the greatest brilliance."[98] Precisely this extinguished promise, the preface suggested, validated the patriotic moral of Brunel de Pérard's brief story. Conveniently, the deceased concluded what proved the last entry in his diary with a valedictory statement:

> In some sense, and from a strictly personal point of view, I will regret these two months that I have just lived through which, alongside very difficult privations, have carried with them emotions of marvelous richness and variety. Although I do not have the slightest fear of death, it would be a shame if I do not return. Up to now, I have known how to make war.[99]

Such confidence might have prove difficult to maintain as the war stalemated. The publication of Brunel de Pérard's journal in July 1915, less than one year after the beginning of the war, was less about commemoration than mobilization. He could rejoin his compatriots by inspiring them from the grave. Such was the reason, after all, for publishing the account in the first place.

Fiction also made it possible for the author to pronounce the rites of passage definitive. René Benjamin provided an overtly propagandistic moral to the story of the initiation to combat in *Gaspard*.[100] Set upon by the Germans in August 1914, the French fought bravely. Those marked for death did so with unproblematic courage and little recorded bloodshed. The dying regretted that they would not see their families again, to be sure. But mostly, they regretted that they would not be physically present for the inevitable French victory. For his part, Gaspard survived his baptism of fire unimpaired in spirit and nearly so in body. He was wounded in the buttock

97. Quoted in Annette Becker, "La Mort des écrivains," *Le Monde*, numéro special, "La Très Grande Guerre," September 1994, 13.
98. Brunel de Pérard, *Carnet de route*, 5.
99. Ibid., 105.
100. See Benjamin, *Gaspard*, 86–136.

by a piece of shrapnel, which made him uncomfortable but did not otherwise change his character. Gaspard's condition gave rise to innumerable ribald jokes, which vaguely titillated the nuns taking care of him. He recovered speedily. Now that Gaspard "knew" death, he could scoff at it with even more assurance than before. He rejoined his unit as soon as he could, to fight with undiminished ardor.

Fiction of a more overtly political point of view produced long after the fact could also portray the initiation to combat as definitive. No author luxuriated in the irony identified by Fussell more than Pierre Drieu la Rochelle, who composed a fictionalized account of his experience in August 1914, "La Comédie du Charleroi" (1934). Drieu's personal defeat on the battlefield reflected that of the army, and in turn the utter defeat of France in the Great War. As we saw, the protagonist began the charge in a rush of almost orgasmic enthusiasm, only to tumble ingloriously into the ditch that saved his life. He suffered a slight shrapnel wound to the neck, which delighted him: "My blood flowed. I recalled my pride. I was a man; my blood had flowed."[101] But once he realized he would live, he became disgusted with himself and with the war. He threw away all his military equipment, including his rifle, and slithered back to the French lines, complaining about modern warfare:

> This modern war, this war of iron and not of muscle. This war of science and not of art. This war of industry and commerce. This war of bureaucratic departments. This war of the newspapers. This war of generals and not of leaders. This war of ministers, union heads, emperors, socialists, democrats, royalists, industrialists, bankers, old men, and women and little boys. This war of iron and of gas. This war made by everybody, except those who actually fight it.[102]

Narrator and narrative, paradoxically, triumphed through the representation of failure. Grandiose expectations and crushing disillusion provided for decadence so profound that Drieu could wallow in it almost joyfully. He did, after all title his story "La Comédie de Charleroi."[103] The initiation to combat as a rite of passage prepared him for impotence. "I have given myself two or three times in battle," he wrote in his famous aphorism on Mars and Venus, "and two or three times in bed."[104] The result was the same.

101. Drieu la Rochelle, "La Comédie de Charleroi," 85.
102. Ibid., 61.
103. *Comédie* may mean "comedy" but may also mean "drama," as in Honoré de Balzac's *La Comédie humaine.*
104. Drieu la Rochelle, "La Comédie de Charleroi," , 59.

The fictional emplotment of a definitive identity formed by the initiation to combat was not the exclusive domain of the extreme Right. Léon Werth shared nothing with Drieu politically, but he emplotted the initiation to combat in a parallel manner. The rite of passage structured a narrative ending in defeat. Whatever happens to the initiate subsequently would simply ratify and perform an outcome determined in advance. For Werth, as for many on the political Left in the interwar years, defeat had its origins in the mobilization itself. When confronted with a choice between a passage to revolution as preached for decades by European socialists and a passage to war, the peoples of Europe had chosen war. As Clavel walked the streets of Paris during the mobilization, he "understood quickly that there would be no insurrection. He guessed that no Socialist deputy was going get himself killed at the head of a band of rioters."[105] Battle simply affirmed the pointless passage to war, as well as the loss of agency implicit in accepting mobilization in the first place. Combat destroyed haphazardly and affirmed nothing.

> The emotions of war are like those at the gaming table. The man takes his chances. . . . The soldier counts on combinations in space. Will his card be trumped? With the shell touch him? . . . The soldier is diminished and shrunken, like the gambler who expects nothing, either of himself or of his comrades. His hopes and fears are fastened by chance to a cut of the cards or to the hand he is dealt. The warrior, like the gambler, gives up feeling, thinking, living.[106]

Soldiers were simply those who understood the defeat of the Great War before everyone else. Their rite of passage made them became a distinct community, party to a special, dreadful knowledge, which the rest of society would acquire only later. In this sense the disillusioned society would eventually become "reincorporated" into the already disillusioned society of veterans.

Roland Dorgelès, a much less overtly political figure than Werth or Drieu, held an even more expansive view of the ability of the author to determine the outcome of the rites of passage. Dorgelès posited a narrator who could solve the seemingly intractable problem of reconciling the authority of immediacy with the requirements of narrative coherence. No one understood the possibilities of narrative better than Dorgelès, who wrote the best-selling novel *Les Croix de bois* (Wooden Crosses, 1919). Ten years later, he published a series of reflections on how he had written the book.

105. Werth, *Clavel soldat*, 24.
106. Ibid., 100–101; ellipses added.

Normally, Dorgelès recounted in 1929, he had nothing but contempt for efforts to emplot experience as it was happening. He disdained keeping daily diaries and had burned all the notes he had taken himself, "so as not to lie."[107] Only narrative, a story strictly regulated by a fully formed narrator, could correctly convey experience. That narrator had been produced by Dorgelès's own rite of passage.

Dorgelès allowed that the writing of liminal experience had a special relationship to immediacy. He recalled his own baptism of fire, in 1915 near Neuville-St. Vaast in the Artois. Dorgelès was lying in a first-line trench under a horrible bombardment. To overcome his fear, he forced himself first to read one of the books in his haversack, then to take out pencil and paper and begin to write about what was happening to him. As he explained in 1929:

> The soldier was perhaps going to die, the man feel himself become a coward. But something still resisted: the writer, this maniac of a writer whose curiosity did not leave him and which in fact even separated itself from him to see him tremble in his skin.[108]

His encounter with the *sacra* in pitched battle, his time of direct encounter with mutilation and death, had to be emplotted immediately, in "real time." He "reproduced" the 1915 version in the 1929 reflections. Indeed, he considered this transcription of the liminal experience so authentic that it could enter the public domain directly, from the consciousness of the narrator to the printed page. The text could speak for itself.

> I had only to recopy what I had written, without subtracting a word, without adding a comma. When today you pick up *Les Croix de bois,* in the chapter entitled "Victory," you will find these notes, hardly changed at all.[109]

Dorgelès's claim is all the more extraordinary for being demonstrably untrue. The "transcription" of his notes in the 1929 reflections and the relevant passage in the novel certainly are similar, but they differ in significant ways. The version in the novel concentrated on an array of bodily reactions to the bombardment—such as a tightened facial expression, a head that felt at once empty and heavy, a curiously regular heartbeat. After summing up this variety of somewhat contradictory responses, he mused: "Is all this

107. Roland Dorgelès, *Souvenirs sur les Croix de bois* (Paris: À la Cité des livres, 1929), 19.

108. Ibid., 31.

109. Ibid., 33.

fear?"[110] The 1915/1929 version is actually more than twice the length of the version in the novel, and it ended with an answer rather than a question. The shells landed closer and closer, and gave his head additional weight on his neck. "A sort of dazed resignation overcomes you," he concluded in the version published in 1929.[111]

It seems odd indeed for Dorgelès to claim that the version in the 1919 novel and the 1915 "notes" published for the first time in 1929 are almost exactly the same thing, when a cursory glance at both reveals that they are not. At stake, I would argue, is not insincerity, but rather a specific authorial position produced by his personal rite of passage. Dorgelès quite overtly subjugated the emplotment of the story to its moral, and the specifics of narrative to the universal truth that narrative sought to illustrate. As he wrote in the 1929 reflections, his goal had been "not to recount *my* war, but *the* war."[112] Here, the truth in question seems to be that the experience of encountering the *sacra* of extreme danger spoke for itself when properly conveyed by the narrator. "My soul, my thoughts, my flesh," he wrote, "were completely full of the war. All I had to do was draw it out."[113] The author represented himself simply as the scribe of experience, rather than its creator and arbiter. According to the authority of this embattled self, if the words revealed the same inner truth, the texts *were* the same.

It is not my purpose here to denigrate fictional testimony, or in some way to proclaim it less "valid" or "authentic" than nonfictional testimony. My point is not to praise or condemn any text as such, but rather to figure out what exactly witnesses are testifying *to* when they put their experience into writing. Practically speaking, everyone who wrote about the initiation to combat pronounced the experience transformative. Yet clearly a tension existed between recounting the immediacy of the experience and structuring it into some kind of coherent narrative. Bloch's diary, which emphasizes immediacy, sits at one end of a spectrum. Dorgelès's 1929 recollections of writing his 1919 novel sits at the other, emphasizing the authority of the narrator who can pronounce two different texts the same because they convey the same message. If there is a caution to keep in mind about fictional testimony, it is that fiction tends to reincorporate experience, narrative, and narrator into the public sphere as though they were solved problems. My argument is that they were not, at least not until long after the war.

The diary of Paul Lintier, and most of the other texts examined here, fall

110. See Roland Dorgelès, *Les Croix de bois* (Paris: Albin Michel, 1919), 221.
111. Dorgelès, *Souvenirs sur les Croix de bois,* 33.
112. Ibid.,
113. Ibid., 34.

somewhere in between those of Bloch and Dorgelès in the ways they try to resolve the tension between representing experience "as it happened" and the structural requirements of narrative. Lintier did not fixate on immediacy. He continued to work on what became the published version of his diary, and saw the page proofs delivered to him at the front on March 11, 1916, just a few days before his death.[114] Lintier provided an indeterminate conclusion to the full story of his initiation to combat. "Experience" would continue to resist narration.

Lintier posited a stable if menaced identity after his first battle. Certainly, he and his comrades, referred to in the third person, had been shocked by the disparity between the beauty of the mobilization and the horrors of the battlefield. Yet this had taught them not irony and bitterness so much as a love of life in its very fragility:

> They were not afraid. But the habit of danger, which had made them brave, did not prevent them from loving life, this life that they felt bubbling up within them and which later, perhaps, would trickle away, like their red blood, across the field of sugar beets. [115]

Lintier even tried to reconcile his goals of personal survival with the successful defense of France. His encounter with the *sacra* of the battlefield had not diminished his patriotism, quite the reverse:

> To live! To still be alive tonight, and above all to have won! To prevent the enemy from coming in, invading our homes, to protect first and foremost the dear and vulnerable beings behind the lines, in France, whose lives are more precious than our own. To be the victors! And to be alive tonight![116]

But Lintier's narrative did not end with what appeared to be a statement of the moral of his story, his optimistic, enduring love of life and country in extreme circumstances. His account actually stopped some thirty pages later, after a dramatic story of his serious injury and evacuation. On September 22, with the French advance following the Battle of the Marne coming to a halt, his battery came under bombardment. Suddenly, Lintier was struck twice—by a bullet in the chest and by a piece of shrapnel that went through his hand near the thumb. The bullet to the chest, presumably fired from some distance away, did not harm him: "My notebook of writing, my

114. See Paul Lintier, *Avec une batterie de 75, Le Tube 1233, souvenirs d'un chef de pièce, 1915–1916* (1917; repr., Paris: L'Oiseau de Minerve, 1998), 273. This is a compilation of Lintier's additional writings published after his death.
115. Lintier, *Ma Pièce*, 253.
116. Ibid., 254.

letters, my wallet, placed in an interior pocket of my shirt, stopped the bullet."[117] The written word, it seemed, quite literally saved his life. He noticed his hand bleeding, but concluded: "Oh, it's nothing." Only at the insistence of his lieutenant did he seek medical attention.

Bit by bit, Lintier began to appreciate the seriousness of his wound. Bleeding profusely, he started to leave the battlefield, still under bombardment. He dove for cover between the corpses of two horses that had just been killed. Lintier left again as soon as he could, now at a much faster pace. "My wounded hand," he now realized, "was contaminated with dirt and horse's blood." A captain from a unit of Moroccan infantry dressed his wound and warned him of infection. As Lintier approached the first-aid station, his happy anticipation of his impending evacuation faded when he finally understood his lieutenant's concern: "The fear of gangrene, and above all of tetanus, of all the putrefactions of the hospital, seized me by the throat." The overwhelmed medical staff recommended a simple, drastic solution common at the beginning of the war—amputation of the thumb. But they quickly moved on to tend to those more seriously wounded, and Lintier departed, in effect to seek an unauthorized second opinion. He walked two kilometers to a larger facility, the division medical station. Along the way, and with darkness closing in, he encountered someone (probably a civilian) stealing personal articles from the corpses. Lintier told him to stop, but when he ran away, the two exchanged pistol fire. When Lintier fired a second time, "it seemed that the man fell in the brambles."

Upon reaching the station, Lintier was seated in the straw waiting for treatment. "A large negro," he noticed, "is stretched out at my side. All I can see of him is two glowing eyes." The wounded man, from Sénégal, talked incessantly. The Sénégalais had his own views of the German kaiser: "William . . . bad chief . . . goes to bed with a lot of women . . . many! Ah!" After listening to him for a while Lintier fell asleep, his exhaustion finally overcoming the pain in his hand. When he woke up, he saw the body of the Sénégalais, no longer breathing. He reached out and touched the man's cold hand: "I notice that my feet are soaked in a pool of blood."

Lintier's own situation improved considerably. The staff concluded that they did not need to amputate the thumb. They bandaged Lintier's hand and tagged him for evacuation, though he would have to walk the eight kilometers to the train. "Finally," he wrote, "the hospital . . . the bed . . . the hands of women, the bandage stiffens the broken-up blood, the silence . . . ah! the silence!" On September 30 he received a letter from a

---

117. Ibid., 274–85.

friend describing the death of their much-admired captain. He had suffered a not particularly heroic death, by a canister bullet through the left eye from an exploding shell. The battery continued to fire, as several of the men wept, including the lieutenant who had taken command. "Since, then," the letter reads in the last paragraph, "we haven't done very much. Moreover, everybody's morale hasn't really gotten over this loss." Like Lemercier as noted earlier, Lintier finally allowed himself a moment of collapse. The last line of the book reads simply: "Me too, I wept while reading this letter." Their experience became his through the written word.

WHAT should we make, then, of the disparity between the moral of Lintier's story and its ending? Or of the stability of the identity produced by the rites of initiation to combat? Clearly, Lintier's short experience of battle (the entire book covered only a period of about two months) had plainly transformed him. He sought to reincorporate into the emerging war culture the transformed identity of a sensitive, persistently patriotic individual who loved the life he was still willing to give to the national cause. Unspoken but presumably still present was his continued willingness to take lives, not just those of his German enemy, but that of his compatriot caught looting the corpses of his comrades. Death, the ultimate transformation, framed his narrative: the death of the ambiguous Sénégalais, a friend more mysterious than the German enemy; the death of his captain, whose passing, learned from a letter, authorized Lintier to express his own sorrow; and most of all, the prospect his own death, which readers would know took place just before *Ma Pièce* was published in 1916. The prospect of death framed the rites of initiation, yet defied narrative conclusion.

Freud identified precisely this uncertainty in his 1915 essay. He argued that before 1914 death in modern, "civilized" societies had been tamed by secreting it in hospitals, morgues, and graveyards, where the dead would not unduly trouble the living. But the scale and horror of death at the beginning of the Great War defied this understanding, just as it had defied the moral of Lintier's story as he tried to tell it. "Death," wrote Freud, "will no longer be denied; we are forced to believe in him."[118] Yet Freud concluded that new ways of understanding death had not yet emerged from the liminal experience of 1914. So far, the war had compelled Europeans to recognize a more "primitive" attitude toward death: "Is it not for us to confess that in our civilized attitude toward death we are once more living psychologically beyond our means, and must reform and give truth its due?"[119] For the present conflict had lain bare what he called the "primal

---

118. Freud, "Thoughts for the Times," 17.
119. Ibid., 24.

man in each of us," who knows and admits that death is ubiquitous: "It constrains us once more to be heroes who cannot believe in their own death; it stamps the alien as the enemy, whose death is to be brought about or desired; it counsels us to rise above the death of those we love."[120]

Just what this reconciliation with the primitive would mean, Freud did not yet feel able to say. He transformed the old adage *Si vis pacem, para bellum* (If you would desire peace, prepare for war) into *Si vis vitam, para mortem* (If you would endure life, be prepared for death).[121] This became the question for the poilus, who would take up the task of narrating experience in what after the battles of 1914 had become a completely open-ended war.

120. Ibid.
121. Ibid., 25.

2

The Mastery of Survival

DEATH, MUTILATION, AND KILLING

Freud's dictum from early 1915, "If you would endure life, prepare for death," can be read as a call to imagine survival in the context of omnipresent death. This chapter examines attempts to imagine survival through mastery. Mastery as a narrative device responds to questions left unanswered by rites of passage. Rites of passage were collective and conventionally demarcated a transition in which the various stages and their meanings were understood in advance by both the initiates and the broader society. But actual experience in 1914 afflicted individuals and invoked myriad internal and external transformations entirely understood by no one, including the baffled Freud. Mastery provided a way to individualize experience, as well as its own justification as a moral to the story.

"A master," wrote Delora Wojciehowski, "is an overlord, a victor, a teacher."[1] Such a figure has triumphed over experience in the sense that he has made it his own and can convey its proper meaning to society and to posterity. He is also an artisan, a master craftsman, able to bring an advanced and proprietary skill to a certain craft. This archetypal narrator had his roots particularly in a certain notion of the male individual in Renaissance humanism. What Wojciehowski called "Old Mastery" revolved around a self-conscious individual directed and demarcated by his own free will. To Jacob Burckhardt, the great nineteenth-century propagandist for Renaissance individualism, a medieval veil, "woven of faith, illusion, and childish prepossession," melted away first in Renaissance Italy, where "man

---

1. Delora A. Wojciehowski, *Old Masters, New Subjects: Early Modern and Poststructuralist Theories of Will* (Stanford: Stanford University Press, 1995), 1.

became a spiritual *individual,* and recognized himself as such."[2] For the first time since antiquity, man existed for himself. In Pico della Mirandola's "Oration on the Dignity of Man" (1486), God informs man that he can operate in a state of complete moral freedom:

> Thou, constrained by no limits, in accordance with thine own free will, in whose hand We have placed thee, shalt ordain for thyself the limits of thy nature. We have set thee at the world's center that thou mayest from thence more easily observe whatever is in the world.[3]

Mastery so construed provided a basic structure for narrating experience at the front, as an ideal and an aspiration. Témoins wanted to believe that the individual as imagined by Pico could continue to exist in the extreme conditions of the trenches. Moreover, he could contain experience in language, thereby stabilizing it and producing a stable identity that has had that experience, which his text could then convey to the world beyond himself. Mastery thus justified itself and the narrative it produced. This was the "truth" or "authenticity" that authors sought across genres to express: a mastery of experience through the establishment of narrator and narrative.

Yet varieties of extreme experience in the trenches—death, mutilation, and killing—defied narrator and narration in any number of ways. The riddles of death proved as unsolvable as they had ever been. Mutilation could result in death, and even in the complete annihilation of the physical body. But the prospect of permanent physical injury could transform and threaten identity in as many ways as there were types of wounds. Although killing might have seemed a straightforward experience for a soldier who had willingly donned his nation's uniform in wartime, it proved to be anything but that.

Wojciehowski argued that discourses of the will in early modern Europe "are structured by a tension between the desire for mastery and the acknowledgement of the impossibility of that mastery."[4] In other words, the very assertion of mastery protests too much, and thus has within it an admission that mastery is impossible. I argue that we can think about explanations of extreme experience in the Great War in a similar way. United in

2. Jacob Burckhardt, *The Civilization of the Renaissance in Italy,* trans. S. G. C. Middlemore (1860; repr., New York: Phaidon Publishers, 1951), 81.

3. Giovanni Pico della Mirandola, "Oration on the Dignity of Man," in *The Renaissance Philosophy of Man,* trans. Elizabeth Livermoore Forbes, ed. Ernst Cassirer, Paul Oskar Kristeller, and John Herman Randall, Jr. (Chicago: University of Chicago Press, 1948), 225.

4. Wojciehowski, *Old Masters, New Subjects,* 10.

the desire of their narrators to master experience, the resulting narratives ended up highlighting the intractability of the very problems of survival they were written down to address. In creating themselves through stories of death, mutilation, and killing, narrators and narratives produced not mastery but a fascinating textual world of contradictions, ambiguities, and peculiarities. The endlessly inventive attempts revealed the impossibility of the task. "Experience," then, comprised the myriad pieces of a puzzle of mastery that never quite fit together. It is the ways these pieces did not fit and why they did not fit that interest me here.

Death: *Le passage est trop atroce*

Paul Dubrulle, the son of a wheelwright, had joined the army as a four-year volunteer in 1901. Upon the completion of his service, he joined the clergy as a noviciate in the Compagnie de Jésus. On August 2, 1914, with France plunging into war, he was ordained a priest. French clergy were not exempt from military service, and Dubrulle was recalled as a private in the infantry. His regiment fought at Verdun and, in September 1916, took part in the later stages of the Allied offensive at the Somme. On the night of September 11, the fragile sleep of his unit was shattered by a German artillery bombardment. The fire did not seem precisely targeted, but was deadly and endless:

> The fraying of the nerves gets worse, soon it becomes extreme and, truly gone to pieces, we begin to let go. Despairing of living through such horror, we ask God not to die—the passage is too atrocious [*le passage est trop atroce*]—but to be dead. We have only one desire, the end![5]

Deeply devout down to the time of his death along the Chemin des Dames in April 1917, Dubrulle could imagine being safely in the care of God once dead. Catholicism promised eventual mastery over death as an article of faith. But believing in the defeat of death at the end of time did not resolve Dubrulle's immediate existential agony. Nor did centuries of Catholic theology on the glorious death of the martyr. The violent passage to death seemed so atrocious that Dubrulle pleaded with God not to have to experience it. Like everyone else, he surely knew that one day he would die. But something was different about dying under enemy bombardment.

Of course, the great paradox of death is its certainty coupled with the

---

5. Paul Dubrulle, *Mon régiment dans la fournaise de Verdun et dans la bataille de la Somme: impressions de guerre d'un prêtre-soldat* (Paris: Plon, 1917), 224.

difficulty of actually imagining it. Nothing in the Great War was more ac-
tuarially certain than death at the front, if one served in active sectors long
enough. Yet even those such as Dubrulle, who believed in an afterlife, found
it impossible to master the prospect of the violent separation of body and
spirit. Certainly, death on the battlefield was not a new form of human experience. What was different was the scale. Never before in European history had so many died on the battlefield so violently in so short a time, or
had so many at risk left so many anxious loved ones behind the lines. In
and out of the trenches, a massive need arose to understand and master
death, and a need to articulate solutions to its existential perils. None
"worked," in the sense of being able to assuage the anguish felt by Dubrulle
and millions of others.

Religious solutions most seriously engaged the anguish of death. From a
German prison camp in 1915, Jacques Rivière wrote: "We make war for a
certain way of seeing the world. Every war is a war of religion." Rivière's
observation served as a point of departure for Annette Becker, who argued
for the centrality of religion to French war culture—how the French understood the war at its deepest levels and how they persuaded themselves
to continue fighting it.[6] Certainly religion, which to the vast majority of the
French meant Catholicism, provided a narrative structure for imagining
mastery over death. Mastery revolved around the traditional Christian re-
quirement to follow the example of Christ, *imitatio Christi*. The believer
serving in the trenches would imitate Jesus by suffering torture and death
to save humanity.

As Carolyn Walker Bynum has shown, Catholicism traditionally did not
insist on the same radical separation of body and spirit as most versions of
Protestantism.[7] Western Christianity had held for centuries that at the Last
Judgment, all would be reassembled and resurrected. Human beings would
meet and be judged by God in their corporeal bodies. The martyr could an-
ticipate eternal life as a superior version of himself, as a sacralized somatic
whole. Belief could confer meaning on earthly suffering, but it was not supposed to alleviate it, anymore than it had for Jesus. After suffering would
come redemption and glorification. This was the tacit bargain of martyrdom—exceptional reward for exceptional suffering. Mastery lay in finding

6. Annette Becker, *La Guerre et la foi: de la mort à la mémoire, 1914–1930* (Paris: Armand Colin, 1994), 15.
7. See Carolyn Walker Bynum, *Holy Feast and Holy Fast: The Religious Significance of
Food to Medieval Women* (Berkeley: University of California Press, 1987); and idem, *The Resurrection of the Body in Western Christianity 1200–1336* (New York: Columbia University
Press, 1995).

a way in language to accept the martyr's atrocious passage to death, in anticipation of what lay afterward.[8]

Some found the prospect of martyrdom unproblematic, or at least claimed to. The Catholic theologian, evolutionary biologist, and Jesuit priest Pierre Teilhard du Chardin served as a stretcher-bearer in the Great War. This was a task fully as dangerous as fighting—to some extent more so, given that the unarmed stretcher-bearers often had to carry out their duties standing up, and thus particularly exposed to enemy and friendly fire. Teilhard imagined the flesh of the future martyrs as already sacralized, rendered holy in a way that would help them withstand the ordeal to come. Just before an attack at Douaumont near Verdun in October 1916, he wrote:

> Dissipated into dust that actuates a halo of energy and glory, substantial reality would remain intact, in which all perfection is contained and possessed incorruptibly. The rays fall back upon their source, and there, I hold on to them still all aglow.
>
> That is why the war does not worry me. [. . .] And if I must not come back from there, I want my body to remain in the clay of the forts, like a living cement thrown there by God between the stones of the New City.[9]

To Teilhard, the spiritual reality of the flesh remained incorruptible, morally beyond anything the war could do to it. From such sacrifice, and from the somatic merging of the human and the sacred, God would build a better world on earth.

Other Catholics pointed to the grim price of *imitatio Christi* and the Catholic narrative of mastery of death. Abbé Albert Bessières spoke the following prayer while administering communion to a soldier under artillery bombardment along the Chemin des Dames: "May the body of Our Lord Jesus Christ keep your soul unto eternal life."[10] As stated, the prayer asked that *body* of Jesus—that is, the somatic whole of the resurrected Christian savior that the Host became upon consecration—protect the *soul* of the communicant unto eternal life. In other words, Bessières called upon the sacralized yet physical body of Jesus to protect the earthly yet metaphysical *soul* of the soldier then in the act of receiving communion. That protection would extend through the soldier's own atrocious passage from this

8. The theology of Christian martyrdom is explored in Nadia Tazi, "Celestial Bodies: A Few Stops on the Way to Heaven," in *Fragments for a History of the Human Body,* ed. Michel Feher, Ramona Naddaff, and Nadia Tazi (New York: Zone, 1989), 3:519–52.

9. Pierre Teilhard de Chardin, "Le Christ dans la matière" (1916), in *Écrits du temps de la guerre, 1916–1919* (Paris: Éditions du Seuil, 1965), 127.

10. Abbé Albert Bessières, *Le Chemin des Dames* (Paris: Bloud et Gay, 1919), 34.

life to the next, until the Last Judgment, when he, like Jesus, would triumph over death through resurrection. What remained conspicuously unprotected was the earthly body of the soldier under bombardment. The living psychosomatic whole of the soldier (and of the priest at his side) could still be mutilated or annihilated at any moment.

Some seemed actively to embrace the physical and spiritual agony of *imitatio Christi*. Etienne Derville had been a young student at a Catholic University in Lille, evidently destined for a career in the Church. He was performing his regular military service as a sergeant in the infantry when the war broke out. Abbé Eugène Evrard published a large collection of his letters and notes, written from August 1914 to his death in June 1918.[11] Derville wrote in a letter dated January 1, 1915:

> I have been wounded twice within fifteen days, and the shock was so violent and the part of my body struck so crucial, that both times I believed I was only a few moments from death. And, you see, I keep an ineffaceable memory of these moments. In full conscience, I have made the sacrifice of my life, with joy, for the rechristianization of our country, for the greater love of God on the part of my parents and my friends, and I do not feel the least bitterness. This sacrifice will be even more easy and joyful now, because I have reflected a great deal on it since then.[12]

To approach death was to approach God, and the more serious the injury, the closer the approach. Through imitating the sacrifice of Jesus, Derville hoped to participate in effecting the salvation of France.

Suffering remained central to his religious mission, and inextricable from his service at the front. After a time at headquarters working in intelligence, he returned to the infantry in 1916, during the Battle of the Somme. He wrote on July 23:

> It is better this way. I would have become too "General Staff" and would not have suffered enough. And what else could we ask for at this moment, and always to suffer as much as possible, as much as we can stand?[13]

After his time at the Somme, Derville's letters and notes recorded increasing disillusion. The cause seems to have been not so much his personal suffering as a gathering sense of disconnection between that suffering and results. France was neither winning the war nor "reconverting" en masse

11. Etienne Derville, *Correspondances et notes (août 1914–juin 1918)*, ed. Abbé Eugène Evrard (Tourcoing: J. Duvivier, 1921).
12. Ibid., 63.
13. Ibid., 293.

to Catholicism. He wrote in a letter dated November 22, 1916, that "the religious level declines day by day."[14] Increasingly in 1917 he turned openly to condemnation of the secular Third Republic. On May 2, 1917, with the Chemin des Dames offensive in ruins and open mutiny brewing in large parts of the French army, Derville wrote in a letter: "How dearly we will pay for our political regime before the war."[15]

Yet even the anguish of personal doubt as to the value of sacrifice could be incorporated into a Catholic narrative of mastery over death. The spiritual agony of Jesus is quite real in Christian belief, as he expressed it in the Garden of Gethsemane and in his anguished cry of alienation to his Father from the cross. This spiritual pain is every bit as meaningful as his physical suffering. Embracing this kind of suffering is part of the *imitatio Christi*. Never, at least in the documents that Abbé Evrard included in the collection, did Derville express any doubt in the Catholic narrative of mastery of death. But neither did he seem satisfied with what that narrative had to say about the meaning of suffering in this world.

Doubt also crept around the edges of the account of Captain Frédéric de Bélinay, a mobilized Jesuit serving as an officer in the Chasseurs à Pied, or light infantry. Like Derville, the captain did not express concern about his personal fate, nor did he doubt survival and salvation as provided by Christianity. His anguish took the form of seeking to intervene with God on behalf of his men.

> Look at my *chasseurs*, are they not heroes? Heroes of endurance, of courage, of confidence . . . Will you let their souls be lost? And me, I do not have the right to speak to them. They do not know You, but if they did, they would serve God as they serve their country . . . Will they remain, through the fault of others, deprived of that which gives force and sweetness to life?
> Make yourself known, oh my Lord . . . Why do you wait?[16]

Like Derville, de Bélinay wanted suffering in the trenches to have social and political meaning in this world. His *chasseurs* had shown themselves spiritually worthy through their de facto *imitatio Christi*, even though he did not take most of them to be believers. They were cut off from the hope of mastering death by the heathen regime, which kept him from proselytizing in the trenches. He wondered if God had abandoned them and begged God to intervene. Such intervention, ultimately, could only be political in nature. God could save the soldiers, who as citizen-soldiers would transform the

14. Ibid., 319.
15. Ibid., 32.
16. Frédéric de Bélinay, *Sur le sentier de la guerre* (Paris: Gabriel Beauchesne, 1920), 111.

secular republic; or God could transform the republic directly. De Bélinay was puzzled and distressed that God had not done so.

What the Catholic narrative of *imitatio Christi* could not guarantee was that suffering would have any meaning or produce any tangible benefit in the temporal world. Anyone who had read the Book of Job knew that the God of Jews and Christians did not operate in ways always intelligible to believers. Anyone familiar with Augustine knew that all things worked out for the best in the City of God, not in the City of Man. France would not necessarily become any more Christian, no matter how many Christian soldiers imitated the agony of their savior. Nor, according to centuries of Christian theology, would France necessarily win the war, even if it rechristianized. To the great consternation of ardent Catholics such as Derville and de Bélinay, the Third Republic remained a resolutely secular regime.

Secular conceptions of the mastery of death tended to focus on collective rather than individual survival. As I argued in the previous chapter, performing the survival of the national community, whatever became of any given initiate, had been one function of rituals of mobilization. Collective survival entailed the submergence of individual identity into a greater cause, whether national or ideological. The death of any individual could be construed as contributing to an archetype, an idealized, universal, yet very male identity that would live forever to inspire posterity. As I will argue further in the next chapter, the citizen of the Republic existed as such through his individual and total implication in the collectivity. After death, he might live on as a name on a monument. His name would be visible up close, but as the onlooker's field of vision retreated he would quickly and beautifully disappear into the collectivity. While not citizens of a republic, the British built the edifice displaying this form of survival most dramatically, in the monument at Thiepval on the battlefields of the Somme. The name of each of the tens of thousands of missing was inscribed on the massive edifice. But when seen as a whole, the only visible words are the famous inscription by Rudyard Kipling, "Their name liveth forevermore."[17] The many individuals, whose corporeal remains were strewn across the huge battlefield, became one in death.

In republican France, this concept of survival offered citizens a latter-day version of the medieval theory of the "two bodies" of the king.[18] Political

17. On this question see Daniel J. Sherman, "Bodies and Names," in *The Construction of Memory in Interwar France* (Chicago: University of Chicago Press, 1999), 65–103.

18. See Ernst Kantorowicz, *The King's Two Bodies: A Study in Medieval Political Theology* (Princeton: Princeton University Press, 1957). My analysis of secular narratives of mastery over death draws from my article "Le Corps et la survie d'une identité dans les écrits de guerre français," *Annales: HSS* 55 (2000): 111–33.

theorists imagined the sovereign as both a mortal physical being and the incarnation of the immortal monarchy. As sovereignty became collective under the Republic, this dual corporeal identity came to belong to all members of the political community, most especially to those who had taken up arms in its defense.[19] With collective sovereignty came collective political identity. Consequently, the republican *patrie* (fatherland) offered transcendence of both the individual physical body and individual identity—in other words, metaphysical and collective compensation for physical and individual sacrifice. The individual body became above all the shell of the self. In the end, this shell belonged more to the patrie than to the individual soldier. Once separated from the physical body, the individual self became submerged into the eternal patrie. Such a notion of survival and mastery over death prevailed across a broad political spectrum of opinion.

The eagerness of the hero in René Benjamin's 1915 novel *Gaspard* to submerge his individual identity in that of the national cause was discussed in chapter 1. Bodies rather than characters changed over the course of Benjamin's book, in that their meaning was reinvented to serve the patrie. The individual dead in the book transcended their bodies, bloodlessly and unproblematically. It thus became possible to sanitize or simply ignore the horrific things war did to the body of any individual, because the locus of survival lay elsewhere.

The patrie in *Gaspard* had a physical manifestation in the sacred soil of France. To die was to merge physically with France by simply disappearing, most often literally, into that soil. En route to the front in August 1914, Gaspard's company passed a field in which two hundred French soldiers had been massacred by German cavalry. The French chose to die where they stood rather than retreat and give up a single centimeter of sacred soil. When they ran out of ammunition, they simply dug themselves into the ground:

> This torn-up field, bruised by mangled shoulders and knees, this was the vivid and poignant image of two hundred men who became cadavers. These men were the first to defend, relentlessly, inch by inch, the French soil. But there remained only the imprint of their efforts, the horrifying pattern of their last expression. They themselves had disappeared, buried in their last furrow, swelling up the turned earth with their two hundred bodies crammed in together, so as to encumber the living as little as possible.[20]

19. On the origins of this notion see Dorinda Outram, *The Body and the French Revolution* (New Haven: Yale University Press, 1989), 75–76.

20. René Benjamin, *Les Soldats de guerre: Gaspard* (Paris: Fayard, 1915), 163.

Gaspard's friend, a university professor named Mousse, met a similar fate. Under Gaspard's influence, he abandoned his efforts to be posted in a desk job behind the lines and volunteered to return to the front. Mousse achieved complete redemption with his death. He was killed and instantly buried by earth thrown up by an exploding shell. The sacred soil itself concealed the gory details of his death.

> The German canons had killed him, and they would bury him. The canister had horribly wounded him; but at the same it had dug him a tomb, laid him in it all curled up. The earth took him back, without the assistance of the hand of man. The war struck him down, but watched over him. Rest straight away, after death. Neither body to touch nor pockets to rummage through; no cries, no words. Soldier Mousse: vanished.[21]

Gaspard found a fleeting success among a public starved for some kind of novelistic structure in which to place the war. But as an explanation of experience, one of its many difficulties was its simplistic solution to the mastery of death. In effect, the novel denied that there was any problem at all. As individuals, the dead were, once dead, out of sight and immortalized in mind. Their bodies had united with the soil of France and their souls with the eternal, spiritual patrie. Individual identity was transcended simultaneously with the individual body.

Although a world away politically from Benjamin, Henri Barbusse imagined survival in a parallel form. His most famous book, *Le Feu (Under Fire,* 1916), remains to this day the best-selling French World War I novel. It was published less than one year after *Gaspard,* and its success illustrated a tremendous change in political perspectives on the war in a short period of time. Barbusse had come to see the war as a global problem, to which his deeply felt if ill-defined international socialism would provide the solution. Yet, as in *Gaspard,* the individual soldier owed himself, body and soul, to the collectivity. His body was the stage upon which the great historical drama of the Great War would play itself out—hence the "realism" for which the book is best known. Survival would be entirely collective, through the inevitable triumph of the socialist cause. The dead would live on as heroes in the hearts of a much-improved posterity.

Even more overtly than the conservative Benjamin, Barbusse imagined the threat to survival and the mastery over death in gendered terms. The political individual was as male to Barbusse as he was to the Third Republic. In his first piece of published war writing, a letter dated August 9, 1914, to the editor of the Socialist newspaper *L'Humanité,* he wrote: "If I

21. Ibid., 283.

make the sacrifice of my life, and if I go with joy to war, it is not only as a Frenchman, but above all as a man."[22] That war threatened the identity not of a genderless civic subject, but of a man in a male body. Bloody stalemate and the moral confusion of the conflict as it evolved menaced not just the soldier's life but his masculinity. Too little aggression rendered the man at war less than manly, too much brutalized him. Barbusse positioned "man" midway on a spectrum between clearly effeminized staff officers and perversely hyper-masculine colonial soldiers, particularly Black Africans: "People talk about the character of these darkies, how ferocious they are in the attack, how they love to put in the bayonet, how they don't like to give quarter." Barbusse assured the reader: "They're real soldiers, in a word." Using a racial distinction to help define gender roles, a white comrade added immediately, "We're not soldiers, we're men."[23]

To create the archetypal identity impervious to death, Barbusse turned to one of the oldest exemplars in the Western tradition. This is the figure of the Just Warrior, as Jean Bethke Elshtain calls him, who can reconcile violence and virtue and kill without murdering—because he fights for an absolutely just cause.[24] One fully developed Just Warrior appeared in *Le Feu*, Corporal Bertrand. After one particularly brutal battle, Bertrand announced, with neither pride nor shame, that he personally had killed three Germans. But, as he lectured his comrades, "We had to—for the future." To Bertrand, the work of the future will be "to efface this present and to efface it more than we think, to efface it as something abominable and shameful."[25] Essentially, the novel emplotted the moral journey of the soldiers in Bertrand's squad from emasculated men to socialist Just Warriors. Contrary to common readings of Barbusse, he never advocated anything but the most ferocious prosecution of the war until it was over. *Le Feu* was anything but a pacifist novel.

Le Feu did not become a huge success because of its familiar gender politics or because of its socialism. Rather, Barbusse's novel offered unprecedented "realism," meaning graphic depictions of bodies mangled and consumed by trench warfare. That realism seemed all the more striking because the book appeared in the middle of the war, despite an increasingly

22. Reprinted in Henri Barbusse, *Paroles d'un combattant: articles et discours (1917–1920)* (Paris: Flammarion, 1920), 8. The analysis here of Barbusse and gender draws from my article "Masculinity, Memory, and the French World War I Novel: Henri Barbusse and Roland Dorgelès," in *Authority, Identity, and the Social History of the Great War,* ed. Marilyn Shevin-Coetzee and Frans Coetzee (Berghan Publishers, 1995), 251–73.
23. Henri Barbusse, *Under Fire,* trans. Robin Buss (New York: Penguin Books, 2003), 42.
24. Jean Bethke Elshtain, *Women and War* (New York: Basic Books, 1987).
25. Barbusse, *Under Fire,* 236–37.

complex and intrusive censorship bureaucracy. But Barbusse never invoked realism for its own sake. He considered himself simply the spokesman for a great and irresistible movement of human progress. In the cosmos of history, physical survival could not be guaranteed to any given individual who did his duty to humanity. But his example could live on, and he would in some ideological sense survive, as the war transformed from a battle among nations driven by capitalist greed into a crusade for a better world.

The great drama of history acted itself out on the male body. Full of religions imagery, *Le Feu* told a secular story of sin, damnation, and redemption.[26] The Fall of Man into the moral abyss of the Great War was occasioned by "the monstrous interested parties, the financiers, the great and small wheeler-dealers, encased in their banks and their houses, [who] live by war and live in peace during war."[27] Their sins created this war, this hell on earth that condemned the body of the soldier to torture, dead or alive. One passage depicts how the squad comes across some dead soldiers in the village of Souchez, home to one of the narrator's comrades.

> We go over to them quietly. They are pressed against one another, each making a different gesture of death with his arms or his legs. Some exhibit half-mouldy faces, their skin rusted or yellow with black spots. Several have faces that have turned completely black, tarred, their lips huge and swollen: Negro heads blown up like balloons. Between two bodies, belonging to either one or the other, is a severed hand with a mass of filaments emerging from the wrist.[28]

The war transformed the bodies of individuals into undifferentiated, rotting flesh. Earth, which had been a comforting and concealing symbol of the patrie in *Gaspard*, became poisoned by mass death in *Le Feu*. Cadavers lined the trenches, physically merging with the cursed earth, itself deformed by thousands of miles of trenches. The narrator himself discovered one night that he had been sleeping on top of the rotting corpse of one of his comrades.[29]

Barbusse never made clear exactly how an international patrie based on socialism would follow from a French military victory, or even what this patrie would look like. Readers, particularly after 1918, have been tempted to focus on the realism of the novel and consider it a powerful protest against the war itself. But all truth is one in Barbusse. The political message

26. See Jay Winter, *Sites of Memory, Sites of Mourning: The Great War in European Cultural History* (Cambridge: Cambridge University Press, 1996), 178–86.

27. Barbusse, *Under Fire*, 315.

28. Ibid., 136.

29. Ibid., 216.

of the book is inextricably linked to how Barbusse construed physicality and survival. Nothing about the reimagined patrie could change the necessity of the war, or what the war did to the body. Dead bodies inhabit the most ideologically insistent parts of the novel. Corporal Bertrand's death both adopted and parodied the crucifixion of Jesus:

> His arms are extended in the shape of a cross, with open hands and fingers stretched. His right leg is reaching to one side while the left, which was broken by a piece of shrapnel, causing the haemorrhage that killed him, is completely turned round, dislocated, soft, with nothing to support it. A sad irony made the last twitches of his dying agony look like the gesticulations of a clown.[30]

Bertrand lived on, not as an individuated being in an afterlife, but as a martyr to an immortal cause. The body in Barbusse's novel, as in Benjamin's, was the physical shell of the self. Both authors expected the individual soldier to sacrifice his body, and his individuality, for the greater cause of the war. Survival, in a diffuse and collective sense, occurred vicariously through the birth of the new and much better world the war was supposed to bring about.

To some extent, the secular mastery of death in Benjamin and Barbusse could both be considered results of the *Union sacrée,* the agreement among the French at the outbreak of the war to focus for the duration on what united them as a political community. This tended to preclude extended public discussions of an afterlife, as far too personal and contentious a subject. Benjamin and Barbusse offered a form of survival in the public sphere that could accommodate a wide array of private views. One could find public comfort in the greater cause, private comfort in religion or spiritualism. But death became too general and too ghastly in the Great War to remain neatly divided between public and private spheres. Individual survival through submersion into the immaterial and immortal archetype, however, was scarcely recognizable as such to most Western sensibilities. In the public sphere of wartime France, the mastery of death ran up against two contradictory requirements: secularism and a need for individuated identity.

These two requirements could be met through imagining a secular resurrection. The best-known attempt to do so came through one of the most famous legends of the war, "Debout les morts!" ("Arise the dead!"). According to the definitive version of the story, on April 8, 1915, Jacques Péricard, a lieutenant in the infantry, was taking part in a disorganized but deadly battle with the Germans. The French had retaken a bit of trench but

30. Ibid., 247.

soon found themselves nearly surrounded by the enemy. Péricard saw French corpses lying all around him, and began to yell at them: "You over there, get up! What are you doing, screwing around on the ground! Get up, and let's get these pigs the hell out of here!"[31] To his great surprise, the dead responded that they would follow him: "And rising to answer my call, their souls mixed with mine and we sent a mass of fire, a vast flood of metal fused together." Crucially, Péricard could not remember exactly what happened next: "There is a hole in what I remember. Action devoured memory."[32] But he clearly remembered some form of bodily transformation:

> As for me, I had the impression of having a body grown immeasurably tall and wide, the body of a giant, with superabundant vigor, unlimited, with an ease of thought that permitted me to look in ten directions at once, to call out an order to one while giving another order by gesture, to fire from my rifle while at the same time getting out of the way of an incoming grenade.[33]

The Germans were finally driven off, thanks not just to fire from the dead, but to sacs of grenades mysteriously found among the sandbags in the trenches. As if any doubt remained, Péricard added: "But it was certainly the dead who had put them there."[34]

Bizarre as the story of "Debout les morts!" seems today, it was taken very seriously at the time as a major media event. Politicians discussed it on the floor of the Senate, newspapers repeated it endlessly, and artists visualized it. But what actually happened in the story remains uncertain in significant details. At no point did Péricard invoke God or any other specific supernatural power. The dead "rose" in some sense, as nameless but clearly individuated human beings. They were not generic spirits sent from the next world, but were attached to the specific corpses on the battlefield. Whether they had physical bodies or not actually remains an open question, as a bit of Péricard's memory swallowed by action. But they could clearly interact with the physical world, by producing sacs of grenades and firing on the enemy. This odd story had its success, I would argue, because it provided for a fleeting, secular resurrection of great usefulness in the ongoing national mobilization. The flexibility of the story meant that it could accommodate a number of views as to the precise relationship between the body

---

31. Maurice Barrès, preface to *Face à face: souvenirs et impressions d'un soldat de la grande guerre,* by Jacques Péricard (Paris: Payot, 1917), 15. The preface is a reprint of the original article by Barrès in *L'Echo de Paris,* 17 November 1915. Barrès claimed simply to be recounting the story of Péricard.

32. Ibid.

33. Ibid., 16.

34. Ibid.

and identity. In whatever form, the dead clearly still lived as individuals somewhere, in a place from which at a special moment they could return to help win the war.

The author and right-wing politician Maurice Barrès, fifty-two years old in 1914, was too old to serve at the front. But he played an indispensable role in popularizing the "Debout les morts!" story, and probably some role in writing it. In his own writings, Barrès went even farther than Péricard by positing a living spiritual identity distinct from the body. "Since the beginning of the war," wrote Barrès in February 1916, "hundreds of thousands of Frenchmen have died, who were worth more than ourselves, who survive them."[35] These dead constituted the elite of the country, and Barrès could not accept "that they should provide no counsel in the reconstruction of the patrie that they have saved."[36] He believed the living had become so ennobled by mourning that the dead somehow lived on in them: "Look at their bearing, listen to their speech, what a transfiguration! It seems as though the soul of the deceased has come to twin that of the survivor."[37] Thus, the dead lived on in the bodies of the living. In recognition of the survival of the soul in the earthly world, he proposed nothing less than giving the dead the right to vote, the *suffrage des morts*. Widows could vote in the names of their husbands. If there was no widow, the father could cast a second vote. The mother could vote if the father were dead. The dead envisaged by Barrès were not ghosts, in the sense of lost and disembodied souls who haunted the living in search of final rest.[38] Rather, they were living, spiritual beings who, for now, did not need their physical bodies. Barrès, here at his most politically imaginative, sought to mobilize them for the war effort as individuated beings. As such, they could play a practical, secular role in daily life on earth.

Secular views of mastery over death sought to include an overt social and political element missing from religious views. The legend of "Debout les morts!" and Barrès's proposal for a *suffrage des morts* showed the lengths to which narrators were willing to go to express the desire for the mastery of death, as well as the problematic results of fulfilling that desire. Secular narratives could prove more odd than religious narratives, which at least admitted that resurrection required supernatural intervention. Solutions to

35. Barrès, Maurice, "Le Suffrage des morts" (2 February 1916), in *Le Suffrage des morts* (Paris: Émile-Paul Frères, 1919), 205.
36. Ibid., 206.
37. Ibid., 207.
38. See also Thomas Kselman, "Alternative Afterlives in the Nineteenth Century," in *Death and the Afterlife in Modern France* (Princeton: Princeton University Press, 1993); and Winter, "Spiritualism and the 'Lost Generation,'" in *Sites of Memory*, 54–77.

the problem of survival such as those of Péricard and Barrès transgressed all sorts of intellectual, religious, and political norms. Secular opinion normally operated in accordance with natural law, which did not allow for the resurrection of the dead. In orthodox Catholicism, resurrection occurs only at the end of time, with the Last Judgment. In addition, two souls do not inhabit one body, ever. Political opinion in a country that did not permit women to vote until 1944 did not welcome the prospect of women casting ballots, on behalf of their deceased husbands or otherwise. In short, secular stories that sought to master death through individuated resurrection did not hold up well because of their internal contradictions.

Mutilation

Mastering mutilation meant mastering not one threat to the self but many. Of course, men for centuries had torn each other apart on the battlefield. Many weapons of the Great War were familiar in the history of warfare—bullets, artillery shells, grenades, knives and clubs. But in addition to a considerable difference in the scale of injury, the Great War also gave rise to new forms of mutilation. Poison gas could mutilate internally, without external loss of blood. Constant shelling inflicted *commotion,* the most common French term for "shell shock," which afflicted the psyches of thousands of soldiers not otherwise harmed. Artillery fire is generally believed to have inflicted at least two-thirds of the wounds in the Great War. Its effects, even more unpredictable than those of bullets, could produce anything from a tiny scratch to a nervous breakdown to complete bodily annihilation. The centrality of artillery in the Great War confused courage and fear and, in many situations, made heroes and cowards interchangeable. Advancing, fleeing, and cowering in place could all prove equally dangerous.

Mutilation might or might not kill the mutilated. But whether the stricken man lived or died, mutilation distorted the intact self by violating the body. Much of the horror of mutilation lay in how public it was in the semi-separate society that emerged at the front. Blood and body parts strewn over the battlefield both defiled the deceased and reminded the living of the arbitrariness of their own survival. Mutilated bodies could putrefy in full view. Mutilated survivors displayed the mark of war every time they stepped out in public for the rest of their lives.

Soldiers had plenty of time to ponder the possibilities and effects of mutilation, given the protracted periods of waiting between major offensives, as well as the grinding and indecisive violence of trench warfare. Anticipation and anxiety became most acute in the hours and minutes before an attack. Never did the flesh seem so vulnerable, or contemplating that vulnerability so horrible, as in the last seconds of relative safety before maximum peril. Jean Bernier, in his novel *La Percée* (The Rupture, 1920), speculated at one such moment that a slow death might be the worst fate:

> And if I catch a bullet in the stomach, if in full consciousness it takes me three days to die stranded in No Man's Land, a ridiculous target, bawling like the wounded at Perthes. "Stretcher-bearers! Have the stretcher-bearers come by here . . . France come to me, I am going to die, come to me, to me!"
>   Pitiless doubling of my being! I see my discolored blue cadaver, hanging from the barbed wire like a fly, bled dry and swaying with the rhythm of the wind in the web of a spider.

Annihilation by a shell, in contrast, would be relatively straightforward and oddly comforting: "An enormous shock, and if I have a beautiful death, annihilating sleep and nothing, forever."[39] For Bernier, the worst thing about such a fate was its permanence, given that he had renounced any form of survival after death. Being nothing for a century seemed somehow fathomable, but not in perpetuity. He envied those who, for religious reasons, foresaw life after death, and even "those made drunk by official mysticism: Alsace, Duty, Patrie!"[40]

More commonly, however, soldiers described bodily obliteration as the most awful potential fate. As a priest, Paul Dubrulle presumably had read countless martyrs' tales depicting the fragmentation of the body as the supreme act of *imitatio Christi*. Presumably, he also believed in the resurrection of the body and in the ultimate mastery of death. Yet he saw the prospect of utter physical destruction as particularly horrifying:

> To die from a bullet seems to be nothing. The parts of our being remain intact. But to be broken into pieces, torn apart, reduced to pulp, there you see an apprehension that the flesh cannot withstand. That is the worst of what suffering is about during a bombardment.[41]

Such anxiety had deep historical roots. As Carolyn Bynum has shown, hell and damnation—beyond which human suffering could not go—for centuries had been depicted in terms of fragmentation of the body and the decay of its parts.[42] The grisly descriptions of Great War testimony thus

39. Jean Bernier, *La Percée* (Paris: Albin Michel, 1920), 219.
40. Ibid., 220.
41. Dubrulle, *Mon régiment dans la fournaise*, xxi–xxvi.
42. See Bynum, *Resurrection of the Body;* and idem, "Material Continuity, Personal Survival and the Resurrection of the Body: A Scholastic Discussion in Its Medieval and Modern

secularized a long religious tradition. At a psychological level, annihilating the body meant annihilating the physical line demarcating the self from the outside world, a primary form of human knowledge. For precisely this reason, theories of survival as part of an archetype or a metaphysical cause proved problematic. There remained something unsatisfying, and to many something impossible, about survival without a body.

In an instant, men could pass from whole, somatic beings to masses of undifferentiated body parts. Soldiers at the time did not spare each other the details of such spectacles. One of them wrote in a trench newspaper in July 1917:

> I see those who previously were two living beings who are not there anymore, now, one a mass of mud and blood, the other a long-stiffened body, the face black, three bullet holes, in the face, in the stomach, and in the legs, and the two fists raised up in defense in front of the face, these two fists who asked for grace and seemed to be rolling like the fists of a boxer to fight off death.[43]

Similarly, a close call enabled infantry officer Maurice Genevoix to imagine in some detail what it would have been like to be killed by a shell explosion.

> It was then that a 210 shell fell on us. I felt it all at once, on the nape of my neck, like a blow from a club, and in front me, like a red and rumbling furnace. Here is how a shell kills you. I did not move my hands, wanting to tuck them into my exposed chest. If I could bring them in toward myself, I would push my two hands into the warmth of my naked viscera. If I were standing in front of myself, I would see my pale trachea, my lungs and my heart through my raised ribs.[44]

Nor did the threat to the body end with disfigurement and death. Ubiquitous rats added not just insult but post-mortem injury by feeding off dead human flesh. In a 1927 novel, René Naegelen wrote of rats paying not quite enough attention to the difference between the living and the dead:

> The cadavers, gnawed up to the tendons, no longer nourished the rats. Still starving, they hid in the shelters, broke into haversacks, attacked provisions, and carried into their holes the scraps of the last meal. They approached

Contexts," in *Fragmentation and Redemption: Essays on Gender and the Human Body in Medieval Religion* (New York: Zone Books, 1992), 239–97.

43. *On progresse*, 1 July 1917, quoted in Stéphane Audoin-Rouzeau, *À travers leurs journaux: 14–18: les combattants des tranchées* (Paris: Armand Colin, 1986), 85.

44. Maurice Genevoix, *Ceux de 14* (Paris: Flammarion, 1950), 596–97.

sleeping soldiers shamelessly, confusing them with the dead and smelling on their faces the odor of the soldier, which is not yet that of the dead.[45]

Of course, all flesh decays once deprived of life. Modern mortuary science evolved precisely to conceal and postpone an inevitable physical process. But the dispersion of the body on the battlefield meant the dispersion of decay. Soldiers could never be sure just when they might come upon broken and rotten body parts. A harrowing poem in the trench newspaper *La Musette* (The Haversack) recounted in 1916:

> The spectacle of them makes us think we are hallucinating
> Tensed up by the supreme effort
> A hideous grimace imprints itself
> On the muddy faces of the dead
> Greenish flesh with pus seeping out
> Eye sockets hollow, heads emptied out
> Stomachs opened when the rats had eaten
> They putrefy, the stiffs.
> On the corpses the vermin
> Each day are born, crawl, and wiggle
> In the mists and the drizzle
> We still hear their death rattle.[46]

Up to a point, witnesses could normalize the most ghastly encounters with the defiled dead. André Pézard wrote in spare language of a "cadaver detail" (*corvée de cadavres*): "all the same, you sleep and you eat near the charnel house, you even work there, and you keep smoking or laughing."[47]

Certainly, authors of many political or ideological stripes used gory depictions of body parts to make a point, as well as to describe life and death in the trenches "as it was." It is not clear that dead bodies and their constituent parts figured quite so prominently in soldiers' daily lives as novels such as *Le Feu* or *Les Suppliciés* might suggest. Whenever possible, and very close to the fighting, armies on both sides went to considerable trouble to bury the dead in marked graves, and even to separate officers from common soldiers.[48] The very fact that Pézard's "cadaver detail" existed at all suggests an attempt to separate the dead from the living as much as pos-

45. René Naegelen, *Les Suppliciés: histoire vecue* (Paris: Éditions Baudinière, 1929), 84.

46. Quoted in Audoin-Rouzeau, *À travers leurs journaux*, 87.

47. André Pézard, *Nous autres à Vauquois, 1915–1916* (Paris: La Renaissance du Livre, 1918), 91.

48. See the collection of articles in "L'Archéologie et la grande guerre," *14–18: aujour-d'hui*, no. 2 (1999): 17–127.

sible. But particularly at the sites of major battles, such as Verdun or the Somme, the mutilated dead regularly made their presence felt.

The Cubist painter Fernand Léger, who knew something about fragmentation, served as a stretcher-bearer during the war. In October 1916, during the later stages of the Battle of Verdun, he made a tour of the battlefields. In a private letter, not published until 1990, he told of bodies rising from the mud into which they had sunk.

> Human debris began to appear as soon as we left the zone where there was still a road. I saw excessively curious things. Almost mummified heads of men emerging from the mud. They were all small in this sea of earth. We thought they were children. The hands were most extraordinary. There were hands I would have wanted to photograph exactly. That's what was most expressive. Several had fingers in their mouths, fingers bitten off with the teeth. I had already seen this on July 12 in the Argonne, a guy who was in so much pain he ate his own hands.[49]

A body in such pain that it inflicted one injury to displace another seemed to tell its own story. As Stéphane Audoin-Rouzeau has noted, Léger observed that the fragmentation of the normal physical world at Verdun seemed like perfect material for what Léger called "my cubist soul" (*mon âme cubiste*).[50] What could cubism add in such a situation, after all, but an attempt through abstraction to detach fragmentation from the pain behind it, and so to master it?

One attempt at mastery of the prospect of mutilation involved a specific reinvention of courage. A soldier could be considered brave, not because he was aggressive or disregarded danger, but rather because he conserved an integrated and self-conscious, embattled self that persisted to the last moment of life. The moral of the story became the presentation of a man who showed himself a man because he remained himself to the end. Mastery was thus individual, fleeting, and highly gendered. Pézard wrote of a gas attack, emphasizing the physical torture of wearing the gas mask itself: "You do not see clearly with the glasses, which make you sweat around the eyelids. You have the mechanism, which dances on your nipples. The air heats up in the box of potassium. That scorches you from the bottom of your lungs to your kidneys. The brain begins to turn. The rubber cannula

49. Fernand Léger to Louis Poughon, 30 October 1916, in *Une correspondance de guerre à Louis Poughon, 1914–1918* (Paris: Les Cahiers du Musée National d'Art Moderne, Hors Série/Archives, 1990), 66.

50. Stéphane Audoin-Rouzeau, "La Correspondance de guerre de Fernand Léger en 1914–1918," *Europe* 75 (1997): 54–55.

makes you want to throw up, and the saliva runs out of the corner of your mouth."[51] Some men could not stand the experience:

> There are the guys who go crazy, who take out the cannula to call for their mothers. They swallow the poison gas, they begin to cough, to spit, to vomit up their guts. They run for the door, they howl, they demolish the partitions by hitting them with the pumps or with their heads, until we go to collect them.[52]

Pézard made clear that he had kept his head while those around him were losing theirs. By remaining "himself," he survived the experience to tell the tale in writing, and to testify to mastery through stoic masculinity.

Likewise, Guy Hallé, in the infantry, framed the prospect of his own annihilation at Verdun with a presentation of a fragile but stoic courage. He sought to direct himself "completely to the feeling one must have; to comport yourself correctly in the face of death. It is not very difficult to say these few words, but what a horrible effort it requires to carry them out, my God!"[53] Heroism in a conventional sense had disappeared. Hallé held no illusion that anything he did was going to affect the battle one way or another. Nor in this situation did he name any cause, national or ideological, that could have rendered his sacrifice meaningful. As he waited to advance, he imagined his bodily annihilation in grisly detail: "There will be a great flame, a cry, next I will be lying there, legs shattered, stomach torn up, all bloody, eyes wide open, and the face completely white!"[54] Yet as the moment to attack approached, Hallé remained "himself," his identity steeped in a male courage frayed but still present: "And always to hang on. I even have a smile on the lips. Oh this smile, how many times have I seen it. This pale smile that trembles just a bit, pulled at the corner of the mouth. You must comport yourself correctly in the face of death."[55]

Jean Norton Cru, a great admirer of Hallé, expanded on this notion of courage. Lecturing at Williams College in 1922, he drew a distinction between "courage" and "heroism." He considered the latter, in the sense of a total disregard for personal danger, a fundamentally irrational and fleeting state of mind. As Norton Cru put it, the hero "was no longer aware of the frailty of his flesh, he moved in the midst of frightful dangers with steadiness and precision, he acted in a sort of hallucination, in a world un-

51. Pézard, *Nous autres à Vauquois,* 296.
52. Ibid., 296.
53. Guy Hallé, *Là bas avec ceux qui souffrent* (Paris: Garnier Frères, 1917), 32.
54. Ibid., 34.
55. Ibid.

real, all his mental powers excited and sharpened, but bent towards one single aim: the mission to be accomplished."[56] He described heroism as a "fit" that is "generally attended by death." "Courage," on the other hand, was a more daily, rational struggle:

> Courage was a painful struggle against fear, an inner strife between body and soul, a breathless wrangle between the rearing snorting animal that shrank from suffering and destruction—and the mind that listened to duty, or stuck blindly to self respect. The torture attending this miserable dispute was intolerable; one would have accepted any physical pain in exchange.

Courage had little to do with physical survival, as shells and bullets brought death to hero and coward alike, most often arbitrarily. Courage was something that happened in time, through the self-construction of a certain kind of mastery, a narrator who could describe a sequence of emotions, tied together with an absolute, internalized notion of stoic behavior in extreme danger. Norton Cru as witness and Norton Cru as a critic of testimony had the same goal—the creation of a narrator and a narrative of courage that could survive, regardless of the fate of the author as a person.

Historical discussions of the body usually turn to discussions of sexuality. Considering the durable stereotype of the oversexed Frenchman, most published testimonies were notably restrained, even chaste.[57] Women seldom figured prominently in wartime novels, including such bestsellers as Barbusse's *Le Feu* or Roland Dorgelès's *Les Croix de bois*. When they did, they were often either angelic or dangerous figures, such as the month-old corpse of Euxodie in *Le Feu*, who in death and decay tried to "kiss" a horrified soldier she had rebuffed coldly in life. The easygoing homoeroticism so familiar in British wartime literature was much more rare in published testimony from France, either during the war or after.[58] Sometimes, such as in *Les Croix de bois*, the misfortunes of combat hurled living and dead men into quasi-kisses, as a symbol of the perversity of the war itself.[59] In

56. Jean Norton Cru, "Courage and Fear in Battle: According to Tradition and in the Great War," lecture delivered 14 February 1922 at Williams College in the series of Weekly Public Lectures by the Faculty, Fonds Norton Cru, Bibliothèque universitaire, Aix-en-Provence, Cote Ms. 75.

57. Postcards, on the other hand, quite exuded sexuality. Pronatalist postcards particularly celebrated sexual reunions during leaves, so that soldiers could impregnate their wives and thus increase the dismal wartime birth rate. See Marie-Monique Huss, *Histoires de famille: cartes postales et culture de guerre* (Paris: Noêsis, 2000).

58. On British homoeroticism see Paul Fussell, "Soldier Boys," in *The Great War and Modern Memory* (New York: Oxford University Press, 1975), 270–309.

59. On these incidents see Smith, "Masculinity, Memory," 254–55.

an intriguing Freudian interpretation, George Mosse argued that Europeans in the modern era channeled sexual energy into nation building.[60] Intact bodies representing the nation might be presented as beautiful and nude, but they had to be chaste, almost cold, for the desires and libidinal energies contained within them had to be repressed and redirected toward the collectivity. Many témoins wrote as though this were the case.

Yet the prospect of battle seemed to put a certain sensuality back into the intact body. Soldiers marveled at the precarious and arbitrary line demarcating their whole physical beings from the mutilation they witnessed all around them. Hallé wrote of waiting to attack at Verdun:

> To say to your self: at this moment I am myself. I am entirely me. My blood circulates and pulses through my arteries. My eyes are where they should be, and all my skin is intact. I do not bleed. If they stopped this horrible war right now, right away, I would be able to stretch out and sleep in the sun. Oh, to sleep knowing that it is over, that I will live, that I will have joys and pains, sorrows and pleasures. That I will not be killed.[61]

The experience of simply feeling intact had conferred a sublimeness which he dreamed of making continuous. Somatic integrity at its most fragile moment gave the most mundane feelings an extraordinary character.

Jean Bernier approached a kind of autoeroticism in paying tribute to the sensuality of his whole but imperiled body:

> Oh the blood inside my body, fluid to the exquisite touch which, returning in its goodness, reeducates my body. My blood that I feel lick with the smoothness of velvet, first at the flesh in my core, then my appendages, the ravaged confines of my empire!
> I find you again, my stomach, and you, my individual fingers, which I name anew one after the other, commanding each to move. I return to my plenitude, and this second universe that is myself, hollow, as it must be so that I can be a man, fills again with life.[62]

Extreme danger created an extraordinary narrative space that slowed time and heightened sensation. To Bernier, his body in this moment became its own self-contained universe, through which he sought to conserve psychosomatic wholeness by the simple act of commanding his fingers to move.

It is perhaps unsurprising that soldiers would become fascinated in a sen-

---

60. George Mosse, *Nationalism and Sexuality: Middle-Class Morality and Sexual Norms in Modern Europe* (New York: Oxford University Press, 1985).
61. Hallé, *Là bas,* 32.
62. Bernier, *La Percée,* 84.

sual way by their own bodies at the moment of extreme danger. Perhaps more surprising is a very sensual fascination with the bodies of colonial soldiers, particularly Black Africans. Barbusse's previously noted characterization of Black African soldiers as natural brutes seems broadly representative of soldiers' testimonies in most situations. The Africans were bloodthirsty savages when fighting the Germans, though many accounts portrayed them as cheerful and friendly, if garrulous and simple-minded, toward their white French comrades. But particularly, accounts from medical personnel illustrated an undisguised erotic appreciation of colonial male bodies. Most French soldiers, it bears noting, had probably never seen a body of color at close range before the war. The "otherness" of colonials' bodies, perhaps, encoded and thus authorized an eroticized appreciation of vulnerable male flesh, an appreciation normally reserved for one's own body.

Abbé Félix Klein helped care for some of the first wounded colonial soldiers in the fall of 1914. The kindly if usually austere Klein recounted bathing a soldier from Guinea, slightly wounded in the head:

> The white bubbles on his bronze skin exaggerated his powerful muscles and the harmonious proportions of his huge body. The doctor greatly admired it. Because there were no other patients waiting, we did not hurry. The beautiful Negro benefited from the operation.[63]

Pierre La Mazière, after having served in the infantry in the Champagne, volunteered as a nurse in the Dardanelles. He went even further in explaining the appeal of Black Africans:

> Their distress, the tender thankfulness they show once the fear we inspire in them passes and they understand what we are doing for them, are hardly the only things that make me love these Negroes. They are beautiful! If you exclude their flat feet and their calves which are too thin, they have splendid forms; the large legs of women, torsos bulging admirably with muscles. As for their skin, it is so soft, and sweet, that you understand, in some way, why the whites were wanting to touch it.[64]

The colonial body was familiar in its maleness, yet "other" in its color and in a certain androgyny. Témoins never wrote about white male bodies in this way, at least not in published testimony.

63. Abbé Félix Klein, *La Guerre vue d'une ambulance* (Paris: Librairie Armand Colin, 1915), 203–4.

64. Pierre La Mazière, *L'H.C.F.: l'Hôpital Chirurgical Flottant* (Paris: Albin Michel, 1919), 111.

Bodies of color, of course, were as vulnerable to mutilation as white bodies. Descriptions of mutilated colonials were underpinned by an assumption that they could have no idea what cause they were fighting for. "Guillaume, michant" ("Mean [Kaiser] Wilhelm," spoken with an African accent) was all they were assumed to know about the war. As La Mazière put it:

> I really think it is the Negroes that make me feel the most compassion and that I would most like to spare from pain, and to make happy. Such distress, such terror is painted on their childlike faces, when they come out to the treatment rooms. They are such ignorant victims of the reasons for which they are being slaughtered![65]

This pity for the infantilized colonial subject authorized particularly sensual depictions of assistance. La Mazière wrote of an episode in September 1915, when he was caring for a Black soldier whose leg was in shreds:

> I took the poor Black in my arms to help him. I leaned over him on the table. He head rested on my chest. He continued to scream. Huge tears rolled down his cheeks. I felt sorry for him, cuddled him, I cradled him. At one point, I told him he was a handsome guy [*beau garçon*]!
> Then, with his lovely smile, he stretched out his arms and kissed me [*m'embrasse*]. I was truly moved. I could even say that few things caused me so much emotion as the gesture of this poor savage who turned to me in his distress.[66]

Colonials in these accounts became simultaneously adults and children, men with some of the appeal and emotions of women. Whether this sensuality amounted to actual erotic desire or not is a matter of opinion. But it does illustrate a curious attempt at mastery, in taking advantage of an unusual narrative space to break through conventional restraints of race, gender, and sexuality. In so tenderly describing the broken bodies of colonials, the author could grant himself permission to confess the vulnerability of the sexed body and the male self more generally. Applied to colonial soldiers, pity also provided a straightforward and even gentle way to remind narrator and readers that colonial hierarchies were still present, even in a situation in which destruction rained down equally on colonizers and colonized.

Pity in general provided its own form of mastery. Accounts from the *mutilés* themselves did not figure prominently in published testimony. Self-pity,

65. Ibid., 108.
66. Ibid., 43–44.

of course, was unlikely to prove a commercially appealing option in the competitive marketplace of testimony.[67] Pity expressed by those not mutilated, however, could reinforce the boundary that was so arbitrary in actual combat between the stricken and the spared, and could somehow enable readers to imagined they experienced mutilation vicariously. Some of the most important writing about the wounded came from women, most often nurses.[68] Perhaps in the gendered politics of publishing, women were deemed "naturally" suited to convey pity. The most famous man to write from a position of pity was Georges Duhamel, a medical officer turned pillar of the postwar literary establishment. His narratives of the *mutilé*, sometimes maudlin and sometimes searingly poignant, sought aesthetically to ennoble them, and thus in some sense to redeem their suffering. As though their rescuer, Duhamel tried to reclaim some traces of humanity on their behalf by skillfully telling their horrible stories. He integrated their stories into his own narrative of mastery.

In 1928 Duhamel published *Les Sept Dernières Plaies* (The Last Seven Wounds), which concluded with a vignette recounting the transition from war to postwar at a medical station near the front. As the war dragged into the late autumn of 1918, the narrator had become an efficient cog in the war machine: "I was operating, better and better, quicker and quicker, on men who remained unknown to me, even their nationality. The triumph of Taylorism."[69] On November 6, what proved the last group of wounded arrived—eleven men, of whom six were only lightly injured. One of the remaining five was in grave condition: "From the first, Choquet gave me the greatest concern. He had a terrible wound—a crushed spinal cord, the lower limbs separated from the rest of the body by an irreversible paralysis."[70] The narrator lied to Choquet, telling him that the paralysis was only temporary.

The war ended five days later, meaning that strictly speaking everyone still alive had survived the war. "The war," the narrator declared with highly mitigated joy, "became brusquely a fact of another age. Each one began to think about his own affairs. Each one sought to leave the gaming table as soon as possible. Human life became once again, for the whole world, a precious thing. It was like money to the prodigal who discovers

67. This would change somewhat by the 1930s, as self-pity became laced with self-loathing in the successful works of Pierre Drieu la Rochelle and Louis-Ferdinand Céline.
68. See Margaret Darrow, "White Angels of the Battlefield," in *French Women and the First World War: War Stories of the Home Front* (Oxford: Berg, 2000).
69. Georges Duhamel, *Les Sept Dernières Plaies* (Paris: Mercure de France, 1928), 273.
70. Ibid., 277.

all of a sudden, after insane dissipation, the extent of his ruin."[71] Yet Choquet's deteriorating form of survival reminded the narrator that he could not disentangle war and postwar experience easily. One by one, the other wounded men recovered enough to be evacuated behind the lines. Choquet's condition continued to worsen, and the body began to break down even before death:

> Great ulcerous wounds rose all over the poor paralyzed body stretched out on the litter. What's more, the man could no longer control his bodily functions. Choquet, despite all our care, lived like Job on his own dung heap. For better or worse, he had become used to the smell of this misery. But he understood that it afflicted the people alongside him and it made him gloomier.[72]

Ever more plaintively, Choquet continued to ask when it would be his turn to be evacuated.

Paradoxically, caring for Choquet clearly had a restorative effect on the narrator. He admitted to the reader that he had become an "automaton." "I can tell you this. Choquet returned me to myself. I understood that he made me a man again."[73] The dying man had awakened enough moral sensibility in the narrator to enable him to carry out a final act of humanity. With Choquet's demise clearly approaching, the narrator came up with a scheme to give him the impression that he was being evacuated. He told Choquet that a car had been arranged to take him away the next morning. Somewhat to the narrator's surprise, Choquet was still alive when the car came:

> We cleaned him thoroughly, before sliding him into a plaster cast that looked a bit like an unconventional sarcophagus. He was laughing. Yes, I can affirm it, he was laughing and his face expressed such great confidence that, since then, I have always thought of it when I hear a man making his plans. He was laughing.[74]

The car left, to return only a short time later. Scarcely three kilometers on, Choquet died. Yet the conspirators had their small triumph over death. As the driver told the narrator: "Go look at him. You might say he is still laughing."[75]

71. Ibid., 281–82.
72. Ibid., 283.
73. Ibid.
74. Ibid., 294.
75. Ibid., 295.

It takes nothing from the poignancy of the story, and is no reproach to the author, to observe that the moral has more to do with the narrator than with the deceased. Duhamel the survivor and witness emerged as a narrator, a figure who could tell the story of the mutilated Choquet and correctly discern its meaning. The story itself was about what Wilfred Owen called "the pity of war," a famous expression from a 1917 poem with which Duhamel by 1928 was surely familiar.[76] The story spoke of both the waste of life and the surprising forms of humanity that could emerge under such ghastly circumstances. In caring for Choquet, the narrator had regained a part of his own humanity, and consequently had mastered his own wartime experience. Duhamel as narrator and author could thus bring that experience and its significance to the public sphere.

Of course, mutilation did not always kill the mutilated. The 1.3 million French soldiers killed in the Great War tended to overshadow some 2.8 million who were wounded, 1 million of them at least twice. Over 900,000 Frenchmen received some sort of pension for a war wound as of 1919.[77] The Great War showed the great resilience of the human body at a time before plasma and antibiotics, when even sterile surgery could not always be taken for granted. The *mutilé de guerre* from the Great War remained a visible public presence in France long after World War II. To this day, the *mutilés* receive the highest-priority seating on the Paris Metro, even though not a great many remain alive from any war, let alone that of 1914–18.

Sophie Delaporte has studied one of the most macabre and famous groups of wounded, the *gueules cassées* (usually translated as "the men with broken faces").[78] Given how much of individual identity is invested in facial appearance, she argued, severe facial wounds challenged and transformed the mutilated in ways not comparable even to those with amputated arms or legs. Sometimes the *gueules cassées* could not imagine survival, in the sense of fitting their injury into some kind of continuing narrative of their lives. Nurse Henriette Rémi accompanied a young father named Lazé on a home leave during his recuperation. Upon his arrival, Lazé picked up his son, who began to scream, "Not papa! Not papa!" Lazé was devastated. As Rémi described his reaction: "Having been a man, having committed all he had fully to realize what this word means, and to have

---

76. See Wilfred Owen, "Strange Meeting" (probably 1917), in *The Lost Voices of World War I,* ed. Tim Cross (Iowa City: University of Iowa Press, 1989), 79.

77. Total figures remain uncertain and controversial. See the sober assessment in Antoine Prost, *Les Anciens Combattants et la société française,* 3 vols. (Paris: Presses de la Fondation Nationale des Sciences Politiques, 1977), 2:22–27.

78. Sophie Delaporte, *Les Gueules cassées: les blessés de la face de la grande guerre* (Paris: Noêsis, 1996).

come to this. An object of terror for his own child, a daily burden for his wife, a source of shame for humanity. 'Let me die.'"[79] Lazé killed himself after returning to the hospital.

It appears as though such responses were relatively rare, though no study exists of suicide rates among veterans, mutilated or otherwise. Certainly follow-up was rare for the psychologically maimed, the *commotionnés* or shell-shocked.[80] Delaporte has shown that unlike them the *gueules cassées* developed networks of support and tended to their brethren from the time they entered the hospital. Hospital wards of similarly wounded men lent themselves to the recasting of primary group solidarities. After the war, many became revered figures in their communities, even if veneration became mixed with an awkward fascination.

Soldiers' and veterans' newspapers provided means through which the voices of the *gueules cassées* could enter the public sphere. These newspapers, in fact, constitute an important exception to the relative silence in the published record of the testimonies of the wounded. More common than suicidal tendencies were stubborn attempts on the part of the *gueules cassées* to master their experience. Sometimes this took the form of self-deprecating humor, such as one soldier's observation that "in the here below, everything passes, beauty is only a plaything."[81] Sometimes attempted mastery took the form of trying to seize and transform beauty itself, as in a poem by E. Poiteau published in a survivors' newspaper in 1933:

> O faces without eyes, O faces without jaws,
> That the infamous trench one day threw out.
> O you who the pestle of glory massacred
> I love you much more than all the beauties!
> Human vomit of the poor patrie,
> Bloody tatters of our days of sorrow,
> Who carry, burned in your flesh, the seal of pain
> Formless rejects of the murderous earth
> I love you more than if you were beautiful![82]

Probably the most famous literary figure in France who wrote about his mutilation was Blaise Cendrars. If Cendrars did not attempt to redefine

---

79. Henriette Rémi, *Hommes sans visages* (Lausanne: S.P.E.S, 1942), quoted ibid., 133.

80. See the articles in "Le choc traumatique et l'histoire culturelle de la grande guerre," *14–18: aujourd'hui,* no. 3 (2000): 23–137.

81. *La Greffe générale,* no. 2, January 1918, quoted in Delaporte, *Les Gueules cassées,* 137.

82. E. Poiteau, "Les Gueules cassées," *Bulletin de l'Union des blessés de la face,* August 1933, quoted ibid., 164.

beauty, he did seek to master his experience through narrative. He interrogated the meaning of his amputation in ways that were both highly abstract and entirely rooted in his own anxiety about psychosomatic wholeness. But by definition, survival remained unfinished business.

In a vignette entitled "Le Lys rouge" (The Red Lily) from *La Main coupée* (The Severed Hand, 1946), Cendrars sought to master survival in a surreal and harrowing setting. The story took an abrupt turn midway through, when he abandoned "realism" in the sense of events empirically plausible. On a beautiful sunny day in June 1915 (a few months before Cendrars lost his arm), he and his comrades were wandering through a very quiet sector of the front, chatting and passing time before lunch. Suddenly one of the comrades started screaming and pointing to something that had fallen to the ground some distance away.

> planted in the grass like a great flower in full bloom, a red lily, a human arm with blood running down it, a right arm severed below the elbow and from which the hand, still living, was burrowing into the soil, the bloody fingers delicately balancing themselves before it to maintain its equilibrium.[83]

At first, they suspected that the arm had somehow fallen from an airplane, even though they had heard or seen no trace of one. They telephoned all around the sector and were told that there had been no amputations that morning. Finally, as insects settled around the hand, the men gave up their search for its provenance. After all, lunch was waiting.

Mutilation, survival, and witness were all bound up in this image. Of course, the severed hand prophesied Cendrars's amputation, but beyond that it remains ambiguous and troubling. We can read the story of the red lily as part of Cendrars's foredoomed quest for wholeness despite his amputation. The lily, of course, is often a symbol of death, though here it is a bright, blood-red lily of the garden variety. The color seems to confuse the image, and further to muddle the line demarcating life and death in the story. For a terrifying moment, Cendrars was *both* the red lily and the surviving body that was observing it. It was explicitly identified as a right hand, the one Cendrars wrote with before his injury. Clearly, the hand had some volition of its own. It struggled for some sort of balance while trying to dig itself into the soil, the soil of the front, as if to bury itself. The red lily was actually upside down; its most visible part of the hand was the bloody stump, the point at which it was severed from the surviving body—unless, of course, one read the stump itself as the flower.

---

83. Blaise Cendrars, *La Main coupée* (1946; repr., Paris: Denöel, 1991), 409.

The story ended with Cendrars's acceptance of his separation from the severed hand. He survived independent of the red lily and the will to death that seemed to guide it. The red lily dug its grave, and bugs crawled over it. It would rot and cease to exist. Cendrars came to imagine survival as inherently ambiguous, like the mystery of the red lily: "Never did we find the key to the enigma."[84] Life went on in its most mundane forms—the men simply wandered off to lunch. Survival, to Cendrars was the unending process of imagining survival. Perhaps the most masterful of French writers of the Great War acknowledged the impossibility of mastering the experience of his mutilation.

Killing: The Defeat of the Just Warrior

Actual killing is surprisingly elusive in Great War testimonies. Millions died; very few indeed seemed to have killed. Certainly, this reticence to discuss the taking of life concurred with a dichotomy of victim and brute. A victim by definition was unable to conserve his own life, let alone take that of another. The brute took life and enjoyed doing so. But brutes were the war's elite, just numerous enough to prove that the vast majority comprised simple victims. Beyond these discursive constructs, the relative silence on killing has something to do with how men actually died in the Great War. The fact that most casualties were inflicted by artillery meant that most of the dead were killed from hundreds, sometimes thousands of meters away. Trench mortars were designed to fire shells at relatively short range, but with a high trajectory, so that they would land directly on top of the enemy trenches. In other words, artillery and mortars were weapons designed to strike at a largely invisible enemy. Machine guns were designed primarily to create a wide lethal zone that would kill anyone who entered it. Much of the killing in the Great War took place under conditions not much less anonymous than those of war from the air today.

What, then, did it mean to master the experience of killing in the Great War? If killing meant firing the weapons that caused death, the more soldiers killed, the less they wrote about it. The challenge to narration seems to have been not killing in the abstract or in the aggregate, but in the material and the particular. Wishing general death and destruction on the enemy, and even firing lethal weapons in his direction, seemed an experience easy enough to master. Taking the life of an individuated human being in an enemy uniform—whose life at that moment closely mirrored one's own—proved quite another. To make clear just who was a perpetrator and

84. Ibid., 410.

who was not, témoins could posit very restrictive definitions of killing. Norton Cru, for example, was quite sure that he had never killed, nor had he witnessed anyone else do so, under the following somewhat cumbersome definition: "I have never seen a soldier commit the act that killed a man who I saw die."[85] Maurice Genevoix likewise defined killing rather obliquely, as a situation in which "I felt as such the presence and the life of the men on whom I was firing."[86]

Yet individuated human beings sometimes did kill other individuated human beings. Infantry-to-infantry combat had been quite common when armies collided into one another in August 1914. Even thereafter, raids and patrols frequently brought soldiers on opposite sides into direct contact. When a trench was taken, the grim business of *nettoyage des tranchées* (literally "cleansing" the trenches) often meant killing enemy survivors.[87] This kind of personalized killing posed a particular narratological problem. Most narrators wanted to present themselves, in effect, as the heirs to Renaissance humanism—rational, self-conscious, morally autonomous beings. Reconciling this self with the experience of killing, or even narrating the killing, of others and thus "mastering" that experience proved surprisingly difficult, and subject to many inconsistencies.

Logically, this should not have been a problem, as it would seem that the act of donning a uniform in wartime should imply assent to the act of killing. On the face of it, killing ought to have been an easily mastered experience. As noted, Just War theory presented a logical calculus of cost and benefit, weighing the evil of killing another human being versus the good of the triumph of the Just Cause. This calculus seemed to work well enough in the abstract, and for those who killed Germans they never saw. Yet Just War theory and the Just Warrior created by it seemed curiously unsuited to killing in the particular. Most accounts of such experience proved circumspect, elliptical, and full of internal peculiarities.

No one killed more men they could not see than artillerymen, but few wrote less about killing. Paul Lintier was a young and very reflective artilleryman who wrote two volumes of recollections before he was killed in 1916. Presumably, he participated in firing hundreds of shells that killed

85. Jean Norton Cru, *Témoins: essai d'analyse et de critique des souvenirs de combattants édités en français de 1915 à 1928* (1929; repr., Nancy: Presses Universitaires de Nancy, 1993), 567. The French reads: "Je n'ai jamais vu un soldat accomplissant le geste qui tuait un homme que je voyais mourir."

86. *Ceux de 14*, 44. The French reads: "j'ai senti en tant que telles la présence et la vie des hommes sur qui je tirais."

87. On the circumstances of killing, see Antoine Prost, "Les Limites de la brutalization: tuer sur le front occidental, 1914–1918," *Vingtième Siècle: Revue d'histoire* 81 (2004): 5–20.

Germans. But he seldom saw any direct evidence of what he had done, and came to describe his duties as a kind of industrial work. For example, sometime during the night of October 19, 1915, Lintier was awakened by orders to fire on Battery Z. They fired some fifteen rounds, then fifteen flares to try to determine what, if anything, their shells had hit. He saw the six men of the German battery "in motion around a rectangular hole, in a vision of a bloody inferno." But he could not tell whether any of the enemy had been killed or wounded, only that fire from the battery had ceased. So his men simply closed up their artillery pieces and went back to sleep.[88] On March 13, 1916, just two days before he was killed, Lintier wrote:

> One of the most certain characteristics of the present war is its fastidious uniformity. Danger and death always present themselves in more or less the same manner. Nothing resembles a shell so much as another shell. [. . .] The abrupt return of danger, the rustling sound of death itself is no longer unforeseen.
> [. . .] If the truth be told, the notebook of souvenirs of a combatant should not be exempt from a great deal of monotony.[89]

Captain Jules Émile Henches was a professional officer commanding a battery of artillery. As previously noted, he had expressed some concern in his letters to his wife as to the damage he had been involved in inflicting during his initiation to combat in 1914. But such empathetic references, in which he never provided details, disappeared afterward, down to the time of his death in October 1916. He recounted one episode that took place on November 15, 1915. After midnight, he telephoned a series of orders to the artillery pieces under his command to bombard a German position some five kilometers away, and then calmly went back to sleep. For the next five hours, he concluded laconically, the Germans received "some shells that must have bothered them—at least I hope so."[90]

Some accounts from the infantry took the formulation of the Just Warrior at face value. A few swashbuckling heroic narratives exist, in which the French killed cheerfully and triumphantly without attention to gory detail. But such accounts proved much more rare than one might think, even in the most patriotic wartime testimonies, perhaps because they had nothing to offer about how to explain or resolve the stalemated war. Somewhat

---

88. Paul Lintier, *Avec une batterie de 75, Le Tube 1233: souvenirs d'un chef de pièce, 1915–1916* (1917; repr., Paris: Éditions L'Oiseau de Minerve, 1998), 61–64.

89. Ibid., 277.

90. Jules Émile Henches, *À l'école de guerre: letters d'un artilleur* (Paris: Hachette, 1918), 121.

less rare and certainly more interesting were accounts that explained killing according to a simple if brutal moral calculus. While these accounts might strike readers today as coldhearted, they did no more than hold the Just War to its own logic. They sought to master killing by rendering it entirely rational. Accepting the war meant accepting fighting it, and accepting fighting it meant accepting killing.

In 1977 the historian Antoine Prost published a short narrative by Daniel Pechmalbec, taken from a collection of 425 unpublished accounts brought together in the 1960s. On the morning of September 10, 1916, Pechmalbec spied a German walking above the trenches with a bucket in each hand. The Frenchman posed his Lebel rifle on the parapet, and fired twice. The German disappeared. Pechmalbec never knew if the German had been killed, wounded, or had simply jumped into a shell hole at the sound of the first shot. By Norton Cru's definition, this would not have even counted as a killing. But Pechmalbec plainly believed that he acted in a way consistent with killing, whether he succeeded in doing so or not. And he drew a simple moral to his short story.

> What I can affirm—not to boast, but because it is the truth—is that I never felt the least emotion or the least moral scruple at firing on a man, and on a man who had done me no harm. We were there to kill the Boche. He would have done the same to me at the first opportunity. It was war. They had given us a rifle, and it was up to us to make use of it. I fired on him as I would have fired on a rabbit. And, should I admit it? I had as much pleasure at seeing my Boche disappear as seeing a rabbit running at full speed roll over on itself after getting hit by a rifle shot.[91]

No less unapologetic in its use of the calculus of the Just Warrior was an account published in September 2001 by Lucien Laby, a medical student mobilized and sent to the front in September 1914. As we saw in chapter 1, Laby had shown compassion toward grievously wounded Germans in his care, though at the same time he confessed to some yearning to kill the enemy in combat. In November 1914 he got his chance during a small but deadly incident while he was trying to make his way back to his medical station. With fire all around from artillery, machine guns, grenades, rifles, and revolvers, Laby got involved in the fighting. Once he reached his destination, he wrote:

---

91. Prost, *Anciens Combattants*, 3:16. Selections from this collection were subsequently published in Roger Boutefeu, *Les Camarades: soldats français et allemands au combat 1914–1918* (Paris: Fayard, 1966).

> Sigh of relief. I killed, I hope, my Boche, and perhaps several of them. I have
> done my duty as a Frenchman. It took me a while to do so. And now, it is
> with a better heart that I will do my duty as a doctor.[92]

Laby presented a simple, highly gendered affirmation of himself as a
Frenchman, a citizen-soldier of the Republic. The active citizen fights and
kills for his country. The national community, in essence, had solved his
moral problem for him by calling him to war for a Just Cause. Like Pechmalbec, Laby personalized the duty of killing—any "Boches" he would kill
were uniquely his own, as though they were hunted prey. Having dis-
patched them legitimized and thus supported his other duty, caring for the
wounded. Killing and caregiving thus became two sides of the same coin.
He killed because he was a soldier and he helped heal because he was a
physician. Both were duties in which he could take a just pride.

This satisfaction at taking human life could prove a potentially difficult
issue, given that the Just Warrior was supposed to be motivated by a strict
cost-benefit analysis. One solution, alluded to by Laby, was to place killing
in a broader context of "duty," the fulfillment of which in its totality could
be a source of just pride. Some stories left out the question of emotion entirely. Philippe Barrès (son of Maurice Barrès) had a thoughtful answer to
the problem of how the killer should feel about killing. The specific act of
killing simply responded to circumstance. Hatred needed to concern itself
only after the fact, and thus to some extent could be separated from the act
itself. In a semifictional novel *La Guerre à vingt ans* (War at Twenty Years
Old, 1924), the younger Barrès recounted an incident in which a soldier
(notably not himself) found himself in a situation similar to that of Pechmalbec. He saw the opportunity to shoot an unsuspecting German soldier
and did so. When asked whether he had killed out of hatred, the perpetrator responded:

> Hatred is the desire for an extreme solution: to strike down, to kill. Hatred
> develops in the pleasure of a peaceful life. But in the domain in which ad-
> ministering death is such a frequent act, this bitterness seldom accumulates,
> being too often satisfied. One kills simply because it is the sole persuasive ar-
> gument.[93]

In other cases, the lack of emotion at the death of the enemy could be expressed coldly. Laby recounted an episode from October 1915 in which the

---

92. Lucien Laby, *Les Carnets de l'aspirant Laby, médicin des tranchées, 28 juillet 1914–
14 juillet 1919*, ed. Sophie Delaporte (Paris: Bayard, 2001), 80.
93. Philippe Barrès, *La Guerre à vingt ans* (Paris: Plon, 1924), 109.

French brought him a German soldier with a bullet in his stomach. According to the Geneva Conventions, enemy wounded were supposed to receive equal medical treatment without regard to nationality, under the supervision of the Red Cross.[94] Laby had indeed intended to care for him, once all the French wounded had been attended to. Seldom one to explain himself in detail, he wrote: "When I went to take care of him the next morning—he had croaked [*claqué*], my stretcher-bearers having had the kindness to offer him chocolate!"[95] Of course, all of the medical personnel knew full well that eating anything with a stomach wound meant certain death. But Laby could recount such a deed in the most matter-of-fact manner. The German had simply croaked. He found no words of reproach for the stretcher-bearers, even after the fact. As Stéphane Audoin-Rouzeau noted, Laby reacted strongly to reports of German atrocities in Belgium. Perhaps in a more immediate sense, Laby did not regret contemplating German suffering, given the scale of French suffering the mobilized medical student had to encounter on a daily basis.[96] Yet the Just Warrior's moral calculus of cost and benefit did not allow for revenge. Those who sought revenge, or who even took satisfaction in the revenge of others, became less just. It seems revealing that blunt assertions such as those of Pechmalbec and Laby tended to be published only decades after the fact.

Both in wartime and in the tortured peace that followed, testimony to killing seemed to require more decorous, or at least more ambivalent, narratives and narrators. Anxiety about killing could take many forms. In a prayer, Frédéric de Bélinay, a mobilized Jesuit, asked God, "If possible, preserve me from having to kill."[97] Yet what was actually at stake in such a request? As a member of an order renowned for its commitment to education, de Bélinay presumably had long been exposed to the theology of the Just War. At no point did he reject the present war, or the implicit necessity of killing in order to win that war. Nor did he request that no one die or that his comrades not have to kill. He asked only not to have to do so himself.

In 1950 Maurice Genevoix published *Ceux de 14,* a compilation of five volumes of témoignage published between 1916 and 1922.[98] The compi-

94. On treatment of the wounded, see Annette Becker, *Oubliés de la grande guerre, humanitaire et culture de guerre: populations occupées, déportés civils, prisonniers de guerre* (Paris: Noêsis, 1998), 273–76.

95. Laby, *Les Carnets de l'aspirant,* 131.

96. Stéphane Audoin-Rouzeau, "Avant-propos," ibid., 11.

97. De Bélinay, *Sur le sentier de la guerre,* 111.

98. *Ceux de 14* comprises *Sous Verdun* (1916), *Nuits de guerre* (1917), *Au seuil des guitounes* (1918), *La Boue* (1921), and *Les Eparges* (1923).

lation comprised nearly seven hundred printed pages recording only eight months of service at the front, narrated with the attention to detail for which Genevoix had become famous. He included two references to his involvement in killing, each in less than one page in length. We have already seen Genevoix's restricted definition of killing, a situation in which "I felt as such the presence and the life of the men on whom I was firing."

The second incident, which took place on February 18, 1915, proved by far the more straightforward of the two. The French had conquered a small piece of ground near Les Eparges south of Verdun. In a bloody German counterattack in which several of his comrades were killed, Genevoix and two comrades found themselves set upon by an enraged German soldier, "all alone, his fists clenched on his rifle, making his way down the collapsed ground, the eyes fixed, the face contracted as though in a kind of orgasm."[99] The three Frenchmen fired: "we saw the German let go a savage cry, drop his rifles while grabbing his stomach with his two hands, and fall over as though into a hole." Two other Germans appeared. The French likewise fired on them, and "they disappeared [*disparu*], both of them." There seemed little more to explain. The enraged German left little doubt as to his intent, and Genevoix and his comrades needed to defend themselves.

But Genevoix's first experience in killing proved another matter altogether. On the night of September 10, 1914, in the first month of the war, Genevoix was trying to get some sleep in his open-air encampment. Suddenly he began to hear bullets flying overhead. He heard boots pounding into the mud and cries of "Hurrah! Hurrah! Vorwärts [forward]!" The scene descended into total confusion, with explosions, rifle fire, and cries of wounded and dying on both sides. Suddenly isolated and surrounded by German cries, Genevoix saw a German corpse right next to him. He took the helmet from the deceased, put it on, and began to follow the Germans: "And like the Boches, I cry 'Hurrah! Vorwärts!' And like them, I mutter a word that they recognize in the dark of night, which is *Heiligthum* [literally, 'holy place'!]."[100] Between the mud and the darkness, Genevoix evidently fit in easily enough with his enemies, who in the confusion failed to detect either a French uniform or a French accent. Genevoix managed safely to restore contact with his French comrades. In the meantime, the French had rallied, and the Germans disappeared as quickly as they appeared.

But the key to the incident lay in a short paragraph, in which Genevoix described actually killing three Germans:

99. Ibid., 572.
100. Ibid., 44.

Yet, before rallying the troops, I came across three isolated German soldiers, each running behind the other at the same pace. I fired a bullet from my revolver into the head or back of each of them. Each one collapsed, with the same strangled cry.[101]

A man who chose his words with formidable skill, Genevoix did not use any form of the verb "to kill" (*tuer*). He shot the Germans and they fell, each with the same strangled cry. Most readers, of course, would infer that Genevoix had killed them. The matter appeared straightforward. Genevoix fulfilled the duty of the Just Warrior—driving off the enemy who had surprised them in the middle of the night and seeing to it definitively that they would not return. He certainly recorded no joy in having done so.

Yet Genevoix's story had its own story. The episode had appeared in the original printings of 1916, was suppressed in subsequent editions, and reappeared in the compilation of *Ceux de 14* in 1950. In a footnote in the compilation, Genevoix explained the deletion of the passage and its restoration. After his somewhat cumbersome definition of killing, the footnote reads in its entirety:

> Happily, such occasions were rare. And when they did occur, they hardly allowed for anything but the inevitable sort of reflex action, devoid of reflection on one's own conduct. It was kill or be killed.
>
> When this book was republished, I suppressed this passage. It was an indication of this "reflection on one's own conduct," which was fated to arise later on. I put back the passage today, taking for a lack of honesty the voluntary omission of one of the episodes of the war that shook me most deeply and that has made an ineffaceable imprint on my memory.[102]

But unlike the episode of February 1915, this was not, strictly speaking, a situation of "kill or be killed." The three Germans he fired upon were running away and did not at that moment appear to pose any immediate physical threat. It made a certain amount of sense to shoot them, simply

101. Ibid.
102. Ibid., 44. I am indebted to Janice Zinser, Daniel Sherman, and John Horne for their help in translating this difficult passage. The French reads:

> Heureusement, ces occasions étaient rares; et, lorsqu'elles survenaient, elles n'admettaient guère qu'un réflexe à défaut de retour sur soi-même que devaient fatalement se produire; il s'agissait de tuer ou d'être tué.
>
> Lors d'une réimpression de ce livre j'avais supprimé ce passage: c'est une indication quant à ces "retours sur soi-même" qui devaient fatalement se produire. Je le rétablis aujourd'hui, tenant pour un manqué d'honnêteté l'omission volontaire d'un des épisodes de guerre qui m'ont le plus profondément secoué et qui ont marqué ma mémoire d'une empreinte jamais effacée.

because they were the enemy and because he saw the chance to do so. The Germans, after all, had fallen on the French in their sleep. The Just Warrior did not have to be in immediate danger to strike at the enemy, merely to be fighting in a Just War. The matter in itself seemed straightforward, much like Pechmalbec's explanation of his own lack of hesitation about firing at a German who posed no immediate threat to him. They were there to kill Germans. But by 1950 Genevoix had come to consider such an explanation inadequate.

The confession in the footnote turned on the phrase "reflection on one's own conduct." This reflection produced different results at different times, but always with the same objective. Genevoix, I would argue, wanted first and foremost to master experience by showing that killing had not altered his essentially humanistic construction of himself. The rational calculus of the Just Warrior proved not up to the task of doing so. After 1918, reflection on his conduct led him to suppress the passage. The return of peace, perhaps, made him feel obligated to omit the rather glaring fact that war had meant taking life as well as losing it. By 1950, more than thirty years later, self-reflection had different requirements, this time the restoration of the "whole" story, out of simple honesty.

Yet in its way, the 1950 explanation also sought to master experience. Killing could be explained as a consequence of the liminal stage of the initiation to combat, and thus the exception that proved the rule for the humane Genevoix. By 1950, self-reflection meant telling the "whole story," with the additional confession as to why part of it had disappeared after 1918. But it was no longer exactly the same story. As Nicolas Beaupré has shown, in the 1916 version the Germans he killed were referred to by the racial epithet "Boches."[103] In the 1950 version, the enemy are "Boches" most of the time, but the men he actually killed become *fantassins allemands* (German foot soldiers). And he had fired on four of them in the original 1916 version, but only three in the 1950 version.[104]

Nor did the matter of just what had happened end in 1950. In 1961 Genevoix published another version of the episode.[105] The basic circumstances were the same as in the 1916 version. The Germans surprised the sleeping French, who nevertheless managed to rally themselves and drive

---

103. I am indebted to Nicolas Beaupré for initially bringing this episode to my attention, and for his work in bringing out disparities between the 1916 and 1950 versions. See "Les Écrivains combattants français et allemands de la Grande Guerre (1914–1920): essai d'histoire comparée" (Doctoral diss., Université de Paris X-Nanterre), 2003, 233.

104. See Maurice Genevoix, *Sous Verdun* (Paris: Hachette, 1916), 66.

105. Maurice Genevoix, *Jeux de glaces* (Paris: Wesmael-Charlier, 1961). I am indebted to Prost, *Anciens combattants,* 3:15, for this reference.

off the enemy. Genevoix engaged in the same bit of trickery by donning a German helmet, whereupon he noticed shadows of the retreating Germans. But by the 1961 version, he seemed have to been trying to convince himself that he had acted appropriately:

> The storm was going away, but the night, at intervals, continued to light up. I recognized the greenish uniform, the pointed helmet. Kill or be killed . . . The man heard me, I was sure of it. He was going to turn around, turn around . . . Understanding this, I raised the weapon in my right hand and fired. I had the impression that he had just stumbled. He tilted forward, his arms open, and fell down on the barrel of his rifle.[106]

He fired on the second German just a few seconds later:

> And right away it began all over again, in a sequence of events so terrible, so like the first time that it left me with the memory of a dive into the completely unreal. Nightmare? A trance? But the two cries, so like each other, which ring in my ears after forty years, I really heard them, that night in the Vaux-Marais, on the plateau of the Meuse where the shooting flared up again, where the clamor of the bayonets broke into the confines of shadows even as the thunder and lightning from the storm, rolling ceaselessly low in the sky, seemed to surround the battlefield with a gloomy dawn which would never break.[107]

Time had not clarified some important details of what happened, quite the reverse. In the 1961 version, he fired on only two Germans, rather than four or three as in the previous versions. Unmentioned in previous versions was his strained conviction that they had become aware of his presence and were about to turn around, so that he had preempted danger by shooting them in the back. The weather in the 1961 version seemed to tell the moral of the story—the storm of self-reflection about the incident within the author which would never end. But the weather had not figured nearly so prominently in the previous versions, and certainly had not been accorded so much symbolic significance. These were not negligible differences for an author famous for his commitment to detail.

By the time he gave a television interview in 1977, just three years before his death, Genevoix said of the episode, as his face turned crimson, with a stricken and doubting look, "I very much hope I did not kill them."[108]

---

106. Genevoix, *Jeux de glaces*, 48.

107. Ibid., 48–49.

108. Prost, "Les Limites de la brutalization," 5. As Prost described his expression, "le visage s'empourprait."

Never in the previous sixty years had he allowed for doubt, at least in print, that he had killed between two and four Germans on September 10, 1914. The various versions of Genevoix's encounter with killing, as they changed in emphasis and even in information over the years, really told a single tale—his attempt to master experience by creating an embattled self in various guises as a humane narrator. The Just Warrior of 1916, the veteran so ashamed of killing that he censored his own work, the long-term survivor who needed to get a critical detail off his chest, and the old man still haunted by the episode as he approached his own death, were all the same figure.

More common than personal narratives of killing were stories about killing done by others. In such stories, the narrator told the story as a witness rather than a protagonist. But because he was physically present, his account qualified as eyewitness testimony, with all the attending and inherent legitimacy. Often, the narrator placed some sort of Just War explanation in the context of what Joanna Bourke called the "theater of war."[109] In such an account, the extreme circumstances of battle created a distinct psychological space in which rules and morals of civilian life no longer applied. Killing thus became situational, determined by specific circumstances rather than by the character of the killers. Such stories provided the narrator with a unique position. He had enough proximity to report the situation faithfully and to empathize with the killers. Yet it was their killing, not his. His intermediary position gave him the authority to counsel readers not to make their own moral judgments unless they had been though something like the experience so construed. In so doing, he could close down interrogation of his own version of the story.

Paul Dubrulle was the priest serving in the infantry who had so feared the atrocious passage from life to death. He had equally conflicted views on the atrocious passage of the enemy. He recounted an incident during the Battle of the Somme on September 12, 1916. The French had clearly beaten the German infantry in his section of the front. Where Dubrulle was fighting, the Germans surrendered, some offering prizes such as water bottles, pipes, or knives, others just throwing their rifles away. Others simply fell to their knees, and "were crying with a voice that broke your heart, 'Partonn, Frannçous, Partonn! Vier kinder' ['Pardon, French, Pardon! Four Children']," in heavily accented French.[110] The French responded, if not gently, at least with restraint. They rejected the trinkets, "landed them a

109. Joanna Bourke, *An Intimate History of Killing: Face to Face Killing in 20th Century Warfare* (New York: Basic Books, 1999). See particularly chap. 11 and the epilogue.
110. Dubrulle, *Mon régiment dans la fournaise*, 238.

few well-placed blows," and sent them to the rear as prisoners. As they filed past, Dubrulle did not conceal his satisfaction: "I could not repress a burst of laughter, a good deep laugh that must have seemed strange to them but that in any event put them at ease."[111] The gesture provided Dubrulle with a simple but effective means of mastering of his own experience. He could express a clearly masculine pride at achieving dominance over his enemy. But through the simple gesture of the laugh, he showed that he not only had preserved the enemy's life but had put him at his ease once out of combat. Like anyone possessing the power of life and death over someone else, he could perform domination by conspicuously refraining from cruelty.

Less fortunate were Germans just to Dubrulle's left, who continued to fire after their comrades had ceased, and certainly after the outcome of the engagement had been decided. The French attackers were only two meters away from the Germans, a particularly dangerous distance if both sides were still armed. Suddenly, "at that moment when there was nothing left for them but to die with dignity, and with very German aplomb, they jumped out of their holes," threw down their weapons, and asked for quarter. Dubrulle warned readers that the Germans had largely sealed their fate, whatever they did at that moment:

> The wretches did not know that the vanquished would never survive a hand-to-hand encounter, and that the man of the sweetest disposition could not forgive, there on the spot, the rifle fire he had just received.[112]

This seemed odd in itself, as Debrulle had just described the successful surrender of German soldiers in circumstances not dissimilar. But the situation seriously deteriorated in this case, when a German who had not thrown down his weapon shot and killed a French officer. A French captain immediately executed him. But his men did not stop there:

> His men, who had not waited for orders to avenge the fire they had just suffered, had already thrown themselves upon them. A few moments later, the wave of men, without feeling and with weapons raised, went for red bayonets.[113]

Dubrulle's explanation of the episode, and the moral he drew from the story (explained in a footnote), is as intriguing as the story itself. The mobilized priest did not invoke any version of Just War theory, religious or sec-

---

111. Ibid., 239.
112. Ibid., 239–40.
113. Ibid.

ular, to justify killing. Nor did he invoke in these extreme circumstances the call of Jesus to turn the other cheek, nor any concept of Christian charity:

> Some generous utopians, who believe in the virtue of humanitarian conventions, might wish to skip reading these lines. However, in writing them, one certainly does not claim anywhere to legitimize under other circumstances the massacre, the assassination—to use the exact term—of a disarmed enemy. My intention simply is to present, in this specific case, the existence of a psychological law that acted with the force and necessity of a physical order.[114]

Having admitted that such a deed could not be explained away in any other situation, he proceeded to explain it in this one. The pride of the conqueror could be easily satisfied, indeed quite literally laughed off, if the Germans threw down their weapons. But if they sought to deceive their conquerors, as the German soldier did in killing the French officer, the matter turned to one of excited revenge. The men could no longer be held responsible for their actions in the theater of war.

Yet after the fact, Dubrulle still seemed evasive on the morality of collective punishment for an individual offense. The French captain administered summary justice to the particular German who killed the French officer. What seemed to need additional explanation was the killing of the rest of the surrendering and disarmed Germans, by the very personal means of the bayonet. Here, Dubrulle called upon a special, situational psychological space, which had the effect of producing a more or less involuntary action. He thus insisted on the continuing humanity of the French as moral beings. Their "failings" in the episode, if they even needed to be referred to as such, were those of the human condition. Consequently, killing in this situation was not only not a mortal sin, but perhaps no sin at all. Nowhere did the priest Dubrulle suggest that the killers need any specific forgiveness. He assumed some readers would remain uneasy with this explanation, a response he politely but firmly dismissed as utopian. Readers, after all, had not been there. Nothing could trump the evidence of experience so construed.

Jacques Meyer, a lieutenant in the infantry, provided a contorted explanation of what, to a convinced Just Warrior, ought to have been a straightforward episode. In the first days of the Battle of the Somme, on July 6, 1916, a group of counterattacking Germans suddenly found themselves exposed in open country. With superior French forces in front them, they could not retreat back into the woods whence they came because of French artillery fire. In desperation, the Germans continued their counterattack, a

114. Ibid.

few reaching the parapet of one company's trench. This presented, as Meyer put it, "the beautiful target so often refused."[115] Two French machine-gun companies firing on two sides mowed the Germans down. As French rifle fire joined in, the previously foggy battlefield cleared, and they saw what had been well-regulated lines of German infantry disintegrate into a few tiny groups of men, whose survival seemed all but inexplicable, given the intensity of the fire. Meyer's men were not directly involved, except as spectators.

Events as told here seemed straightforward. The Germans advanced, got caught in the open, continued to advance, and got killed en masse. What Meyer did believe needed additional explanation was how much his own men as spectators enjoyed the encounter. His men, "during this uncommon spectacle, worn down by inaction, wanted, even the most peaceful ones, to take part in this massacre—because we were at one of those moments, always quite rare, in which reigned the insane bloodlust of killing. It was a paroxysm of joy and excitement, which played itself out in the most unconsciously cruel thoughts. [. . .] They cheered on their comrades with such cries as 'And the grapeshot, don't you think it's doing good work? Ah, old buddy, it must be a pleasure to work like that. That I don't call wasting munitions.'"[116]

In explaining his men's reaction, which in retrospect seemed to him so indecorous, Meyer invoked *both* a Just Warrior explanation and the "theater of war." But the two explanations did not need each other and even seemed contradictory. On the one hand, the Germans deserved their fate: "We must administer justice to these Brandenburgers, these Pomeranians, these Saxons. They could, without seeming cowardly, have hit the ground and waited for nightfall to rejoin their lines."[117] But they continued to advance. Consequently, "our overexcited men, intoxicated with murder, could no longer hear the cries of '*Kamarad*.' Even less could they hear the words of Father Saint Marie who, still with them, had been trying to make them listen to him about how to treat an enemy who was valorous but now was powerless."[118] The Germans had attacked hysterical men, who were past hearing either cries of surrender (widely presumed to be tricks in any event) or pleas of restraint from their own priestly comrade. The most difficult problem, for Meyer, was the unseemly joy of the French.

Like Dubrulle, Meyer provided his own commentary and his own somewhat confused moral to the story:

115. Jacques Meyer, *La Biffe* (Paris: Albin Michel, 1928), 223.
116. Ibid., 223–24.
117. Ibid., 224.
118. Ibid., 225.

I note what I have seen, without approval or blame, and I do not want to seem to excuse these men, who in any event are well above excusing. But I believe that they were living up to their role as men, overexcited by weariness and the death of so many of their companions, just as was the pastor, Father Saint-Marie, this admirable figure.[119]

Meyer thus placed the men who killed, the men who cheered them on, and the priest who tried to restrain them all on the same moral plane. The men simply behaved "like men" who had experienced loss and massive stress. But no less praiseworthy was Father Saint-Marie, who had kept his head while all those around him had lost theirs.

But Meyer seemed to explain more than he needed to. As stated, the Germans were attacking, and defenders at war were supposed to kill attackers if they could. The French under Meyer's command were paying their share to win the war. If they expressed joy at doing so, and if they really were "well above excusing," what exactly about their behavior needed explanation? And if the French really were blameless Just Warriors, why did he need to praise the priest who tried to restrain them? Were there relevant details missing from the story as told? Meyer's narrative of "what happened" and its meaning raises as many questions as it answers.

The insufficiency of the Just Warrior permeated all of the narratives of killing examined here. None of the stories questioned the Great War as a Just War, yet the most logically consistent explanations of killing seem the most unsettling to readers today because of their cold reasonableness. Pechmalbec and Laby accepted the logic of the Just Warrior in so many words. Barrès simply drained killing of passion, almost dismissing it. Genevoix tried so hard to conserve his humanity as a narrator over so many years that the story itself became less clear with time. Dubrulle and Meyer both found the logic of the Just Warrior insufficient. They posited alongside it the existence of a distinct, temporary psychological state that explained killing as something that happens beyond conscious volition. The narratives thus explained more than seemed necessary. If the good of killing in war outweighed the evil of taking human life, why should one have to enter a space beyond conscious volition in order to carry it out?

THIS chapter has explored how *témoins* imagined survival through the mastery of experience through narrative. In so doing, authors sought to establish themselves as arbiters of experience, figures who had properly understood what had happened and who could convey its meaning to the

---

119. Ibid.

outside world and to posterity. There was, of course, something circular in this way of constructing meaning. Experience created the narrator, who in turn created experience and the author as arbiter of that experience.

"Real" experiences of death, mutilation, and killing resisted mastery—hence the tensions, contradictions, and irresolution within the stories. Death has resisted mastery ever since people began writing about it, and death in the Great War simply cast this oldest of problems in particularly agonizing ways. Neither religious nor secular explanations of survival after death could master the anxiety of those who faced it in the trenches. Mutilation likewise resisted mastery, reducing heroism to unconvinced stoicism. It also authorized a morbid fascination with the decayed body, as well as an uninhibited sensual fascination with the male body, whether one's own or that of a colonial soldier. Surviving mutilation meant engaging it and the ways it altered identity for the rest of one's life. Stories about killing were either brutal assertions of the cold logic of the Just War or embarrassed, contorted, or self-contradictory stories of exceptions that prove the rule of an underlying humanity. Imagining survival and mastering it proved to be very different projects.

3

The Genre of Consent

As we have seen, the mastery of survival as a set of narrative tools produced unstable narratives and narrators. Survival, simply put, had to be structured further, typically by some higher meaning that could provide a moral to the story. Survival had to figure in some broader narrative pattern making the war comprehensible. Consent provided such a framework and its own set of narrative tools. Observers have long noted that in the nineteenth century, stalemated war pointed the way to a compromise peace. But stalemate in the Great War pointed the way to the total mobilization of individuals and societies. Consent provided an answer to the problem of total war.

As a category for understanding just why Europeans kept slaughtering one another for more than four years, consent is largely the creation of historians, myself among them, connected to the Historial de la Grande Guerre in Péronne, in the battlefields of the Somme. The term "consent" is simply a literal translation of the French word *consentement*. We have construed consent as a variety of commitment that intensified along with the Great War itself. The more ghastly the war became, the more committed the protagonists became to prevailing in it. Consent in the Great War had various components, such as an affective attachment to the national community, various kinds of political loyalties, redirected religious fervor, a hatred of the enemy, and brutalization, meaning an abandonment of the norms of civilization itself as the war radicalized.[1] Together, the argument goes, these components intensified the conduct of war and paved the way for the still greater catastrophes of World War II.

---

1. See Stéphane Audoin-Rouzeau and Annette Becker, *14–18: Understanding the Great War*, trans. Catherine Temerson (New York: Hill and Wang, 2003), esp. pt. 2

Consent has come under strong criticism in French historiography, and has become a subject of considerable controversy.[2] Nicolas Mariot has questioned the assumptions underpinning the use of the term *consentement*, notably whether it implies a capacity for individual choice.[3] Rémy Cazals and Frédéric Rousseau have found the very concept of consent little more than nationalist coercion under another name. They have contended instead that the whole foucauldian array of disciplinary institutions inculcated in the soldier what they called a "culture of obedience," the prelude to victimization at the front. "Education and instruction," they wrote, "did not just make patriots, they made obedient patriots. Whether they came from the countryside or the working-class neighborhood, all soldiers interiorized at the most profound level this culture of obedience."[4] Of the ensuing controversy, and perhaps himself a bit carried away by military language, the journalist Jean Birnbaum has written of "fortified conferences, editorial ambushes, academic assassinations, and targeted reviews" to describe the resulting war-about-the-war over consent.[5] So well-tempered a scholar as Jay Winter has agreed that "when you touch the First World War in France, you are playing with fire."[6] Why should consent prove so divisive?

The political implications of consent help explain why the concept became so contested in France, as well as why the resulting controversy has had so little resonance elsewhere. Mariot, Cazals, Rousseau, and others have raised important issues, such as the ideological content of consent, and the need further to articulate the relationship between consent and coercion. But equating consent and coercion means assuming a political identity formed almost entirely externally. Agency in such a context can mean only resistance, usually futile. At the end of the day, this constitutes another formulation of the soldier-as-victim truism that I have argued against ever since *Between Mutiny and Obedience*. Missing in the analysis is the self-construction of the individual, precisely the subject of the present book.

2. See, for example, the essays by Antoine Prost, Mario Isnenghi, Rémy Cazals, and Antonio Gibelli, "Controverses," *Le Mouvement Sociale*, no. 199 (April–June 2002): 95–119.

3. Nicolas Mariot, "Faut-il être motive pour tuer? Sur quelques explications aux violences de guerre," *Genèses* 53 (2003): 157–59.

4. Rémy Cazals and Frédéric Rousseau, *14–18: le cri d'une génération* (Toulouse: Éditions Privat, 2001), 145. See also Rousseau, *La Guerre censurée: une histoire des combattants européens de 14–18* (Paris: Seuil, 1999); and *L'Affaire Norton Cru* (Paris: Seuil, 2003). The most relevant work by Michel Foucault is *Discipline and Punish: The Birth of the Prison*, trans. Alan Sheridan (New York: Vintage Books, 1979).

5. Jean Birnbaum, "1914–1918, guerre de tranchées entre historiens," *Le Monde*, 11 March 2006. http://www.lemonde.fr/web/article/0,1-0@2-3230,36-749539,0.html.

6. Jay Winter, "P vs C: The still burning anger when the French talk of the First World War," *Times Literary Supplement*, 16 June 2006.

At stake in the debate about consent, I would argue, is nothing less than the political legacy of the Third Republic, and perhaps even the legacy of French republicanism itself. To equate consent in the Great War with coercion is at some level to indict the regime that waged the war. If consent and coercion were really the same thing, then something had to be wrong with the whole republican project after 1871. This implicit debate about the republican legacy has helped keep the debate about consent "French." So radical a critic of Britain's participation in the Great War as Niall Ferguson never expressed much doubt about British institutions, or about the political evolution of Britain up to the time of the Great War.[7] Many American historians have doubted Woodrow Wilson, but few indeed the United States Constitution. The Russians, Austro-Hungarians, the Turks, and Germans, of course, overthrew their institutions in the wake of defeat in the Great War, and were thus unlikely to interrogate them thereafter in the same ways as the French.[8] Consequently, and perhaps in disagreement with some of my Péronne colleagues, I have come to conclude that there is something very French after all about consent as we have construed it. Only France among the European Great Powers was a republic, and only the French had to deal with the dramas of the collision between total war and a specific kind of republican identity. Certainly, *something* kept the other protagonists fighting so desperately for so long. But perhaps it was not consent.

Whether or not the whole French nation came under the sway of consent cannot be definitively demonstrated one way or another using soldiers' published testimony. What I can demonstrate, however, is that consent existed as an ideological system. In so doing, I intend neither to praise nor damn as such the Third Republic, let alone French republicanism more broadly. Rather, I want to show how republicanism operated at a certain time in a certain body of historical evidence. Consent must to some extent be disentangled from patriotism, particularly from the mindless nationalism of the schoolmaster that drove Paul Baümer from *All Quiet on the Western Front* into uniform in the first place. If Benedict Anderson is correct, nationalism is primarily an affective attachment to the "imagined community" of the nation.[9] Such attachments mattered deeply to French soldiers, who maintained a keen sense of the nation as an emotional and geographic space. But con-

---

7. Niall Ferguson, *The Pity of War: Explaining World War I* (London: Allen Lane, 1998).

8. Italy, on the other hand, a "victorious" but factious constitutional monarchy, presents an intriguing comparison with the French case. I am indebted to Winter, "P vs C," for encouraging me to think about the uniquely "French" aspects of consent.

9. Benedict Anderson, *Imagined Communities: Reflections on the Origin and Spread of Nationalism,* rev. ed. (London: Verso, 1991).

sent spoke to logic more than affect, and rested on a certain idea of what it meant to be a member of the political community.

In France, consent revolved around the Republic at war—not simply the Third Republic, but the Republic as the repository of a political identity under evolution for more than a century before 1914.[10] Citizen-soldiers were expected to obey an authority whose source and legitimacy lay in themselves and their compatriots. In this sense, the Republic implicated citizen-soldiers individually and totally in the collectivity. To be sure, this collectivity remained hierarchical and highly gendered. The guardians of the Republic, the all-male community of citizen-soldiers, had an exceptional status that conferred exceptional responsibilities. I interpret consent as the function of internalized absolutes vitally connected to the war and to continuing it. The citizen-soldier could not surrender these absolutes without in some form surrendering who he was as a political being. Consent rendered all social relations a matrix on a national scale. Families, comrades, compatriots, all made up one big community of the French, to whom each citizen-soldier owed an essentially unlimited commitment. Through this logic of necessity implicating every Frenchman in uniform, we can detect traces of the Republic, even in those accounts from soldiers who appeared to have little use for it.

The content of consent produced a specific form of témoignage—first-person nonfictional testimonies, typically published during the war or shortly thereafter.[11] The language of this form was often the spare, grammatically correct French of the republican schoolroom. Most often, such

10. On the philosophical origins of consent, which in fact long predated French republicanism, see Frédéric Gros, *États de violence: essai sur la fin de la guerre* (Paris: Gallimard, 2006), 68–75. A word about capitalization is in order here. Capitalized, *Republic* is used as a proper noun, to indicate an abstract ideal. In lowercase, *republic* or *republican* refers to a regime, typically the Third Republic.

11. This notion of content leading to form helps explain the modalities of publication. The following comprise calculations based on the information in Jean Norton Cru, *Témoins: essai d'analyse et de critique des souvenirs de combattants édités en français de 1915 à 1928* (1929; repr., Nancy: Presses Universitaires de Nancy, 1993). Although Norton Cru's choices were notoriously idiosyncratic, we can glean from his work general patterns of what was published when.

The production of war books peaked during the war. Of 294 volumes Norton Cru considered, he classified fully 234 (79.6 percent) as some form of nonfiction. Of the 294 volumes, 218 (74 percent) were published between 1915 and 1919. Of 234 nonfiction books, 175 (or 74.5 percent) were published during the same period.

It is important to include 1919 in these figures, given that the armistice was not concluded until November 1918, and the Versailles Treaty was not signed until late June 1919. Many of the volumes published in 1919 would consequently have been prepared during the war. Contemporaries also anticipated historians' subsequent doubts that either the armistice or the treaty actually ended the war.

texts—redacted diaries, memoirs, or reflections written in relatively close proximity to the events described—lacked closure, because the war did not yet have an end. By definition, narratives of consent told a story "to be continued" until victory. It rested on sacrifices accepted and hopes deferred. In wartime, necessity provided its own explanation. Testimonies that articulated consent seldom had an explicit "moral" beyond the necessity of continuing the war. Individual stories could have an end, such as the death of the author or his personal evacuation from the war because of some serious wound. But the war itself could not have an end in this genre of testimony, at least not one in the present. The "end" would be the yearned-for victory, in itself presumed to be total and redemptive. In first-person, nonfictional testimony, we can find the internalized absolutes of consent—in their variety, their confusion, their intensity, and their underlying logic of necessity, at times carried to the point of pathology.

The Republic in Small: The Individual and the Group

As imagined in French political history, the Republic sought to reconcile authority and freedom. Individual citizens would hold power, even as it was held over them. The Social Contract itself posited government through the General Will, a collective, metaphysical source of absolute authority, at once comprising all individual wills and creating something far greater than the sum of its parts. The collectivity existed in the individual, and the individual citizen existed politically only through his personal and total implication in the collectivity. As Jean-Jacques Rousseau put it, "Each one, while uniting with all, nevertheless obeys only himself and remains as free as before."[12] The Republic, in short, had to exist in each male, active citizen, who would then be bound to each other as to themselves.[13] In practical terms, constructing republican identity in France became about constructing commensurability among the active citizenry—through universal male suffrage, the continuing massive investment in primary education, and conscription. Rousseau himself, after all, had coined the famous phrase "Every soldier a citizen, every citizen a soldier." "France" as a political community would exist as the collectivity of politically identical male individuals.

By 1914, republican identity had even infiltrated French military tac-

12. Jean Jacques Rousseau, *The Social Contract,* trans. Donald A. Cress (Indianapolis: Hackett Publishing, 1983), 24.
13. The gendering of republican citizenship in France is admirably explored in Joan W. Scott, *Only Paradoxes to Offer: French Feminists and the Rights of Man* (Cambridge, Mass.: Harvard University Press, 1996).

tics.[14] Charles Ardant du Picq had decreed even before the Franco-Prussian War that discipline had become horizontal rather than vertical, the product of mutual surveillance on the battlefield. Long gone were the days when soldiers could be driven forward by pistol-bearing officers. Only men who felt individually and totally implicated in the fate of one another, and in the authority ruling over them, could be relied upon under fire. Nothing seemed better suited to republican citizenship. The Third Republic before 1914 proved far more successful in inculcating political cues in soldiers than impressing military ones. Yet as the war dragged on political cues created their own reality in the field. The Republic as a conceptualization of political power replicated itself at multiple levels. Individuals and groups functioned according to a logic of necessity, expressed in terms of absolute and personal accountability to the collectivity. This logic then reproduced itself at the national level.

Consent expressed itself through public gestures and was to some degree performative. In this book I draw a distinction between assent, a single act such as accepting mobilization in August 1914, and consent, a much more complex and continuing series of gestures. The critics of consent argue that consent assumes a morally free agent—a republican citizen precisely as republican rhetoric itself imagined him. Elaine Scarry, on the other hand, sees consent as a far more complicated interaction between belief and bodily comportment. The soldier "picks up a gun, he puts on a uniform, not once, but each morning, day after day, he re-puts it on, renewing each time his act of consent." While assent is a single act, consent is incremental. As Scarry puts it, the soldier's "fundamental relation between body and belief takes many degrees and radiates out over thousands of small acts." This does not mean that the soldier operates in complete moral freedom, rather that he has internalized some form of ownership of his behavior through connecting it to some belief. That belief may not be the same as that represented in the propaganda all around him. He may internalize none of it, all of it, or part of it; but, as she puts it, "he will have some belief for which he performs the work he performs, daily recertifying its importance."[15]

Jean Marot's *Ceux de vivent . . .* (Those Who Live, 1919) articulated this relationship between gesture and belief at the level of the individual citizen-soldier. He structured his témoignage according to a three-part narrative of situation-crisis-resolution—here, emplotting an ideological journey to con-

14. See Leonard V. Smith, *Between Mutiny and Obedience: The Case of the French Fifth Infantry Division during World War I* (Princeton: Princeton University Press, 1994), 27–31.

15. Elaine Scarry, *The Body in Pain: The Making and Unmaking of the World* (New York: Oxford University Press, 1985), 153.

sent. A beginning section on *émotions* described a collection of responses to life and death in the trenches. A middle section on *devoirs* (duties) demarcated the internalized expectations of the national community, which had to be fulfilled at whatever cost. A concluding section entitled *pensées* (thoughts) began to provide a resolution, by explaining consent as a synthesis of emotions and duties. But full resolution would have to be deferred, replaced for now by a call for redemption of the sacrifice resulting from consent. Only redemption could provide real closure.

Under *émotions* Marot described in familiar terms how the ever-present prospect of death and mutilation haunted daily life in the trenches. Yet it is important to highlight the dehumanizing isolation that accompanied this suffering, which had consequences for the political message of the book. Not just insult but also additional injury came through the torture of alienation from the group. One day, Marot came across a stretcher with a corpse on top of it. The stretcher-bearers had left it there, so as to provide minimal, if macabre, cover for themselves from incoming artillery fire. For Marot, the alienation of the deceased did not end with death. Flesh once dead became an object, perversely still necessary to the war. The dead body could perform its own gestures: "A weariness overcame the emaciated face, the pinched nose, the dull eyes, the grimace of the clenched teeth. An arm dragged, weighted down in the mud." Marot tried to restore humanity to the corpse, and thus somehow to reincorporate it into the collectivity, by imagining it as a person:

> You poor guy! You even had to accept the penalty of abandonment, resign your heart to loneliness, to the forgetfulness of the men, as in the trench. You were so undemanding, so little accustomed to being handled carefully, loved, to having other people take care of you! The comrades hid behind you, and even you would say, if you could, that they did the right thing, that it was not worth it to expose yourself for a cadaver.[16]

The brute rationality of survival, he posited, compounded injury by dehumanizing not just the dead but also the living, who had to shield themselves with dead bodies. Even the deceased would have been forced to admit that his comrades were right to abandon him.

More than once in the book, Marot appropriated Christian belief for secular purposes. In the first section of the book, he turned the crucified Christ into a citizen-soldier. While investigating the destroyed Eglise Saint-André in Reims, Marot and a group of comrades came upon sculpture of Jesus,

---

16. Jean Marot, *Ceux qui vivent . . .* (Paris: Payot, 1919), 54–55. Hereafter cited by page number in the text.

"crucified in the emptiness." The cross had been destroyed, and lay in pieces on the floor. Of the shadow cast by light coming through what remained of the windows of the church, Marot wrote: "His silhouette, liberated from the rigidities of the cross, reclaimed the sinuous movement of tormented bodies." A comrade observed that this peculiar sight seemed to humanize the tortured God who had become man: "like that [without the cross], it's more true to life, he looks just one of the guys [*il a tout d'un bon-homme*]." To Marot, the episode seemed to simplify the complicated metaphysics of the war, not just by humanizing but even by politicizing the crucified Christian savior: "He showed himself to the simple souls of those sacrificed to the war, as well as his fraternity with the sufferers. He teaches to men the mystical law of solidarity, which, through Pain, elevates them to the divine, and which requires that a God suffer to be worthy of men" (55–56). Suffering made men and the Son of God commensurable beings in the present war. Such an appropriation of the sacred, I will argue later, placed religion at the service of articulating consent.

The central section on *devoirs* (duties) asserted what Marot saw as the irrefutable reasons for continuing the war. As Marot signaled readers in his preface, the French soldiers of the Great War "submit to the domination of things, the implacable tyranny of Necessity" (9–10). The imperative of national salvation provided the starting point:

> The salvation of the Patrie is the supreme Law. Success is a necessity, an imperious duty. It conditions every act. It defines, to say as much, the truth inclusive in every intention, in every thought. (82–83)

An imperative of national salvation would hardly have been unfamiliar to readers by 1919. But Marot's exposition of this theme was unusual in the way he connected necessity to reason itself. The rational had become rational because it explained the salvation of France. Likewise, the "real" had become whatever would save France: "This species of superior realism is in the process of substituting a perpetual experimentation for old critical methods." Marot's unconventional, patriotic metaphysics had transparent behavioral implications:

> It is the logic of men of action, for whom the war is a responsibility. Empiricism sublimated by the play of risk, audacious logic, whose rules decipher themselves in letters of blood written on the reconquered land.

Commitment to the war, driven by reason and reality, was both individual and total. Each soldier in facing violence and danger would obey himself and his comrades by adhering to military order: "The essential fact, this miracle of the new era, is the adhesion of all to social discipline, conceived as the condition first of productive action, then of Victory" (120).

Indeed, individuated identity itself continued through a paradoxical submersion into the collectivity. Millions of Frenchmen experienced an extraordinary transfiguration of personality, through internalization of the common task, "to forget [themselves] in order to melt away into the collective will." From this submersion of the individual in the collectivity, from the smallest primary group to the national community itself, would come an extraordinary form of courage. The bloody, murderous, and indecisive battles of the trenches became "rational" matters of thought and action precisely through this ability to conceive the self as collective:

> The squad is me; it is even my responsibility. And so is created a paradoxical form of the instinct of self-preservation, reinforced by all the energies of personal interest, but suddenly transformed into a sublime collective egoism. (157–58)

This was an argument about consent and the meaning of sacrifice, rather than about personal survival. That Marot had doubts about consent as he construed it became clear by the end of his book, as we will see below. But it is important to highlight here that according to Marot's logic, a soldier could not become alienated from the war without becoming alienated from himself as an individual and as a component of the collectivity. And yet nothing about the submersion of the self in the collectivity could mitigate the physical tortures of the war and the highly individuated pain they inflicted.

The third section of the book, on *pensées,* tried to resolve the ideological narrative by reconciling the emotions and the rational duties of war to form a complete articulation of consent. Consent, in other words, combined emotions and duties. Even military discipline, Marot argued, remained staunchly republican—more horizontal than vertical. As we will see in chapter 4, the courts martial became the symbol in antiwar literature of capricious domination by military command. But to Marot, the court martial served primarily to correct and clarify an identity already there—in an individual completely implicated in the collectivity. The relative handful of soldiers who found themselves before a court martial almost always proved pliable: "nine times out of ten, the accused confess, and acknowledge what is expected of them" (176–77). Resistance to the logic of necessity tended to be situational. In every convicted soldier lay the promise of future consent: "In the backs of eyes dulled by anguish, I insist on seeing the glimmering reflection of the flame of truth." The vast majority, already obedient, not only accepted the implacable tyranny of necessity, but consented to the indefinite deferral to the future of the happiness and hopes of civilian life: "You no longer dream, you no longer build castles in the sky. You persuade yourself of universal relativity. You understand the necessary inadequacy you accept in life right now. You express it in prudent and reserved phrases" (193–93). But as we will see, this articulation of consent in the third section of the book would prove neither unproblematic nor sufficient, even to Marot.

There is a vast literature in military sociology on small-group dynamics that has greatly influenced the military history of combat effectiveness.[17] Historians have tended to posit what I would argue is a false choice between the importance of the group as a nearly autonomous entity and the importance of ideology and indoctrination. Rather, the small group can simply reproduce the ideology in microcosm. For example, in *Nous autres à Vauquois* (We Others at Vauquois, 1918), André Pézard described a miniature version of the Republic, based in a small group of men totally and individually committed to one another. Pézard had been a student of literature just admitted to the École normale supérieure at the time the war broke out.[18] *Nous autres à Vauquois* was one of the most demanding but rewarding published testimonies from French soldiers of the Great War.

Most striking is the account's apparent narrowness of vision and its apparent detachment from the great issues of the war. Yet expressed in its dense but spare language was an explanation of consent as a function of total war. Consent in Pézard detached commitment from most typical conceptions of utility. The more Pézard and his comrades suffered, the more they considered themselves committed to one another and through one another to the war. They construed experience itself in terms of this commitment. This experience became an essential attribute of what made them themselves, individually and collectively. Consequently, they could no more yield in their commitment to the war than yield in their commitment to one another. As we will see, Pézard's seemingly microscopic vision had macroscopic consequences, as this logic of necessity and consent replicated itself on the national level.

On June 3, 1915, Pézard and his friend Fairise visited a second lieutenant hospitalized not far from their sector. From his hospital bed, Second Lieutenant B—— boasted of burning some Germans alive: "As a reprisal, we went to launch burning liquids on the Boches. I watched it fly, in open air,

---

17. For a fine summary of present debates, see Hew Strachan, "Training, Morale, and Modern War," *Journal of Contemporary History* 41 (2006): 211–27.

18. See the biographical sketch by Jean-Charles Jauffret in André Pézard, *Nous autres à Vauquois* (1918; repr., Nancy: Presses Universitaires de Nancy, 1992), i–xi.

near ——. It was marvelous, whole trees on fire, like straw. Marvelous!"[19] Walking back from the hospital through the mutilated countryside, Pézard and Fairise reflected on their brutalized comrade. "What shocks me the most," complained Pézard, wondering whether he held some responsibility as mentor, "is to watch that ideologue speak so coldly of such horror. Will what we have learned—him, you, and me—end up making us all that depraved?"[20] Fairise responded with a certain compassion for the second lieutenant that articulated the nature of the bond between himself and Pézard. Second Lieutenant B—— could well enjoy the hideous destruction of the enemy, because he had endured so little of it. But the likes of Fairise and Pézard had to perceive matters quite differently:

> Is that how you'd see yourself, under a *real* bombardment! With the *real* thing? Not on your life. No one will really know about the fear and the suffering, once it is all over. The people behind the lines will never be able to see us in all our horror. You represent poorly the suffering of others. Quickly, you resign yourself to their unhappiness. You resign yourself almost as quickly to your own, and you forget it more quickly than that of others—almost! So much the better, if you like. You need that, no doubt, to make war as they want us to make it; as they show it to us in history. And all that is preferable, if you still judge that it wouldn't be worth it to sign a peace treaty right away.[21]

Experience in the "real war," according to Fairise, had become the property of the citizens of the republic-within-the-republic, the initiates who rites of passage and survival had rendered a different kind of being. Construing the war in a certain way had made them citizen-soldiers in a very specific sense. They formed a community that understood the real nature of fear and suffering at the front, and the delicate balance between the repression of emotion and the self-awareness needed to continue fighting. Indeed, Fairise seemed to posit a kind of mastery of experience. The likes of Fairise and Pézard might indeed throw flaming liquids at the Germans if the situation so required, but they would never enjoy it. They would do what they had to in order to continue a war that had become entirely their own. And continuing, not in spite of their suffering but almost because of it, proved the only course of action these citizen-soldiers considered thinkable.

Pézard responded to Fairise that he shared his microscopic vision of the

19. Pézard, *Nous autres à Vauquois* (Paris: La Renaissance du Livre, 1918), 140. Names and places had to be obscured in wartime, per censorship requirements.
20. Ibid., 141.
21. Ibid.; italics in the original.

war. Pézard confessed that he seldom thought "about those great ideas, those noble sentiments that you find in the speeches." But this did not alienate him and the other citizen-soldiers of the micro-republic from the larger struggle, quite the contrary:

> You might find it long and ignoble and stupid, the war. That doesn't prevent you from *wanting* it, one day, the first time, in knowing why, and regardless of the consequences. You hardly remember and don't suspect it. That is what prevents us from being bastards, whatever we do. And what's more, this ignoble thing, we are the ones doing it, it is our thing, and we do not want others to permit themselves to speak ill of it.[22]

The war might indeed be stupid and ignoble, and the totality of the soldiers' consent to it might not be altogether coherent. But no one, save the citizen-soldiers fighting it, had the right to say so. They had become the war, and the war had become them. Mutual commitment had become the point of continuing the struggle, more or less as an end in itself. Their commitment to the war had become as open ended as their commitment to each other. The mutual surveillance that Ardant du Picq had posited fifty years earlier as essential to modern warfare had created itself in the trenches, though perhaps not exactly in the sense he had imagined.

As his narrative for that day concluded, Pézard further reflected on experience, personal friendships, and consent to the war. Fairise asked Pézard why he found himself in so contemplative a mood. Fairise speculated that something was not right with him, and that perhaps he had received some bad news. Pézard responded that he had just been notified of the death of his best friend from the *lycée,* who he had expected to join at the École normale before the war broke out. Certainly, Pézard reflected, such friends from their earlier lives would be irreplaceable. But the shared experience in the trenches, as he and his comrades had understood it, had created qualitatively different, more intense friendships. Experience bound them to one another as it bound them to the war:

> There are times when I say to myself that I will miss it, the war, because of the two or three friends I made in it, and even because of all the comrades. It is a friendship so vivid, it is the best of us. Listen, I don't know how to put this, but you are one of the ones—and there aren't many of them—for whom I would voluntarily do something crazy, if it would save your hide. I would go look for you on the Boche barbed wire![23]

22. Ibid., 142.
23. Ibid., 143.

The war, presumably the worst thing to happen in their lives, had brought out the best in them through the creation of a particular kind of commitment. Fairise's life, in some sense, had become Pézard's own—so dear to him that he vowed with deadly seriousness to save him from separation from the collectivity, even if doing so meant that Pézard would have to join him in death. The war, in its horrors and its pain, had brought about this union of souls.

The tiny homosocial republic in Pézard had a spatial component parallel to that of the national community, France itself. The collectivity of joined souls existed as such in part because it occupied a specific geographical space. Their devotion to their miserable, all-but-indefensible sector became the physical locus of their identity, as he recalled in a conversation in December 1915 among his comrades:

> Do you think that a regiment that came here from another sector would agree to live as we are living? Here we are, after ten months at Vauquois, and we have not yet succeeded in putting the sector in order. Everything is destroyed before being finished. And how to measure something correctly in materials beyond usage and in ruins forever! [. . .] We are so much made to live in a nonexistent sector that we no longer find it implausible to live here and to hang on here. We are so addicted to this atmosphere that we find it breathable. It is the same thing for the terrain and the protection of the sector. The strength to hold on well under the crazily crazy bombardments [*crapouillotages follement fous*], without having anything to hang on to, we find it natural to remain on this ridge of implausible ruin, in equilibrium underneath the storms that turn up again on all sides, even behind us.[24]

Pézard began to hint here at the radical nature of consent as an ideological system. He and his comrades proudly proclaimed that their fierce devotion to their sector could not be explained through a rational calculus of cost and benefit. Their specific bit of the front had become some sort of new natal soil, the land of their rebirth through the unique and horrible experience that bound them to one another. So intense and personal was this bond that it separated them, not just from their civilian compatriots (a separation generally taken as a given), but even from comrades elsewhere in the army, who ipso facto could not share their devotion to this sector. Indeed, the very irrationality of their stubborn devotion to duty emphasized the proprietary nature of their experience. A comrade named Lateulère proclaimed:

24. Ibid., 204–5.

We live in a sector stupidly contradictory and criminally impractical. We know this. We know there is nothing to be done. And what then? To hell with peace!

All the same, we do something, dammit. We will defend ourselves![25]

In *Là-bas avec ceux qui souffrent* (Out There with Those Who Suffer, 1917), Second Lieutenant Guy Hallé explained consent in his microcosm of the republic through a description of a military ritual. His short book comprised a series of vignettes arranged chronologically, from September 1914 (a vignette examined in chapter 1) to January 1917. But the last vignette in the book disrupted this chronology and returned to June 1916, just after Hallé's unit had been rotated out of the front lines after eight days of intense fighting during the Battle of Verdun. A great many of his comrades had not returned. This last chapter, titled "A Beautiful Memory," recounted a ceremony awarding medals in a village near the front lines. The description of the survivors of Verdun must have already seemed familiar when it was published in October 1917:

> The hunger, the thirst, the fear, the horrible weariness of these hours of hell made of these men, who came here robust and full of life, strange spectral figures, with dark rings under their eyes, wracked with fever, thin cheeks, with the slow and weary walk of old men.[26]

Life in some sense had been stolen from the haggard, prematurely aged soldiers hobbling about the village. Visibly ill and exhausted, they seemed already to muddle the boundary demarcating the living from the dead. Yet Hallé did not want readers to see them purely as victims.

The decoration ceremony began at 10 a.m., with the men lined up in front of the mayor's office. In the center of a square formed by soldiers presenting arms were the officer (Hallé's company commander) and the three soldiers to be decorated. All of the civilians in the village attended, the same people who fifteen days previously had given these soldiers and their now-deceased comrades an enthusiastic if anguished sendoff. As the bayonets glistened in the sun, the colonel shouted the command "To the Flag." Hallé recalled that in normal times, such ceremonies acted out a generally ridiculous military pomposity.

25. Ibid., 208.
26. Guy Hallé, *Là-bas avec ceux qui souffrent* (Paris: Librairie Garnier Frères, 1917) 81.

We often laughed at military parades, I along with the others, because of the falseness of their glamour and their conservative attitudes. I assure you that not one of us wanted to smile at that moment.[27]

The casualties suffered by the regiment gave this particular ceremony a terrible gravitas: "The thoughts of everyone were out there, on the slopes of Douaumont, in the grey powder smoke, with those who are dead."[28] This performance of consent united the living and the dead. In the profound quiet, Hallé heard the scattered, repeated words of the citations—"in the name of the president of the republic . . . powers . . . Legion of Honor"— against the sobs of a woman weeping behind him. Many of the dead, he added, and not as a trivial detail, had "lived their last love in this village." As the ceremony concluded, the men presented arms to the regimental flag. Hallé found the occasion profoundly moving, as he wrote in the last words of the book:

Rarely have I seen as on that day so much goodwill in men. The companies marched by in splendid fashion and the soldiers put their whole heart into the brutal gesture of putting down their rifles to salute.
Truly, that time was beautiful.[29]

Superior authority could require the second lieutenant to be present at the ceremony. But it could not compel the usually skeptical Hallé to take it seriously, still less to find it beautiful. Certainly, previous vignettes spared the reader nothing in descriptions of suffering, or in the expression of deep doubt as to just what was being accomplished by this war. Hallé had written of his state of mind in the Eparges sector in October 1916: "What are we doing there, we poor numbed creatures, our hearts broken and crying with our very blood for peace, for love, for light, and the sweetness of seeing again everything that is so faraway, so faraway. We feel separated from all this by distance without limit and by infinite suffering."[30] Yet in the description of the decoration ceremony, he disentangled despair from commitment. Sacrifice at Verdun was not alienating, quite the reverse. Commitment was profound, almost *because* it hurt and killed.

In these few pages, Hallé evoked a vivid performance of a wartime social order, and of his deep implication in that order. His vignette encompassed both the exhausted soldiers in the town and the civilians who lived

27. Ibid., 83.
28. Ibid.
29. Ibid., 84.
30. Ibid., 57.

there. Enveloping the occasion was the army, the institutional expression of the sovereign people in arms, awarding honors in the name of the republic. Like the Third Republic, the political community represented at the ceremony was hierarchical. The male citizen-soldier clearly constituted the core of the national community. Women appeared as devoted but intrinsically passive supporters. They provided love (presumably carnal as well as emotional) for the doomed heroes before battle and wept for them when they did not return. The ceremony performed the indestructibility of the social matrix created by consent, and the commitment of the community to prevail in the present struggle. The patriotic conclusion of the book did not renounce the despair of the earlier vignettes; rather, it tried to incorporate that pain into an anguished rededication to the grim task at hand. Consent had such grave consequences after the war precisely because of this paradox of despair and ever-deeper commitment.

In *Territoriaux de France,* Francisque Vial, like Pézard and Hallé, explained consent from the point of view of a small group of comrades. But Vial went on to generalize his version of consent to a specific category of soldier, the territorials, who he considered uniquely suited to representing the social matrix produced by consent. The Territorial army comprised men toward the end of the age limit for military service, some of the oldest soldiers in the French army. Most territorials were men with families in their late thirties and forties. As such, Vial argued, they were little swayed by propaganda or abstract military doctrine. They considered themselves full-grown men, fathers of families who saw the world and the war realistically. Territorials remained unimpressed either by a foolish external discipline or by the passions of war that might brutalize their younger regular-army comrades. Discipline among territorials was at once more diffuse and more intrusive than in the regular army, because it was more horizontal than vertical. Formal discipline was simply consent to the war in its specific military sense. Territorials had never really left the civilian society from which they came.

> It thus happened that discipline no longer came from the grip of wills from above on the wills from below. It came from below, spontaneously, from the effect of respect and affection that the soldier felt for conscientious and good leaders, who took care of him and who worked alongside him on the same task. No, one did not come to the territorials at the front to talk about class struggle. They are an egalitarian and democratic army, and we cannot say often enough, a fraternal army.[31]

31. Francisque Vial, *Territoriaux de France* (Paris: Berger-Levrault, 1918), 34. Hereafter cited by page number in the text.

Éditions Berger-Levrault, known mostly for books in military tactics and military history, published *Territoriaux de France* in February 1918. Like the books by Pézard and Hallé, Vial's was published under wartime censorship. His volume appeared as part of a series called "Collection France" claiming to disseminate the "authentic" experience of combatants. For all these reasons, *Territoriaux de France* is an unlikely text in which to seek opposition to the war. But the semiofficial character of the book does not mean that it represented consent in sanitized or simplistic terms, quite the reverse. Consent in Vial's account was refracted through gore, filth, and immense personal and collective suffering, the extent of which the author did seek to spare readers. Consent caused pain and suffering. But the horizontal bonds of comradeship, together with bonds of devotion to family, formed a web linking them to the national community and to the war writ large. To the territorials, duty to the family and their former and future lives as civilians served as the conduit between them and the national community.

At Verdun on July 10, 1916, the same month as the ceremony described by Hallé, Vial's unit was ordered to take up positions in one of the supporting lines of trenches under a heavy bombardment. It some respects, he observed, relieving another unit under a bombardment was actually worse than attacking, because by definition it was a passive exercise. They were exposed to artillery fire but could not respond by firing back: "you were only a miserable tramp, groaning and sweating under the weight of the pack, tripping over stones, falling in holes, and under the shelling, always advancing without knowing where you are being led, not even sure of arriving, in short, a miserable beast" (55).

When they got to their sector, they found it mostly destroyed. They would have to dig for several hours under enemy fire to repair it. At the intersection of the trench and the communications trench leading into it, Vial encountered "a cadaver, not even that, half a cadaver, only a trunk and a head. On the swollen face, on the glazed eyes wide open, on the frothy dribble on the violet lips are packets of green flies" (57). It was impossible to enter the remains of the trench without somehow climbing over "this terrifying heap of decomposed flesh." He tried but failed to find a way around it. There turned out to be more corpses in the communications trench. Vial wondered what his men were thinking as they marched forward among the dead, as shells continued to explode around them. Finally they arrived at their assigned position, or what remained of it. The dramatic climax of the story came when one soldier finally put words to their suffering:

> Suddenly a voice raised up, raucous and strained, and shouted out these simple words, more bitter than a curse:
> Ah! If our poor wives could see us now! (58)

From this fleeting cry of the heart, Vial drew a portrait of the territorials' concept of the war and their own consent to it. Particularly in their darkest moments, what supported them "was the old images of what you left back there, the image of wife and children." War was not for them any kind of adventure, and they sought no glory from it. Consent as they understood it was profound in its practicality.

> [The war] was an austere, imperious, unavoidable necessity; the necessity, having founded a family, of defending it. And in fighting, they thought first of their sons and their fields, just like in the "Marseillaise," of their homes and those sheltered there. These are their "war aims," this is what helps them to live the hard life of the front and, when necessary, to die. (59)

While censors no doubt delighted in the explicit mention of the French national anthem this far into the war, it is important not to read such an explanation as simply another repetition of wartime propaganda. *Bourrage de crâne* (literally "head stuffing," usually translated as "eyewash") depended on sanitizing experience at the front, certainly not the case here. Here, consent and "realism" appeared side by side, and indeed seemed to depend on each other.

As Vial described it, a logic of necessity rooted in family and comradeship precluded alienation from the war, even in extremis. He recalled the death of a comrade in June 1916. Shot in the chest, the man cried out, "I got mine . . . Ah, my poor children!" His last words were "You must tell my wife that I died bravely" (60). The man, a joiner from Lyons described as a rude fellow even among his fellow territorials, always carried a photograph of his wife and two children in the interior pocket of his coat. From seeing him look at the photograph, Vial understood "the foundation of his being, and which explained to me the cold hatred of the Boche that I had always noticed in him" (59). His dying words, for Vial, revealed "the secret of his energy, his bravery, of his stubborn commitment to a war he detested" (61). Like Pézard's explanation of consent, Vial's had its element of conceit, rooted in a proprietary sense of their collective, horrible experience. Vial's deceased comrade embodied, for him, uniquely "territorial" virtues, and a uniquely "territorial" logic of necessity:

> Not having felt enthusiasm, he does not feel discouragement. The longer the war continues, the more clear and pressing the reasons become to hold on. He does hold on. He will hold on to the end. (61)

Clearly, at the level of the individual and the group, there was much more to consent to the war than the mindless, reflexive patriotism of the *bourrage de crâne,* which no one disdained more than the soldiers themselves.

Whether one uses the term *consent* or *coercion,* scholars largely agree that the Third Republic had laid the ideological groundwork for the persistence of France in the Great War.[32] What Péronne historians call consent drew from the most elemental components of republican ideology—the totalized and individualized identification of the political self with the collectivity, extending from the nearest comrades to civilian society to the national community writ large. In obeying the dictates of those collectivities, soldiers were obeying themselves. For better or worse, the regime had done its work. But consent need not imply a neo-positivist interpretation of the Great War. Consent was drenched in blood. It came into existence through horrible circumstances of death, mutilation, humiliation, and pain. Consent also meant violence perpetrated as well as suffered. In its military variety, consent created an exclusionary male community, affirming the link implemented since the French Revolution between full citizenship and military service. Consent certainly reinscribed the masculine character of the Third Republic, a regime closely associated with war from its birth in 1871 to its death in 1940. Exactly how consent operated vis-à-vis the regime of the Third Republic and the affective national community needs further explanation.

The Republic and the National Community

The French have long been accustomed to construing their affective notions of France in about as many different ways as there are French people. In the Great War, monarchists (whether Bourbonists or Orléanists), Bonapartists, and untold varieties of republicans and leftists could all imagine their national communities very differently, and could imagine very different connections and disconnections between those communities and the regime of the day, the Third Republic. Certainly before 1914 many right-wing Catholics, secular reactionaries, and more than a few senior military officers tolerated the regime in daily life but did not see it as a legitimate representation of France. Many on the Left envisaged an international socialism that, if triumphant, might not displace "France" but would certainly displace the Third Republic.

At its founding in 1871, the Third Republic embodied a compromise that did not end revolutionary turmoil in France but gave it a protracted respite. The Third Republic rested on male popular sovereignty and social conservatism. It cared deeply about a few things, such as its schools, its railroads,

---

32. This is not in itself a new observation, given the old French aphorism that the Great War had been won by the schoolmasters of the republic.

and its military, but it treaded lightly on hierarchies of class and staunchly defended those of gender and race. Privately, and to a great degree publicly, its citizens construed "France" as they chose. The ability of the regime to tolerate different conceptions of the national community, perhaps, contributed to the resilience of the Third Republic, to this day the most durable regime in France since the monarchy of the Old Regime.[33]

The Great War joined the Third Republic and the various affective national communities as did nothing else over the life span of the regime. The war effected a powerful combination of republican logic and nationalist affect. The Union sacrée under which French went to war in 1914 united them as a citizenry and as a people. Former Communards shook hands with former soldiers who fired on them, monarchists embraced the tricolor, and workers, facing the prospect of a general European war, shelved their long-held intentions to strike. Certainly, the threat from the invader helped focus affections. France had lost Alsace and Lorraine in the Franco-Prussian War of 1870–71, and saw several of its northeastern departments occupied by the Germans in the present one. For practical purposes, all of the French agreed that France would no longer be France if it failed to prevail. This was precisely what made the whole question of a negotiated peace so intractable. France and the French had nothing they could negotiate.

Yet there was more to the Union sacrée than hatred for the invading Other. The Republic provided a conceptual framework in which to represent France as an integrated political community absolutely dedicated to victory. It bound together all French people, at once equally and hierarchically. In this specific political sense, the Union sacrée created its own reality, which endured long after its affective attributes dissipated as the war dragged on. Logic often merged seamlessly with affect, with some peculiar results. In some cases the Union sacrée produced commitment that bordered on pathology. At the very least, it produced a total commitment, which would require a commensurately total redemption at the war's end.

The *égalité* of Third Republic ideology notwithstanding, male citizens were certainly more equal than female citizens, and white citizen-soldiers were much more equal than their colonial counterparts. Metropolitan soldiers constituted an elite, the guardians both of the regime and the national community. Soldiers whose testimonies were published became an elite within this elite. Some wrote from this position in an encoded, almost inverted way. They saw themselves as absorbed by the evolving republican

---

33. The Fifth Republic (founded in 1958) will not match the sixty-nine-year life span of the Third Republic (1871–1940) until the year 2027.

political culture around them, which assimilated them into a "people's war." They claimed to write simply as instruments of a certain war culture.

Gaston de Pawlowski's *Dans les rides du front* (In the Furrows of the Front) comprised newspaper articles written in 1915 and 1916, when French fortunes in the conflict were steadily declining. That these articles were themselves wartime propaganda is obvious. But as we saw with Vial, propaganda and *bourrage de crâne* did not need to be the same thing. Flamboyant rhetoric did not obscure an intriguing argument explaining consent among citizen-soldiers. In "La Guerre 'civile'" (The "Civil" War) de Pawlowski noted that in the past, armies had been raised and led by subsectors of the population. These armies then made war. In the present conflict, war had made the army. Like Henry Barbusse, though from a more centrist political position, de Pawlowski concluded that the politicized army of the Republic would not just win, but make an end to war: "*the army* is born of *the war*, not an army of career soldiers, but an *army of civilians* who, quite justly, have taken up arms to make war on war and to exterminate it."[34]

Certainly, de Pawlowski had read his Clausewitz, particularly on the "people's war."[35] But if Clausewitz had been a bit perplexed by the *Volkskrieg* as the Spanish had fought it against Napoleon, de Pawlowski saw the French people's war as the teleological outcome of the development of the French as a nation since 1789. Consequently, the war, in the end, would complete the work of the Revolution: "It is that, for the first time perhaps, we have a republican army, a *civil army* that the Revolution itself at its most developed did not know."[36] The army of the Great War represented, and was represented by, the entirety of the French national community. The Union sacrée had become an accomplished fact. Soldiers had become the distillation of the Republic, unshakable in their commitment to victory:

> To speak to this army of peace without definitive and complete victory, that would be a calamity one could imagine only in dreams. And we do not dream. Truly, for all of our soldiers of the front, the months do not count anymore, and the abandoned private affairs are forgotten. There is a great *civil affair* to realize at the front.[37]

34. Gaston de Pawlowski, *Dans les rides du front* (Paris: La Renaissance du Livre, 1917), 32; italics in the original.

35. See Carl von Clausewitz, *On War*, trans. Michael Howard and Peter Paret (Princeton: Princeton University Press, 1976), 479–83.

36. Pawlowski, *Dans les rides du front,* 34.

37. Ibid., 34–35.

Together, and totally implicated in the fate of one another, the French and their army would change the world.

Indeed, de Pawlowski continued, the Union sacrée had managed to appropriate French antimilitarism, and to direct it against war itself. In peacetime many Frenchmen had found military service an annoying inconvenience. But war had transformed grumbling conscripts into devoted warriors: "The same soldiers who, in time of peace, counted the days they had left in the barracks and waited for the release of 'the class' now have teeth clenched like mastiffs, and will not let go, even if one announced to them that this war would last forever."[38] This militarized antimilitarism was precisely what made the French army so powerful. The Germans "had not foreseen, in the greater sense of the term, our formidable *antimilitarist force,* or at least, did not understand that it would be directed against them."[39] The result had become a European crusade against militarism: "it is a *civil army,* and conscious of being so, which, in this struggle of giants, alone can overthrow the old idol of militarism that dishonors our planet."

"The France of 1914–1917 is more sincerely democratic than it has ever been, and she is in love with command," wrote Alfred de Tarde in January 1917. Georges Bonnet read these words while correcting the page proofs of his *L'Âme du soldat* (The Soul of the Soldier) and considered the citation important enough to include it in the final published version of his own book.[40] Bonnet had arrived at the front with some social standing. His father had been a lawyer at the Cour de cassation (Court of Appeals), and the son had studied at the Lycée Henri IV and later at the École supérieure des hautes études and at the École des sciences politiques. After the war, Bonnet became a high civil servant.[41] Bonnet had a particular interest in the ways his social and educational inferiors interpreted the war and their consent to it. He plainly envied at some level their variant of war culture and saw himself as their scribe.

Bonnet could not get out of his mind a story told to him by a friend concerning a certain Lauteu, an electrician who Bonnet's friend barely even knew. One day, the usually laconic Lauteu was holding forth about how happy he had been before the war, living with his wife and two children, and about how anxiously he awaited his next leave. "Above all," the friend recounted, "he repeatedly mentioned his inexpressible fear of death, the thought of which, I could tell, haunted all his thoughts."[42] Lauteu con-

38. Ibid.
39. Ibid., 36–37; italics in the original.
40. Georges Bonnet, *L'Âme du soldat* (Paris: Payot, 1917), 241.
41. Biographical information from Norton Cru, *Témoins,* 420.
42. Bonnet, *L'Âme du soldat,* 112–16. Hereafter cited by page number in the text.

gratulated the friend on just having returned from a dangerous mission, but then chided him for having accepted it in the first place. Lauteu told him "that he wouldn't have done it, that it was too stupid to work for glory when you have your own hide to save." After continuing in this vein for some while, Lauteu received urgent orders to make some repairs, under heavy artillery bombardment, on telephone wires that had been cut in a part of their sector. The friend looked at him with curiosity.

> So what was this man going to do, indifferent as he was to glory and so worried about his own existence?
> My curiosity was disappointed. He listened coldly, took a look at the necessary tools, and then, despite the bombardment which had resumed more ferociously than before, he left our shelter without apparent emotion.

Immediately upon completing his task, Lauteu was killed by shrapnel. The story made Bonnet recall similar examples, such as that of a childhood friend of his who at school had constantly provoked their teachers with antimilitarist diatribes. In time, the friend became a valiant officer who was wounded, decorated, and finally killed. Of course, a chasm of educational and social rank separated the two dead men. "But all the same," he concluded, "I found in both of them the same fight against the same knee-jerk resistance, conquered right away by one, with more difficulty by the other." The less-sophisticated man, it seems, simply proved able to grasp the essence of consent more speedily.

Bonnet embarked upon an anecdotal poll of his comrades to try to explain "the strange and invisible force that animated them and that brought them to where they are" (120). Some provided an abstract explanation—such as wanting the present war to be the last, or defending justice and civilization. But Bonnet remained generally unconvinced of the power of such abstractions over the mass of French soldiers. After all, was it realistic to believe that this war could actually remove the human affliction of war itself? Rather, most hoped simply that the "the present combat will ensure the survivors a good number of peaceful years." Moreover, "the poilu of today thinks first of himself and his children, before dreaming of his great-nephews" (122). Certainly, the soldiers were horrified by German atrocities of 1914. Most were aware in a general sense of "the difference that existed between our civilization and their *Kultur*," but most found "these words too complex for their simple minds" (123). In any event (and somewhat contradicting himself), Bonnet concluded that this highly literate population had read with enough sophistication enough civilian newspapers to doubt such oversimplifications anyway. Some identified a kind of aggressiveness unique to the French as a race. He himself felt some inclination "toward this combative instinct, which long heredity has particularly bestowed upon us, the French." How else to explain "the intense joy that wells up, in the trench, at well-directed fire from the artillery?" "I do not say that this pleasure is very noble," he admitted, but neither did he condemn it. His point rather was that this joy was general, independent of educational or social background (125–26).

But to Bonnet, neither ideological abstraction nor hereditary *furia francese* adequately explained the story of Lauteu. His was "an individual mission, which required sangfroid, not enthusiasm" (130). Repairing a telephone wire under heavy artillery fire involved danger but not aggression. A bit earlier, Bonnet had hinted at an affective explanation for "the strange and invisible force" that drove men such as Lauteu forward:

> Joseph de Maistre responded: God.
> Today, we say: Patrie. (120)

But Bonnet's version of the patrie had specific logical characteristics. Lauteu did not see himself as a hero, let alone a patriotic fanatic, quite the reverse. His frame of reference was his nuclear family: "in his male self-centeredness, he could see no farther than his small familial corner." Yet he did his duty instinctively.

> He had wanted to submit himself to social discipline, of which military discipline is but one of the forms. But the order came, imperious, inflexible, which recalled in him the most intimate links that attached him to society, making him forget for a moment his status as father and husband. And then he left without hesitation, as a soldier. (136–37)

The apparent contradiction between the family and military duty was just that. The family constituted the link between Lauteu and the broader society, the social matrix linking the individual and the affective collectivity otherwise known as the patrie. When the order came, he did what the regime, its schools, and its army had told him to do—see his duty to his family in terms of his duty as a citizen-soldier.

Immediately thereafter, Bonnet recounted a conversation among some other comrades, evidently of a higher educational background than Lauteu. They waxed philosophical on the insignificance of a few years of life before all eternity. "Death, is it such a great evil," they opined, "when one has an awareness of having lived?" No less than Lauteu, these "latter-day Stoics" loved life as they had lived it before the war, Bonnet concluded.

They would love it still more if they survived. But, like Lauteu, "they understood the vanity of all resistance. They found excellent arguments for making the task easier." Like their less-educated comrade, they responded immediately to an internalized sense of duty. They simply invented sophisticated rationalizations, at once philosophical and affective, after the fact.

To Bonnet, a common social discipline linking all citizen-soldiers provided the bedrock of consent. The electrician and the graduate of an elite *lycée* both had the same relationship to authority, the essence of republican *égalité*. Earlier in the book, Bonnet quoted with approval an article published in *L'Oeuvre* in November 1915 that defined what characterized a French soldier: "The poilu in time of war is simply a former civilian who remembers what he was and hopes for nothing so much as becoming one again" (38). Whatever his educational background, a poilu would remain a civil creature—male and otherwise commensurable with his countrymen in rights and responsibilities. To recall the words of de Tarde quoted by Bonnet, it was precisely this quality that made France in some of its darkest hours of the Great War more democratic than it had ever been. The poilu, whatever his class or educational background, could be "in love with command" because the authority behind that command originated in himself.

Nothing about a republican identity in France precluded affective inclusions and exclusions by race. The notion of France as a racial republic dated at least back to the Revolution. The chorus of the "Marseillaise," after all, called for the watering of French furrows with the impure blood of the enemies of the patrie. But by the early twentieth century, decades of low birth rates, which sank even further during the war, heightened anxieties about the strength of the French in the Darwinian struggle for national survival.[43] It is not surprising, then, to see the national community in the Great War articulated as a racial community, in recognizably republican terms. For André Maillet, a private in the infantry, race bound all of the French to one another in a single living but endangered organism. This was precisely what made the stakes in the war as high as they were. The Great War had become nothing less than a life-or-death struggle among biologically antagonistic peoples.

The coercive force driving *Sous le fouet du destin* (Under the Whip of Destiny) was biology itself. To be sure, Maillet's reading of social Darwinism was neither novel nor particularly sophisticated. He began with a melodramatic prologue, in which the dreaming, amorous men of France were called to their biological duty of war:

43. See, for example, Jean Marc Bernardini, *Le Darwinisme social en France (1859–1918): fascination et rejet d'une idéologie* (Paris: CNRS Histoire, 1997).

War, this monster, which was sleeping under the blue sky of your dreams, has come to break its chains and bellow across the mountains and plains. And hideous hatred, at its signal, lets go its bloody mobs, across the human grave-yards.

The gutters of blood already redden the harvest beaten down by the storm. The cadavers rot in the middle of the astonished crops, under a gray sky de-lighted by the black flight of voracious and joyous vultures . . . And the en-emy works away to destroy your race.[44]

As a figure of myth, War could be imprisoned from time to time, effectively enough so that the naturally peaceful Frenchmen could nearly forget that it was there. But eventually, the biological necessity of war would impose itself. Indeed, war seemed as "natural" as the mountains and plains across which it issued its bloody cries. Blood and the shedding of blood were part and parcel of this natural drama. War would determine the survival of the French race. Human volition could not stop the natural drama of war any more than other natural phenomena, such as death or putrefaction.

In Maillet's biological republic, blood linked all Frenchmen to one an-other as mutually responsible guardians of the race. Race both transcended the individual and implicated him totally in the outcome of the war, just as an individual cell is individually and totally implicated in the organism. Bi-ological necessity required natural obedience to the collectivity:

You no longer exist for yourself. Individuals exist only for *those* who remain and for *those* who will come. This is the era of great sacrifices!

Go on, then! Hurry up! I am the soul of your patrie, I am its destiny, your destiny. (2)

Maillet's destiny, and those of his millions of comrades, was to live and die for the future of the race and for French blood. "I know that in this life of struggle and suffering, all of my deeds are useful," he assured himself, "and are necessary to save my race. I feel pride in marching to sacrifice, almost a savage pride."

The survival of the race, of course would have to depend on both gen-ders. Race met gender in a crucial episode almost buried in Maillet's lengthy text. He described his entry into the tiny bit of Alsace reconquered in 1914. He had been raised on nationalist fables of the abduction of the "Lost Provinces," steeped in gender symbolism:

Alsace and Lorraine! They were for me two adorable young girls that brig-ands had taken from their families. Alsace above all had my love; a blond child coiffed with a large moiré ribbon in black, with a tricolor rosette pinned on, who they made do work that was beneath her and who they brutally mistreated. (64)

But as his squad entered the village of Urbès, the men met only disappointment. They saw practically no one at all, only a few old women and one young girl, indistinguishable from females in France proper. He complained: "What happened to the Alsace of our dreams? The Alsace of legend with its picturesque chalets and its native holiday costumes?" His comrades became convinced that they had been tricked, that real *Alsaciennes* could not have looked so familiar, and that they had walked into a German trap. Some concluded that all civilians should be shot immediately. When a comrade brusquely asked Maillet how to say "hello" to the Alsatian women, he immediately responded with "Fraulein, ich liebe Sie!" (Miss, I love you!). The men repeated this phrase endlessly, unaware of its meaning and, it seemed, peculiarly unconcerned that they were speaking German (74–75).

This proved a rare example of irony in heavy-handed text. But embedded in this fleeting episode was a view of the mission of the racial national community. The Alsace of fantasy was geographically French, its inhabitants presumably French by race. But many flesh-and-blood Alsatians spoke either German or an Alsatian dialect not intelligible to the French. France as a nation, and the French as a race, had to "reconquer" Alsace biologically as well as militarily. For now, the love of the French citizen-soldier for Alsace and for Alsatian women would have to express itself in the language of the racial enemy. But *Alsaciennes* became their own kind of battleground. Consummated victory, presumably, would mean that they would be able to woo them with "Mademoiselle, je vous aime" (Miss, I love you). In a postwar mating dance between Mars and Venus, the male conquest of the impressionable and subordinate female would at once echo, domesticate, and redeem the original "abduction" of the "Lost Provinces" back in 1871.

In the meantime, however, the French had to defeat their biological enemy. Both French culture and German *Kultur*, it seemed, had their origins in national blood. Maillet admitted to having studied in Germany before the war. At the time, he concluded in his innocence that the Germans "were men, like the men of my country—workers, perseverant and methodical" (66–67). He confessed to a partial seduction by *Kultur*—whether the sonatas of Beethoven or the "fearful theories" of Schopenhauer and Nietzsche. Yet Maillet had never truly been duped. The waves of the beautiful

Rhine themselves "spoke only of the hatred of the two enemy peoples, always alive, insurmountable" (68). The monster of war simply brought this hatred into the open. Maillet asked himself rhetorically: "Do we obey the same law which, inside our bodies, commands the phagocytes to run to the assistance of cells attacked by the invading hoard of microbes? Are we the phagocytes of the race?" (99). In perhaps a feigned moment of anguish about the prospect of actually having to kill a German, he pondered "what fates at the beginning of time and at the foundation of our races brought us to this, to make of me a hunter lying in wait, of him a prey that I will strike down?" Yet he concluded that the experience would prove easy to master when the time came, *"because that is my duty"* (161–62).

Race war grounded in biology was not necessarily ennobling. War, like other forms of natural conflict, was filled with suffering and gore. Near the end of the book, he recounted a costly and indecisive attack in Hartmannswillerkopf in Alsace in December 1915. His friend Corporal Christin died like a cornered animal, fighting an enemy greatly superior in numbers. All of the men he commanded had been killed or wounded:

> All alone, he fought like a lion, up to the moment when a grenade blew up right in his face, putting him out of action. The explosion mangled his face. It put a hole through one eye, seriously wounded the other one, broke one arm, and crushed his chest. But he did not want to let *them* have his carcass and, blind, managed to crawl back.
>
> He was there, in a hole, his face red and black, unrecognizable, the eyelids closed by the swelling, the eyes swollen as well, planted in his face like two baked apples. (201)

Indeed, they had all come to resemble Corporal Christin, one way or another: "I am no more than a wreck, a bloodless piece of human flotsam, a skeleton that crawls, moving by what remains of my will. [. . .] I am no longer a man. [. . .] What sort of monster am I then?" (204–5). Yet man's own nature had brought him to this state. Consequently, he could not rise above his biology any more than any other creature of nature. Man was simply cursed with an awareness of his bestial condition. War would always be, "like death, a law of our animal nature. It is an original defect that makes our intelligence more terrible. We are the most unhappy of animals" (219).

Yet Maillet's suffering did not alienate him from the war, quite the reverse. The more bitter he became, the more convinced he was of the necessity of the war. Indeed, in the same passage recounting the death of Christin, he scoffed: "This war is the last one, say the monsters who make it" (217). What he had earlier referred to as "this sacrifice, active and a matter of consent" concerned a stubborn eagerness to relinquish his own life for the eternal life of the race.

> Death is nothing; only life matters. And the life of the race, the life of the nation is superior to individual life. What is needed to save the race in danger is not to die, but to live and to fight, regardless of the suffering that comes from it, and regardless of death if it comes to that. (171–72)

Maillet's accounts ended with a somewhat melodramatic description of his evacuation from the front, in some kind of semidelirious state. He had a vision of all the heroes he saw fight and die in the engagement. He gathered all his remaining strength to salute "all these martyrs who fight, who suffer, and who die so that the race may live, so that what is right may live, so that France might live" (235). Maillet could no more renounce his implication in the war than his biological identity as a man of the French race. Toward the end of his book, Maillet expressed no desire to renounce either, as a proud member of a racial republic.

The argument that consent is simply disguised coercion excludes the possibility, shown in various témoignages examined here, of some sort of self-conscious embrace of the conflict. Indeed, to a radical partisan of consent such as Maillet, misery and commitment seemed to reinforce each other in a vicious circle. Louis Mairet's *Carnet d'un combatant* (1919) is the published version of his diary, supplemented by some of his letters home. He explained consent in terms that were not overtly like racial like those of Maillet, but in their way no less extreme. To Mairet, consent had morphed into a kind of existential dilemma. He neither rejected his intolerable situation nor saw any resolution of it in the foreseeable future.

The best-known section of the book is a diary entry dated July 2, 1916, the second day of the Allied offensive at the Somme. The entry took the form of a meditation comprising about three printed pages on why soldiers fight.[45] Mairet certainly took no hope from the greatest Allied offensive of the war to date: "Here and now it opens, this new race to death. A new graveyard takes its place in the illustrious line." Mairet was nevertheless intrigued by the willingness of millions of British and French with no apparent stake in the matter to take part in the present conflict: "Do they fight for the patrie? They hardly know about it. Great ideas remain inaccessible to the common people," he (like Bonnet) observed somewhat condescendingly. Few, he maintained, held any real animosity for Germany or for Ger-

45. Louis Mairet, *Carnet d'un combattant (11 février 1915–16 avril 1917)* (Paris: Georges Crès, 1919), 172–75.

mans. He doubted that the young and unmarried would really fight for the wives and children of others, or that those without property had much enthusiasm for giving up their lives to protect that of others. "Very well," he assured his readers, "the soldier of 1916 fights not for Alsace, nor to ruin Germany, nor for the patrie."

Why then did he fight? At a certain level, the resilience of the soldier of 1916 seemed abstract and apolitical: "He fights out of honesty, out of habit, and out of strength. He fights because he cannot do otherwise." Enthusiasm in August 1914 had given way to discouragement in the first winter, which in turn had become a grim but unshakable resignation in the third year of the war. The war had rendered the abnormal all too normal:

> That which you hoped would be only a transitory state, this suffering, these dangers, the risk of death, all this, in time, became a situation stable even in its instability. You exchanged your home for a foxhole, your family for friends made under fire. You measured life in misery, as you once did in well being. You calibrated these feelings at the level of daily events, and found equilibrium again in disequilibrium. You don't even imagine anymore that all this might change. You no longer see yourself going home. You still hope for it; you no longer count on it.

By 1916 the war had created its own world—an affective dystopia. Otherwise stated, the war had reconfigured daily life through warping existing categories, those of space, family, rhythms of action. Indeed, the war had created its own seemingly permanent temporality. One might hope to return home, as the agnostic might hope for a life after this one. But one would not count on it.

Yet at every turn Mairet declined to denounce the war as unnecessary, because he considered himself so implicated in it. The poilu of 1916 remained inseparable from the national community of which he had become the exemplar. That community, which he referred to as *le peuple* (the people), "possesses to the highest degree the conviction of necessity. We must make war. For what cause, or why, they do not know. But they feel obscurely that it is necessary." Mairet concluded his meditation for that day in an intriguingly arrogant tone, which spoke to the deadly embrace of suffering and commitment as well as to the proprietary nature of experience. The Republic as an abstraction had provided a language binding together the national community, particularly each poilu to every other poilu, and through this union to every other French citizen, active and passive. But the poilu had a unique and unimpeachable ability to speak for that community:

Finally, the fundamental uprightness of people who have suffered so much, the indignation they feel at all baseness, the hatred of the shirkers, the right to speak and command that they claim for later, the satisfaction of duty accomplished, the pride they keep inside themselves, this is the poilu of 1916. I have told the truth. May someone contradict me if he dares!

Consent had become an intractable state of political being in Mairet, but not a static one. It had its own temporality, which seemed to expect an ever-worsening situation. After forty days in the Somme front, Mairet was lightly wounded by shrapnel on the day his unit was relieved. He continued to ruminate on the poilu's plight into the fall of 1916 while recuperating in Paris. Militarily speaking, he opined, there was no reason for the war ever to end. The German offensive at Verdun and the Allied offensive at the Somme had clearly demonstrated that, to both sides.[46] Soldiers, it seemed, could continue to make war forever: "Accustomed to suffering, submissive to discipline, ready to die, the foot-soldier of this war no longer knows fear. [. . .] The end of the war is prevented by the warrior."[47]

In December 1916, Mairet returned to active duty, apparently more fatalistic and discouraged than ever. "The canon has made me stupid," he admitted; "the enormous emotions of combat have made me blasé, and ill-treatment has dried out my heart."[48] The strategy of attrition on the battlefield continued to achieve little in a military sense. But at least it appeared to be wearing down the body and soul of the poilu, its instrument as well as its apparent victim. "Reason gets lost before the spectacle of scientific struggle," he added in a letter to his parents dated December 19, "in which progress serves the return of barbarism, before the spectacle of a civilization which directs itself toward its own destruction."[49]

Yet attrition in this sense never eroded consent, indeed the reverse. Mairet kept close tabs on the national and international politics of the war, and commented on them frequently. He dismissed a public offer of the Central Powers in December 1916 to consider peace negotiations. Such an offer, he scoffed, was simply a ploy to pull German chestnuts from the fire. "Let them burn," he answered, "they are too close to 'just right' for us to take them out. Our sacrifices require a consecration."[50] In his December 19 letter to his parents he wrote bitterly of neutral parties who talked of peace. In reply to Woodrow Wilson's statement that the protagonists had

46. Ibid., 249.
47. Ibid., 249–50.
48. Ibid., 256.
49. Ibid., 271.
50. Ibid., 260.

never precisely stated their war aims, Mairet wrote: "A mistaken point of view, Monsieur Wilson." He believed the Germans had in fact been quite clear about their war aims from the outset—the subjugation of Europe. Likewise, the Swiss had called for reasonableness when necessity required irrationality. The year 1917 would show that the answer to the dilemmas of the war of attrition was more attrition:

> It is necessary, then, whatever they say, that the struggle continue until one of the two parties is finished. This is what we must convince ourselves of, on this New Year's Eve. [. . .] It would be strongly commended this year to persuade ourselves of the following: It is not caresses that stop the wild boar running in the field; *it is not words that will make an end to the war.*[51]

In different ways, Maillet and Mairet pointed to the pathological potential of consent. At the very least, they showed how problematic it was ever going to be to justify or demobilize consent once the war was over. Maillet considered the French individually and totally connected to one another as a race. As such, they would fight the war as a Darwinian struggle for survival. But this, in effect, made the Great War a race war. What kind of an end could such a conflict have? In Mairet's case, the irresistible force of consent faced the immovable object of the stalemated war of attrition. The total and individual commitment of the poilus, as logically and affectively constructed, was open ended, and it deepened with adversity. He could not give up on the war, because to do so meant giving up on a system of power whose legitimacy lay in himself. He could thus curse the war as morally bankrupt in one sentence and insist it be fought to the finish in the next. If Maillet lacked confidence that war as a human affliction could ever be overcome, Mairet seemed to doubt even that the present war would have an end. Any conceivable end would require a total victory over the foe. Even assuming such a victory was feasible, what could redeem the cost of totalized and individualized commitment? By definition, consent as a principle of narrative posed problems of conclusion and closure.

The Logic of Redemption

Thought of in terms of a standard, three-part narrative of situation-crisis-resolution, consent had beginning and a middle, but not a proper end. The situation was the war, and the crisis was consent as explained here—a commitment that deepened with suffering and despair. Yet how could the crisis find resolution, and the war end in a way that would make consent

51. Ibid., 273; italics in the original.

explicable as somehow "worth it"? Narratives of consent stop, but by definition do not "end" in the sense of containing closure and a moral. Some texts trail off inconclusively, or finish simply with a restatement of consent as already explained. Vial, for example, ended by asserting that "you must seek these humble and strong virtues, through which we will be worthy of victory, among the territorials of France."[52] As we saw, Hallé ended his account by backtracking in time, with a tortured affirmation of consent performed in a ceremony of decoration.

Some narratives of consent simply stopped because of something that happened to the author. Maillet, as we saw, finished his narrative with a somewhat contrived description of thoughts he mistakenly believed to be his last. Some accounts were cut short by the death of the author, such as that of Mairet, who died on the first day of the offensive at the Chemin des Dames in 1917. Other témoins simply stopped writing their recollections without trying to compose a proper conclusion. Marc Bloch, as we saw in chapter 1, terminated his "souvenirs" in 1917 and returned to his work in medieval history, apparently never expecting them to enter the public domain. Pézard's last chapter provided an extended meditation on death and mourning, written from his hospital bed. He described not so much closure as an amputation of suffering: "If an adolescent sobs hysterically into his pillow, he finally calms down and falls asleep exhausted. His throat, still hard and dry, relaxes. His breath trembles a bit less in the night, and the blood in his veins softens. In grave and serene waves, as in silence, he listens to a single chord droning incessantly in the hollows of his burning ears."[53] The best-known passage in the book testified to his abrupt, even brutal farewell to his experience at war:

> Let me say this slowly, for a pain-wracked thought is slow. Let me speak slowly, letting fall, with regret, the dear murderous syllables: "Farewell, my poor war!" And that is all.
> *Adieu, ma pauvre guerre.*[54]

Like Bloch, though perhaps more transparently, Pézard preferred to ruminate on the Great War after 1918 through the encoded means of academic scholarship. He became a distinguished authority on Dante.

Narratives of consent have an implied form of closure deferred to the indefinite future. Consent, in a word, required redemption. Reflections with which texts finished often took the form of more or less precise demands

52. Vial, *Territoriaux de France*, 64.
53. Pézard, *Nous autres à Vauquois*, 348.
54. Ibid., 350; italics in the original.

made on the national community of the future to redeem the sacrifices of the present. "Victory" could not simply restore the *status quo ante bellum*, for too many lives had been shattered. As consent radicalized, so too did its deferred price. The national community and the regime had engineered and required absolute commitment. Absolute commitment, in turn, required absolute redemption. However diffuse, complex, or intractable the problem, the Third Republic and the national community would have to provide the solution after victory.

As we saw, Marot's *Ceux qui vivent* had a kind of narrative structure, which developed consent in terms of emotions and duties synthesized into rational thoughts. We also saw Marot put Christian theology at the service of interpreting consent. The book ended with a return to religion, in perhaps the most agonized pages of the book. His format was an agnostic's prayer, each part of which began, "O my God, if you exist."[55] He begged God simply to hear the tortures of the dead, the dying, and those who may yet die in the trenches:

> Oh my God, if you exist, listen to the groaning from the lungs full of holes, the roar of grinding flesh, the agony of souls torn from bodies, from those bodies that you have formed in your image, and that are tortured by the wicked.

Their agony threatened to turn them against God. Marot asked this God, who in the prayer may not even exist, "to hear rise in their voices their resentment, their doubts, their blasphemies, the hymn of despair and anger that they shout toward you, Lord." Marot identified soldiers as reenacting the sacrifice of Jesus, here at its most alienated moment, when, just before his death, Jesus became convinced that his Father had forgotten him. Near the end of the prayer, Marot begged God to restore the means of faith among his victims: "Turn away from your closed skies their gazes and their prayers; make them return to themselves and find you there. Give them faith in themselves, so that they may have faith in you." Consent seemed almost to fall apart because of its own internal contradictions. Only supernatural power, whose existence was by no means certain in the prayer, could redeem their sacrifice.

Yet is redemption in the book really religious in nature? If so, why is Marot's prayer so uncertain about the existence of God? Ultimately, *Ceux qui vivent*, published in August 1919,[56] just weeks after the signing of the Versailles Treaty, was much more about salvation in this world than the

55. Marot, *Ceux qui vivent*, 250–52.
56. See Norton Cru, *Témoins*, 449.

next. Marot's narrative of identity, a journey from emotions to duties to consent, stopped with a desperate call for redemption. Reading the book as a narrative requires returning to the beginning. Marot opened the preface with a poem which began:

> Those who live are those who struggle. There are
> Those who for whom a firm design fills up heart and head
> Those who because destiny requires it, climb the harsh peaks
> Those who walk thoughtfully, carried away with a sublime goal,
> Having it before their eyes, ceaselessly, night and day
> Or some holy toil or some great love.[57]

This poem, perhaps, imitates Charles Péguy's famous 1913 poem "Heureux Ceux," discussed in chapter 3, which praised as redeemed in advance those who willingly sacrificed their lives for the national community in a Just War. Marot's book spoke to survivors, to those who had lived. While the poem in his book certainly lacked the easy, untested assurance of Péguy, the connection between redemption and national community was just as clear:

> Thus the soil, fertilized with the blood that repurchased it, nourishes the seed
> of a better humanity, renewed by courage and simplicity.
>   Those who live are those who struggle for this Renaissance.

The blood of the martyrs and the survivors had provided the seeds for the renewal of the affective national community. The virtues of consent, bred in the agony of the trenches, could nourish this renewal. The rest was up to France itself. The war had created an elite of those who died and suffered, to whom the national community was massively indebted. The sacrifices of that elite had to be rendered meaningful in this world. The content of that renewal had to be political. This was Marot's most frantic hope in August 1919, for a national renaissance that alone could provide real closure to his narrative.

Bonnet concluded *L'Âme du soldat* with an extended section about a hundred pages long, titled "If ever you have the joy of returning home," in which he speculated on the future. He formulated the relationship between consent and redemption in essentially the same terms as Marot, though in a manner that was at once more down-to-earth and more innocent in its positivism. He had an unquestioned, and in retrospect unrealistic, confidence in the continuity of the regime and the national community in the af-

---

57. Marot, *Ceux qui vivent*, 9–10.

termath of the Great War. The war, he believed, had not fundamentally altered human nature. For example, he doubted that the religious revival of the war would long outlast it: "after the war, as before it, we will find unbelievers and believers, rebels against all religious practice, as well as the assiduously faithful, timid people and fanatics."[58] Social conflict in France would not end even among the community of veterans, because "the ties created by the common life amid perils and the constant threat of death were more of comradeship than true friendship."[59] But the war had shown the Frenchman at his best as a citizen. The regime and its citizen-soldiers had not only survived their supreme ordeal, but had affirmed themselves through winning it: "in returning home, the combatants will be more attached than ever to our democratic institutions."[60] The surviving citizen-soldiers would return home to enrich the lives of their compatriots.

The war had made the poilu a "pacifist," to use Bonnet's own term, but in a very narrow sense. He had become more aware of the broader world, of "the consequences that the treaties and the deeds of our diplomats could have for their property, their families, their own peace of mind." In the future, the cautious but clearly Wilsonian poilu would want "less intrigue, more frankness, and more light let into the conduct of foreign affairs." Bonnet foresaw "a 'pacifism' less blind, less confident, but more active, which wants new methods and sturdy barriers."[61]

But as this somewhat vague conception of the new world order suggested, Bonnet's idealism rested on his confidence in the present regime and the existing social and cultural structures governing the national community. He believed that the war had not fundamentally altered the nineteenth-century teleology of national progress. Redemption would occur through the normal evolution of France. The war had made the national community and the Third Republic purer versions of what they already were. It had also raised an exemplar, the poilu and future veteran. Some might worry, he argued, that "after having lived this life in common in which each one sacrificed himself for all, he would return to the egoist motto of every man for himself."[62] Yet such fears would prove unfounded. The strength of the poilus lay in their ability forged at the front to reconcile the individual and the collective. "They will feel how closely individual interests are tied to those of the nation," Bonnet wrote confidently. Indeed, the French soldier's ferocious individuality had enabled him to triumph over his homogenous

58. Bonnet, *L'Âme du soldat,* 165.
59. Ibid., 204–5.
60. Ibid., 192.
61. Ibid., 227–29.
62. Ibid., 229.

German foe: "This spirit of independence made our men incomparable soldiers. They have in them the means, if they know how to use them, of becoming the best citizens in the world."[63] The renewal of postwar France had already begun in the trenches. Redemption would come naturally and with time. But it would come all the same.

More overtly utopian was the imagined global community of Albert Thierry's posthumous *Les Conditions de la paix* (The Conditions of Peace).[64] Thierry had been a friend of Charles Péguy and a pupil of Frascisque Vial at the École normale superiéure de Saint-Cloud. Thierry had been killed during the Artois offensive of May 1915. A heavily censored version of his manuscript had been published in 1916, and a complete version in December 1918, with the deleted selections restored and identified. Thierry's text thus provides an unusual window onto wartime censorship practices. Much of the content of *Les Conditions de la paix* would have been recognizable to readers at the time as a very French version of Wilsonian idealism, if read not just on the stage of world diplomacy, but inward, touching the deepest levels of the human soul. Certainly, Thierry's friends pursued publication of the complete work as a monument to their deceased friend, and as documentation that the precocious hero had anticipated much of the idealism swirling around France immediately after the armistice.

But at another level, Norton Cru is correct to view the book as testimony rather than as simply a political manifesto.[65] Indeed, reading it as a narrative of experience makes it possible to engage the text today beyond an ironic amusement at its naiveté and its French nationalism masquerading as universalism. For Thierry had dared to carry the redemption of consent through to a complex series of logical conclusions. Self-consciously, *Les Conditions de la paix* was a book written from a certain position, that of a citizen-soldier of the Great War. The position of the author as a combatant conferred legitimacy both on him and on the contents of the text. Thierry's book was written at or near the front, and he noted scrupulously where and when he wrote each section, as though he were writing a kind of ideological diary. He provided a blueprint for the redemption of consent, within the individuated self and as well as in the world as a whole. Logic met affect in Thierry's easy identification of ideals of the French with those of humanity itself.

Like Marot's *Ceux qui vivent*, Thierry's book has an implicit narrative

---

63. Ibid., 233.
64. Albert Thierry, *Les Conditions de la paix: méditations d'un combattant* (Paris: Ollendorff, 1918).
65. See Norton Cru, *Témoins*, 469–72.

structure recording the development of an ideological construct. It took the form of an elaborate peace treaty, with numbered clauses organized into five broad categories.

I. Declaration of the Rights of Peoples
II. The Conditions of European Peace
III. The Conditions of French Peace
IV. The Conditions of Universal Peace
V. The Conditions of Interior Peace

Together, these categories comprised concentric circles, with the narrative proceeding inward, from the global to the European to the French. The last two categories concerned the components of the individual, the universalized (yet specifically French) poilu who had internalized the ideological means of redeeming the horrific sacrifices of the war, whatever its duration and whatever its cost.

In world affairs, a redeemed, republican France would serve as exemplar for other nations. Thierry's Declaration of the Rights of Peoples was overtly "an imitation of the Declaration of the Rights of Man, here proposed in homage to France as a model for the nations."[66] The "confederated powers" comprised both the victors and the vanquished in the present conflict, the latter presumably chastened and reeducated. Together, they would remake the world in the image of France. As under the Third Republic, the guardians of world peace would seek to reconcile equality and hierarchy:

> The confederated powers would say first of all that all peoples are born equal in rights, even if this were not apparent and even if the war had not recalled to them that peoples are not born, but form themselves over the course of painful labor, and that their rights [in practice] are not equal but increase or diminish according to the development of their abilities. (6)[67]

Thierry classified peoples of the world as: "civilized"; "savage" (economically underdeveloped); "barbarian" (politically underdeveloped); and "immoral"[68] (morally or religiously underdeveloped) (7). As under the Third Republic, education would provide for the advancement of the improvable. While education could follow national guidelines, its core and ultimate objective would be as universal as it was French:

---

66. Thierry, *Les Conditions de la paix*, 5. Hereafter cited by page number in the text.
67. Janice Zinser provided help with translating this somewhat cumbersome passage.
68. Thierry evoked this last term provisionally, "until such time as a less-pejorative expression is accepted."

> It would be desirable, however, that one kind of education complete another, and that though the study of the French language, impartial history, and religious philosophy, all of the reasons that peoples throughout history had or imagined they had to hate would be dissipated among free peoples. (17)

The peace would be forever maintained by the policy implementation of the Declaration of the Rights of Peoples. European organizations would administer the peace, working in French, the quintessentially European language.

Thierry would have the map of Europe redrawn through the Principle of Nationalities, his version of national self-determination: "according to which an independent people or an enslaved fragment of a people have an absolute right to arrange their affairs, their constitution, and their alliances" (24). Like Wilson a few years later, Thierry assumed that the application of such a principle would lead to less conflict in Europe rather than more. Thierry believed that nationality would prove as unproblematic everywhere as it had in France. Nationality would be determined in "a precise and constant way" with the French example again universalized:

> The French nation comprises all those who declare themselves French, implicitly or by formal plebiscite, whatever their birth, their religion, their race, or their language.

As the postwar publication showed, this proved by far the most heavily censored part of the book. To cite only one potentially incendiary example, he proposed that German-speaking Austria be permitted to join Germany if the inhabitants so chose in a plebiscite (181).

The French would redeem their collective national sacrifice through a kind of internal rebirth. Before 1914, they had governed themselves through hatreds based in religion, politics, and class. In the present war, however, they had refounded themselves as a people, and in doing so had made the Union sacrée an accomplished fact:

> Whatever had been their economic interests, their political opinions, their religious beliefs, their ideals, they no longer persecuted nor tormented one another. The old French hatred that had its own kind of nobility bequeathed itself to a French tenderness that neither France nor the universe had yet known. (59)

France, he argued, would give the world the universal Republic and universal Republicans. The key lay in continuing the Union sacrée into peacetime. In the future, the French would limit themselves to four political parties—royalist, socialist, center-right, and center-left. All would incline themselves toward a republican consensus. Royalists, for example, would renounce the aspiration of returning France to monarchy, though just how they could remain royalist while doing so seems unclear. Socialists would recognize the importance of those who, in addition to industrial workers, contributed to national prosperity (that is, holders of capital). The ideal Republic would be staunchly secular. Catholics would accept the separation of church and state, and Jews would renounce "that form of nationalist ingratitude that they call Zionism" (77). Peace would continue and deepen the profound moral transformation effected by the war. All of French, the dead as well as the living, would serve the nation in perpetual union.

> One sees well that such an integration of war and revolution in the peace supposes a profound moral transformation—an effort of purification and impartiality in which the deceased French deserve to guide the living French, and in which the living French deserve to follow the deceased French. (72)

Because Thierry's radical vision joined logic and affect, it was a small jump from the universal Frenchman to the universal human being. The two innermost circles in the book, Universal Peace and Interior Peace, were really two complementary means to the same end—the restructuring of the self so as to end war forever and create a kind of paradise on earth. The Universal Peace would provide the preconditions for the Interior Peace. The deadly conflicts within each man, "the offensive of the spirit against the flesh, of love against egoism, of generalizing generosity against specializing analysis, ultimately of morality against brutality—are ancient conflicts renewed each time a baby is born" (100).[69] These all-too-human inner struggles could only be resolved through external intervention. "The problem of interior peace," Thierry maintained, "would therefore be a pedagogical problem" (140). Remade and redeemed man would create utopia: "The men so pacified from within would surely find themselves disposed to collaborate, for the good of their patrie, their Europe, and humanity" (138). Through education, the total remaking of human nature would occur at the level of the individuated self.

The Universal Peace, in effect, called for a global republic. Just as the Third Republic had created citizens of France, the global republic would create citizens of the world. Thierry posited strong affinities between the

69. Thierry did not particularly develop the point, but he did indicate that women had their own right to inner peace (164). His scheme banned prostitution and adultery, both considered by him specific crimes of men against women.

two republics. The "Confederated Nations of the Universe" would conduct its business in French, and would adopt the decimal system of money and the metric system of measurement, "instituted by the French Revolution" (105). The confederation could have different capitals for different functions. London might make sense as an economic capital and Rome as a spiritual one, but "the intellectual capital, for the universe thinking and speaking in French, would remain Paris" (107–8). Enlightened colonial rule would extend the blessings of universal and interior peace throughout the world, such that "when this evolution is complete, if it is complete, each people enters equal to every other one into a great human family" (109).

To Thierry, in short, only the remaking of the world and the individual who inhabited it would be enough to redeem the sacrifices required by consent. But it bears reemphasizing that his blueprint was a direct consequence of his experience in the trenches. The subtitle of the book, after all, was "meditations of a combatant." The legitimacy of both narrative and narrator rested on Thierry's position as soldier of the Great War. Experience at the front made him a war author rather than just another literary idealist. To those who brought Thierry's account into the public domain, his service and martyrdom for France and for humanity made him a special kind of commentator. Like Péguy's, his voice became more powerful after his death than when he was alive. In Thierry's analysis, consent had revitalized both the Third Republic and the affective French national community. Consent in the Great War had given the French a modern formulation of a universal political message. Total commitment among the French, he hoped, would ultimately be redeemed across the globe.

As the complete version of Thierry's *Les Conditions de la paix* found its way into print in December 1918, victory appeared to have vindicated the regime and the poilu who exemplified it. Consent seemed to have "worked" in an immediate and practical sense. As René Rémond phrased the matter at the beginning of the twenty-first century: "If France this time defeated the enemy who had conquered it the last time [1871], how not to think that the credit for this accrued just a bit to the regime which had conducted our soldiers to victory, but which above all had also prepared them to withstand the ordeal because it knew how to form citizens?"[70] This chapter has explored some of the deeper issues at stake in consent. I have argued that republican citizenship in France forged total, individualized, horizontal links within the French national community. At an ideological level, these

70. René Rémond, *La République souveraine: la vie politique en France, 1879–1939* (Paris: Fayard, 2002), 410–11.

links made soldiers the authors as well as the subjects of power exercised over them, and implicated them individually and collectively in winning the war. The regime had done its work. It had provided the rhetorical and logical means of understanding the war at the levels of the individual, the group, and the national community. Consent as so construed became irrevocable, no longer even a matter of individual will. Relinquishing the war meant relinquishing a fundamental aspect of one's own being. To no small degree, the soldier was who he was because he represented and was represented by republican ideology. Consequently, consent actually deepened with suffering and despair. "Coercion" is simply not nuanced enough as a category to explain French tenacity in the Great War.

Yet consent both addressed the problem of the totalization of the war and presented its own logical and affective tangles. Whatever its provenance, all commitment has its price, existential and sometimes moral. The more témoins to consent hated the war, the more tightly they considered themselves bound to it. To some, consent could border on the pathological. And radical commitment does not always have a positive balance sheet. Nothing about consent precluded perceiving the affective national community as a racial community. At the very least, consent reinscribed the idea of the Republic at its most pure as a male community based in military service. Consent carried a heavy price in pain and death, and in an absolute dedication to inflicting as much of both as possible on the enemy.

Looking forward, consent made it highly problematic to imagine anything but a "total" victory—something quite different from what actually happened as the war ended in November 1918. Yet redemption through total victory would shortly prove elusive. As the wartime publishing wave of first-person, nonfictional testimonies came to an end in 1918 and 1919, it was already becoming difficult to see how these stories could find the sort of conclusions their underpinning logic required. Justifying consent after the war would prove quite a different matter from engineering it during the conflict. As consent radicalized in the last years of the war, so too did the demands that the poilus, as exemplars of the national community, would make on the future. When the regime, the nation, and the individual failed at the clearly impossible task of the total redemption of total commitment, consent eventually would become trauma.

4

The Novel and the Search for Closure

A central problem of any kind of narration is closure, which pronounces experience "over," at least to the extent that it can be fit into a narrative with a distinct position as to past, present, and future. As Hayden White put it, narrative requires "'the sense of an ending,' which links a terminus of a process with its origin in such a way as to endow whatever happened in between with a significance that can only be gained by 'retrospection.'"[1] Of course, finding closure in the narration of experience in the Great War concerned diverse collective and individual temporalities. Blaise Cendrars's war ended with the shell that took away his arm in 1915, yet that event really only began his encounter with his experience through narrative. This being said, the armistice of November 1918 altered the temporalities of narration for everyone. The war itself appeared to have ended with the establishment of winners and losers. The focus immediately shifted from winning the war to winning the peace—in short, to building a nation and a world that would redeem the sacrifices of consent. It became not just possible but necessary to draw some kind of "moral," not just to the experience of the *témoin*, but to the story of the war itself.

But how to find closure to experience in a war that, most assuredly, did not bring about the utopia required by wartime consent? The French certainly did not seek to forget the war. They maintained a vivid commemorative culture throughout the interwar period, notably through the relentless construction of *monuments aux morts* (monuments to the dead).[2]

---

1. Hayden White, "Narrative in Contemporary Historical Theory," in *The Content of the Form: Narrative Discourse and Historical Representation* (Baltimore: Johns Hopkins University Press, 1987), 52.

2. See Daniel J. Sherman, *The Construction of Memory in Interwar France* (Chicago: University of Chicago Press, 1999).

But the publication of wartime testimony in France slowed dramatically, though it never stopped entirely.[3] While historians may not be able to prove or disprove collective repression, it seems clear that publishers and readers turned away from experience in the trenches. "Consider, I beg of you, this problem simply from the point of view of current events," said an editor to the would-be war author of Joseph Jolinon's novel *La Tête brûlée* (The Burned Head, 1924): "don't count on making money these days if you re-hash the war, an unmentionable subject."[4] As we will see, "closure" in the 1920s often amounted to a simple rejection of the war.

After 1929, testimony reemerged in the novel. The importance of the novel is shown not so much in the number of volumes published as in the cultural significance of those that were. The tenth anniversary of the end of the war, coupled with the stunning worldwide success of Erich Marie Remarque's *All Quiet on the Western Front*, inaugurated a new period of reflection. Benedict Anderson has argued that since its origins, the novel has been uniquely suited to the collectivization of experience and temporalities among people who never knew each other directly. The novel, whether highbrow or lowbrow, "is clearly a device for the presentation of simultaneity in 'homogenous, empty time,' or a complex gloss upon the word 'meanwhile.'"[5] Through the novel, whole peoples can vicariously live through the "same thing." Consequently, the novel along with the newspaper "provided the technical means for 're-presenting' the *kind* of imagined community that is the nation."[6] Certainly, the country of Stendhal, Balzac, Flaubert, Hugo, and Zola had long been accustomed to having national experience mediated through the novel. It is perhaps unsurprising that the novel should have the final say on the experience of the combatant of the Great War.

Literary scholars can prove reluctant to define precisely what makes a novel a novel, though most seem to agree that the novel is an extended narrative in prose. Mikhail Bakhtin described the novel as "plasticity itself."[7]

---

3. Of the 294 volumes Jean Norton Cru considered, 53 (or 18 percent) were published between 1920 and 1923; and 23 (7.8 percent) between 1924 and 1928. Calculated from Norton Cru, *Témoins: Essai d'analyse et de critique des souvenirs de combattants édités en français de 1915 à 1928* (1929; repr., Nancy: Presses Universitaires de Nancy, 1993), 683–84 and passim.

The literary review *Mercure de France* continued to have a category titled "Ouvrages sur la guerre de 14–18" in its section "Revue de la quinzaine" summarizing recent publications. After 1929 this category comprised almost entirely memoirs of generals or politicians and scholarly works about the conduct of the war. Novels were classified under "Littérature."

4. Joseph Jolinon, *La Tête brûlée* (Paris: Redier, 1924), 169.

5. Benedict Anderson, *Imagined Communities: Reflections on the Origin and Spread of Nationalism*, rev. ed. (London: Verso, 1983), 25.

6. Ibid.; italics in the original.

7. Mikhail M. Bakhtin, *The Dialogic Imagination: Four Essays*, in *Theory of the Novel:*

Certainly, the genre could dispense with the spare, grammatically correct French of firsthand, nonfiction testimony, the genre of consent. After the armistice, the novel was required to dispense with that genre's open-ended temporality of suspending closure until the end of hostilities. Bakhtin and others have sometimes written about the novel as though it were as an aggressive and acquisitive character in its own novel of literary criticism. "The novel can do what it likes with literature," wrote Marthe Robert. "It can exploit to its own ends description, narrative, drama, the essay, commentary, monologue and conversation; it can be, either in turn or at once, fable, history, parable, romance, chronicle, story and epic."[8] Whether "the novel" had this level of self-consciousness and agency is a question of textual criticism beyond my concern here. What seems demonstrable, however, is that the novel of experience in the Great War came to dominate testimony, and altered testimony itself along the way.

As témoignage, the novel of experience in the trenches is about the management of temporality. More specifically, it is a genre that testifies to a search for closure, which would give experience an end that would make it historically specific. There proved formidable challenges to doing so in the postwar world. It became all too clear within a few years of the Versailles Treaty that the war had not solved the problem of French national security.[9] The unstable 1920s would give way to the disastrous 1930s with economic crisis of the Great Depression, the rise of belligerent fascism, and the looming threat of a new war. How to find closure to the meaning of experience in the Great War in this context? Bakhtin wrote that "form and content in discourse are one, once we understand that verbal discourse is a social phenomenon."[10] There remained a great deal about the Great War to explain to French society. The novel proved uniquely able to provide explanation and to resolve the problem of stabilizing narrative and narrator.

In considering the novel of experience in the Great War as témoignage, it is important to consider how novels ended, or failed to end. The attempt at closure at the end of a given novel, whether successful or unsuccessful, said something about how experience in the Great War figured into historical time. There were two broad forms of closure, roughly corresponding to the two interwar decades. Novels of the 1920s often ended in some form of abrupt rejection of the war. Novels of the 1930s could end with a

A Historical Approach, ed. Michael McKeon (Baltimore: Johns Hopkins University Press, 2000), 330.

8. Marthe Robert, "From *Origins of the Novel,*" in McKeon, *Theory of the Novel,* 58.

9. See Leonard V. Smith, Stéphane Audoin-Rouzeau, and Annette Becker, *France and the Great War* (Cambridge: Cambridge University Press, 2003), 182–83.

10. Bakhtin, *Dialogic Imagination,* 338.

"solution" that restated the problem, meaning the diagnosis of irresolvable trauma. Accordingly, the Great War had "broken" historical time in some way, thus setting up a future in which a new war would prove inevitable. The novel testifying to trauma could incorporate a wide spectrum of political opinion, from the pacifist Left to fascist Right. By the end of the 1930s, testimony to trauma could prove sufficient in itself. Through the novel, the author could dispense with his own experience, testifying instead to a self-evident metanarrative of tragedy and to a traumatized soldier as victim.

From Consent to Rejection

A war ends not as an event but as a process. John Horne has coined the term "cultural demobilization" to encompass the myriad discursive fields that must change in order for a war actually to end.[11] Cultural demobilization implies diverse temporalities, and numberless individual and collective emplotments. As Horne observed, "any linear chronology that led from war to peace, any certitude, even the inevitability of the transition, was inevitably broken up."[12] I argued in the previous chapter that consent could find proper closure only through redemption, meaning a transformative peace. Even before the ink on the Versailles Treaty had dried, such a peace came to seem unlikely. Consequently, the issue became demobilizing consent, reconciling the extreme expectations resulting from total and personal identification with the war with the actual conditions of the postwar world.

Of course, the novel was not entirely a postwar genre of testimony. Readers clearly found something compelling about narrative explanation through the novel even during the war. Indeed, the three best-selling French war books were all novels: René Benjamin's *Gaspard* (1915), Henri Barbusse's *Le Feu* (1916), and Roland Dorgelès's *Les Croix de bois* (1919).[13] All three were published either during the war or in its immediate aftermath. As might be expected, *Gaspard* ended with a presentation of consent as self-evident and unproblematic. The title character lost a leg but found lucrative employment selling American-made artificial limbs. The last scene found him strolling with his family in Paris toward the Pont Alexandre III,

11. See the articles in "Démobilisations culturelles après la Grande Guerre," *14–18: Aujourd'hui* 5 (2002): 43–157.
12. John Horne, "Introduction," ibid., 46.
13. According to Norton Cru, *Gaspard* sold 168,000 copies within an unidentified initial time frame (*Témoins*, 570). *Le Feu* sold 300,000 copies within two years of its publication, and *Les Croix de bois* 100,000. See Roger Chartier and Henri-Jean Martin, *Histoire de l'Édition française: le livre concurrencé, 1900–1950* (Paris: Fayard, 1986), 218, 559.

near the Hôtel des Invalides. He found a certain perspective on his misbe-
having progeny, finessed by a concluding comment from Benjamin as
narrator:

> As for them [the children of the victors], they will inherit, they will fatten up
> and eat the stuffed turkey, but the Boches . . . well the Boche, we will always
> get them, tan their hides.
> And raising his head, he said all this proudly alongside the glorious dome
> of the Invalides.[14]

Benjamin affirmed the patrie as the guarantor of temporal continuity. The
great dome of the Invalides symbolized the continuity of the past, present,
and future of the special relationship between France and those whose bodies had been broken in its defense.

Le Feu ended in a group meditation affirming Barbusse's version of
wartime consent. The narrator, a minor character in the novel and an ob-
server in the scene, concluded:

> War is made up only of the flesh and souls of ordinary soldiers. We are the
> ones who form the plains of dead and rivers of blood, all of us—each one
> silent and invisible because of the immensity of our numbers. The empty
> towns, the ruined villages, are the desert of us. Yes, it's all of us, and us
> entirely.[15]

Yet their misery only deepened their commitment to the war, convinced as
they had become in the historical inevitability of a better world. As the tiny
group of survivors rose, the narrator pronounced:

> An understanding between the democracies, between immense powers, a ris-
> ing of the peoples of the world, a brutally simple faith . . . All the rest, all of
> it, in the past, the present and the future, is entirely unimportant.[16]

Present horrors would purify humanity for the new day of the international
socialist patrie. Like Benjamin, Barbusse, used sunlight as the symbol of
eventual triumph, here by daylight trying to break through the clouds of
the battlefield: "this line of light, so tightly enclosed, so edged with black,
so meager that it seems to be merely a thought, brings proof none the less

---

14. René Benjamin, *Les Soldats de la guerre, Gaspard* (Paris: Fayard, 1915), 319.
15. Henri Barbusse, *Under Fire,* trans. Robin Buss (New York: Penguin Books, 2003),
310–11.
16. Ibid., 318.

that the sun exists."[17] The transformative peace, like the sun, would one day break through in full splendor. As we will see, emplotting this outcome became an increasingly desperate enterprise in Barbusse's later work.

Les Croix de bois was the first important Great War novel to take up the question of demobilization and to ponder postwar temporality. Its publication came at a particularly opportune moment, April 1919, between the signing of the armistice and the Treaty of Versailles. The politically cautious Dorgelès did not consider consent as such, though he certainly never renounced his own or his country's participation in the war. The soldier Larcher, the narrator and a second-tier figure in the story, is a thinly veiled surrogate for the author. He had arrived at the front in the fall of 1914, and by the end of the war all of his friends were either seriously wounded or had died gruesome deaths.

The title of the last chapter, "Et c'est fini" (And it's over), must be read as ironic, because it is about anything but closure.[18] In just four skillfully written pages, Dorgelès meditated on the impossibility of incorporating his war experience into a single coherent narrative unfolding in time. Larcher had not expected to survive the war: "There had been too many shells, too many dead, too many crosses. Sooner or later our turn was going to have to come." But having survived, inevitably, "life took up once more its happy course."

The narrator wondered whether, as time passed, "we will forget, and the time will come, perhaps, when, confusing the war with our bygone youth, we will heave a sigh of regret in missing those years." The narrator was sure that the normal passage of time would gradually reimpose itself, in that the past would become the past. Consequently, life eventually would prove the enemy of grief, and would commit its own cruelties:

> We will forget. The veils of mourning will fall, like dead leaves. The images of the dead soldiers will disappear slowly from the consoled hearts of those who loved them so much. And all the dead will die a second time.

Yet even in this forgotten or repressed state, his dead friends would continue to exercise enormous power over him, as long as he committed them to the written word:

> I feel you all present, my comrades. You have all arisen from your precarious tombs, and you surround me. And in a strange confusion, I can no longer distinguish which I knew out there at the front, and which I created to make the humble heroes of a book.

17. Ibid., 319.
18. Roland Dorgelès, *Les Croix de bois* (Paris: Albin Michel, 1919), 341–44.

The dead and the memory of them threatened to confound his ability to distinguish between past and present, or between reality and fiction. He imagined them with him as he relived the past while writing: "In the mud we waded through during rotations, under the crushing labor details, before death itself, I heard you laugh, never cry." Yet normal time intruded on this liminal state, confusing life and death: "One friend less, who was quickly forgotten, and you even laughed; but the memory, with time, eats into you, like the bite of an acid." Now shocked into the present, the narrator grieved anew. He could not both live "normally" and keep faith with the dead, whose wounds lived on in him: "And now, arrived at the final stage, a wave of remorse comes to me, to have laughed at your pain, as though I had carved a pipe out of your wooden crosses."

Les Croix de bois ended not with closure but with two competing conceptualizations of the future. The narrator could not live with the dead, nor could he live without them. There was no patrie in Dorgelès to guarantee the continuity of time, whether the mystical timeless France of Benjamin or the future international socialist patrie of Barbusse. Dorgelès ended pondering two flawed temporalities—a present that would not remain the present, and a past that would not become the past. The war had fractured time in some fundamental way.

If Dorgelès pondered demobilization with a certain anxiety as to just how time could move forward, Henri Barbusse, in effect, refused demobilization by clinging tenaciously to a certain idea of transformative time. He sought continued mobilization for a war against war. Down to the end of his life in 1935, he relied on what Frank Kermode called an apocalyptic concept of time, in which time "ends" or is reset with the transformation of the world.[19] Barbusse clung tightly to the liberal notion that people would do what was right once they knew what was right. Consequently, the revelation of truth would lead to enlightenment, which in turn would lead to the apocalypse. Such a temporality, after all, was what made it possible to give the title "Dawn" to the grim last chapter of *Le Feu*.

As the most famous war writer in France at the armistice, Barbusse sought to spend some of his immense cultural capital by founding an international socialist patrie in the Republic of Letters. On May Day, 1919, he announced a literary circle that would produce a journal, *Clarté* (Light, or Enlightenment).[20] Yet the disharmonies of the postwar Left intruded right away, notably over the relations between the Clarté group and the

19. See Frank Kermode, "The End," in *The Sense of an Ending: Studies in the Theory of Fiction* (London: Oxford University Press, 1966), 3–31.

20. See Nicole Racine, "The Clarté Movement in France, 1919–1921," *Journal of Contemporary History* 2(1967): 195–208; and Annie Kriegel, "Naissance du mouvement Clarté," *Le Mouvement Social* (1963): 117–35.

emerging Soviet Union. Barbusse joined what became the French Communist Party following the Congress of Tours in 1920, but he tried unsuccessfully to keep *Clarté* open to a wide array of leftist opinion. It certainly never wielded the kind of political influence in the postwar period that Barbusse had envisaged in 1919.

Barbusse's apocalyptic conceptualization of time became increasingly problematic after *Le Feu*. As Kermode argued, apocalyptic time must sooner or later be either reinvented or abandoned. In Barbusse, transformation still occurred through enlightenment, but at the level of the individual rather than the collectivity. Like his self-confessed role model Émile Zola, Barbusse as a social realist sought both to describe and to alter.[21] But after the war, "reality" became increasingly invested in the message, and enlightenment came to take place in increasingly paranormal situations. Barbusse neither abandoned apocalyptic time nor properly reinvented it.

The Clarté group took its name from Barbusse's novel *Clarté*, published in February 1919. Like *Les Croix de bois,* Barbusse's second war novel was published between the armistice and the signing of the Versailles Treaty. At the time, Barbusse's public utterances were full of optimism for the postwar world, as though the promise of the war to end war were fulfilling itself.[22] This confidence in the future proved somewhat at odds with the plot of *Clarté*. Clearly a more personalized work than *Le Feu*, it told the story in the first person of a certain Simon Paulin, a somewhat superficial provincial who had dabbled in letters before the war. Paulin experienced an extended vision after being wounded during a bombardment. "I am dead," he assured himself. "I fall, I roll like a broken bird, in the dazzling light, in the shadowy gorges."[23]

Paulin's delirium effected his enlightenment. Most of the vision comprised dialogues with dead French soldiers across generations. These conversations forecast a future hell if the present war only affirmed the status quo. The dead were certainly not at rest, and had even carried their grievous physical wounds beyond the grave. As in the 1919 silent version of Abel Gance's film *J'accuse,* the dead served as the conscience of the living, to terrify them into making a better world.[24] In *Clarté* as in the film, only the living could rescue the dead. A voice continually asked them what they were

21. See Jonathan King, "Henri Barbusse: *Le Feu* and the Crisis of Social Realism," in *The First World War in Fiction: A Collection of Critical Essays,* ed. Holger Klein (London, Macmillan, 1978), 51.

22. See Henri Barbusse, *Paroles d'un combattant: articles et discours (1917–1920)* (Paris: Flammarion, 1920).

23. Henri Barbusse, *Clarté* (Paris: Flammarion, 1919), 173.

24. See Jay Winter, *Sites of Memory, Sites of Mourning* (Cambridge: Cambridge University Press, 1995), 15–18.

fighting for, only to receive the plainly inadequate answer "To save my country." The present war threatened to become as morally bankrupt as wars past.

> Universal soldier, man taken by chance among men, remember: there was not a moment when you were yourself. Never did you cease to be bent under the brutal command to which there was no response: "It is necessary, it is necessary." In the grip of incessant labor in peacetime, in the factory of the machines or in the factory of the office, slave to the tool, to the pen, to skill, or to something else, you were hounded without respite, from morning to night, by the daily tasks that barely enabled you to go on living, and that enabled you to relax only in your dreams.[25]

The vision reached its paroxysm when Paulin encountered Jesus Christ along the edge of a lake. He appeared as an ordinary man, without a halo. He told Paulin of the evil done by the war in his name, and he begged believers not to rebuild ruined churches, because "they are not what you thought they were."[26] A short time later, Paulin awoke up from his near-death experience. The last lines of the book revealed that the vision had done its work: "I woke up letting out a soft cry, like an infant being born."

Barbusse's most extreme *cri du coeur* came in his last war novel, *Les Enchaînements* (The Logical Sequences, 1925).[27] By that time, enlightenment took place in an altered state of being because it had to, because the war against war seemed to have been lost. "Real life" had produced a vindictive peace at Versailles, the conservative *Chambre bleu horizon* majority in the Chamber of Deputies, the bitter division between Socialists and Communists all over Europe, and civil war in the newborn Soviet Union. In two volumes comprising some six hundred not very readable and seldom-read pages, Barbusse imagined himself stretching the genre of the novel to the breaking point. He admitted in the preface:

> If I have sought to build an artificial structure by giving to the framework of the "novel" exceptional proportions for which literature has not provided me a model, it is because I wanted to include more scattered experience than the usual and used-up procedures could provide for, and also because I wanted the framework to be of the same scale as certain great obvious facts that manifest themselves from collective deeds.[28]

25. Barbusse, *Clarté*, 179.
26. Ibid., 196–98.
27. *Enchaînement* usually refers to some abstract form of linkage. But the verb *enchaîner* can also mean "to enchain."
28. Henri Barbusse, *Les Enchaînements*, 2 vols. (Paris: Flammarion, 1925): 1:vii.

Written in the first person, *Les Enchaînements* told the story of a twenty-year-old poet serving as a secretary on an army corps general staff (as Barbusse had done at twice that age after he left the front lines). In the course of his duties, the narrator became subject to a variety of visions which transported him from antiquity to the present, and which instructed him as to the historical flaws of humanity. Above all, he learned of the "bestial consent" (*le consentement bestial*) which led perpetually to war.[29] The vision continued into the Great War, and indeed into projected wars of the future. The narrator emerged enlightened, as in *Le Feu* and *Clarté*. But by 1925 the moral had taken on a scolding tone, administered to a diminishing number of readers.

More common than Barbusse's frantic insistence that time could be transformed was a simple abandonment of apocalyptic time, resulting in a total rejection of the war. Emplotting experience thus revolved a personal journey from consent to rejection, not just of war in the abstract but the war of 1914–18. Total rejection constituted both the end of the story and its moral. As the twice-wounded veteran Émile Chartier, more commonly known as the philosopher Alain, put it in a justly famous 1921 essay: "Deny war, firmly, without any concession of spirit, before making it, while you make it, after you have made it. Because you understand that war lives from approbation, begin by not nourishing it."[30]

In narratives emplotting rejection along these lines, closure amounted to a confession that the protagonists' prior consent to the war had been self-defeating and morally wrong. In the novel of the 1920s, rejection was more about the past than the future. It established an ironic, sadder-but-wiser position for the author that provided for few specifics about the future. Rejection simply stopped time and narrative abruptly. Some novels simply halted time for the main character at the moment of complete self-realization. Others directed attention toward a sacrificial victim that would resonate in critiques of the Great War for decades to come—the *fusillé*, or soldier executed after a court martial. In both kinds of endings, time stopped almost as an amputation of suffering.

Jean Bernier had been a founding member of the Clarté group. But he emplotted rejection in *La Percée* (The Breakthrough, 1920) without a conspicuous moral, by terminating the narrative as abruptly as violence cut short the life of the main character. The youthful Jean Favigny "hated Germany with the ingenious hatred of a young male who must hate to prove

---

29. Ibid., 2:296.
30. Alain, "Mars ou la guerre jugée," *Nouvelle Revue Française* 16 (1921): 52. This essay comprised excerpts from a book under the same name published later that year.

his strength to himself."[31] His friends all died the kinds of gruesome deaths familiar to readers by 1920. Favigny himself was killed in the French offensive in the Champagne in October 1915, when the French command's strategy of the rupture (*percée*) of the German position was demonstrated unrealistic. Bernier emplotted the young man's death as an execution, full of sound effects representing the impersonal forces wrenching life from the body. Favigny tried to resist to the last as a somatic whole, but combat tore his soul from his body even before he was killed: "It was not him speaking, acting, it was his body, his envelope voided of him, inspired by military necessity. As for him, he was dead."[32] In the last sentence of the book, Favigny became absorbed in the last sound emitted from his condemned body as he "rushed forward without consciousness, taking refuge in his cry: Haa-a-a-a-a-ha-a-a!"[33] Consent had become a vortex, and agency limited to the last-minute awareness of entrapment.

René Naegelen's *Les Suppliciés* (The Tortured, 1927) likewise did not take an overt political position, apart from a vague sympathy for the efforts of "a few courageous buggers" who tried to renew ties of class among the warring nations.[34] Jacques Feroul survived the war diminished in soul more than in body, as what gender historians would call an emasculated soldier of the trenches.[35] The war had made sex, a topic seldom mentioned in wartime testimony, an inglorious encounter between an animal and a whore. Before battle, Jacques longed to have sex "one more time in life, one last time, perhaps, with a women, a professional in love, of course, but who is still a woman, to whom the male in rut is irresistibly attracted."[36] Male agency had become reduced to tawdry fantasy. As a warrior, he was both defeated and saved by the Spanish flu: "when the time came to depart, he was vomiting something black, and the aroused dysentery [*la dysenterie excitée*] twisted his entrails."[37] The armistice found him recovering in bed at his parents' home. An enthusiastic crowd of civilians and soldiers marched by, crying, "We have won the war!" But as the novel ended, the defeated survivor realized that he had to contemplate the meaning of the war in isolation:

> Then Jacques got up, and to leave them [the revelers] a bit nearer to the one who is out there, cold, all alone, in an unknown trench, he tiptoed over to

31. Jean Bernier, *La Percée* (Paris: Albin Michel, 1920).
32. Ibid., 253.
33. Ibid., 256.
34. René Naegelen, *Les Suppliciés* (Paris: Éditions Baudinière, 1927), 259.
35. See Mary Louise Roberts, *Civilization without Sexes: Reconstructing Gender in Postwar France, 1917–1927* (Chicago: University of Chicago Press, 1994).
36. Naegelen, *Les Suppliciés,* 53.
37. Ibid., 273–74.

the casement window, and in the light, and in the cruel joy of outside, he closed the blinds.[38]

Another way to emplot rejection relied on a figure that would inspire leftist criticism of the Great War until the end of the twentieth century—the fusillé, shot by a firing squad after a court martial and the quintessential victim of wartime injustice. He might have faced trumped-up charges stemming from an all-too-human moment of weakness under fire, or he might simply have been selected at random for judicial murder. Either way, he served as the sacrificial victim in a performance of arbitrary and irresistible military authority. As Nicolas Offenstadt has shown, the fusillé had already emerged as a figure in wartime literature.[39] When *Le Feu* was published in one volume in December 1916,[40] Barbusse added a previously unpublished chapter recounting an execution. Dorgelès included a chapter in *Les Croix de bois* that drew from a controversial case from his 39th Regiment in May 1915.[41] Neither attached any exceptional significance to the fusillés, who seemed simply a specific variety of victim. But as the political Left revived in the early 1920s, the fusillés became a flash point in the political war to right the wrongs of 1914–18.[42] Clearly, more was at stake than their statistical significance. The generally accepted number of six hundred French soldiers executed between 1914 and 1918 constituted only a tiny proportion of the 1.3 million French military dead.

The fusillé had a critical symbolic role to play if the answer to total war was total demobilization. The most profound rejection of the Great War among the French came after the fact. In retrospect, the correct ethical position for a radical pacifist would have been to accept punishment (including execution) rather than to participate in the war. After all, had the workers of Europe taken such a position in August 1914, as thousands had promised, there would have been no war in the first place. Willingly or not, the fusillés became martyrs to the radical pacifist position. Ironically, they could be sacrificial victims in two completely opposite senses. Their execution affirmed the inherently arbitrary and one-directional nature of military authority. But their involuntary sacrifice also paid for the sins of millions in submitting to consent. In telling their story, the author could ennoble and

38. Ibid., 284.
39. Nicolas Offenstadt, *Les Fusillés de la grande guerre et la mémoire collective (1914–1999)* (Paris: Odile Jacob, 1999), 109–15.
40. The novel had previously been serialized in the newspaper *L'Oeuvre*.
41. Barbusse, *Le Feu*, chap. 10, "Argoval"; Dorgelès, *Les Croix de bois*, chap. 9, "Mourir pour la patrie." On the latter case, see Leonard V. Smith, "The Disciplinary Dilemma of French Military Justice: September 1914–April 1917: The Case of the 5e Division d'Infanterie," *Journal of Military History* 55 (1991): 57–58.
42. See Offenstadt, *Les Fusillés*, 69–107.

redeem their suffering, not unlike George Duhamel and his stories of the *mutilés*. At the same time, the author could establish himself as the arbiter of their experience, the figure who properly conveyed its meaning to the public. Two novelists with connections to the Clarté group did just this.

We saw in chapter 1 how the hero of Léon Werth's *Clavel soldat* (published in May 1919) found himself drawn into the vortex of the mobilization of August 1914. The book ended with Clavel in Paris on leave, disgusted with the self-absorption of the civilians around him. Finally, he encountered a woman whose grief deserved his sympathy. Her twenty-year-old son had been killed at the front, and she showed Clavel his last letter. While technically not a fusillé, his total rejection of the war could have marked him for the firing squad: "What I have seen is too horrible, too horrible. I do not want to get wounded, recover, and see all this again. I would rather die. Thank you for all you have done for me."[43] His death by German rather than French bullets was arbitrary.

Clavel chez les majors, the sequel, was published in November 1919. Clavel had been seriously wounded in the leg, and while recovering in the hospital he heard the story of a true fusillé, a man shot for openly refusing to advance into the trenches. A father of three children and popular among his comrades if not among his commanders, he had tried unsuccessfully to evade service by declaring himself ill. Twice sent away by doctors, he still refused to go into the trenches. Clearly, the man was no coward. While drinking wine with his comrades the night before his execution, he told them that "it was not out of fear that he did not want to go into the trenches, but out of disgust." For Clavel, the fusillé posed the dilemma of collaboration versus resistance to the war.

> That one there, he thought, is a comrade . . . He carried his disgust to its logical conclusion . . . But is it necessary to get yourself shot? And me, here I am, stuck in the bog with those who accept the war. That one there . . . others still . . . How many were they? And how unhelpful was their nobility. That one there was a comrade . . . But the others?[44]

Certainly the unfortunate fusillé had the courage of his convictions if only involuntarily. But was it not Clavel's first duty to survive, and above all to avoid death by execution? Clavel, and by implication many of his comrades, felt able to desert mentally though not legally. He had to live with the fact that he could not, in effect, take his own life out of disgust for the war. But he would admire someone who could.

43. Léon Werth, *Clavel soldat* (1919; repr., Paris: Viviane Hamy, 1993), 376.
44. Léon Werth, *Clavel chez les majors* (Paris: Albin Michel 1919), 142.

Perhaps inevitably, the fusillé as a figure for témoignage straddled the line demarcating fiction from nonfiction. It has seldom been easy to determine just why a given soldier was or was not executed. The French army did not and does not grant easy access to military justice records.[45] In any event, authors narrating the stories of the fusillés considered themselves guided by an underlying truth that transcended specific juridical circumstances—the truth that firing squads had executed compatriots unjustly. Indeed, for the fusillés resulting from the mutinies of 1917, specific circumstances could get in the way, if my argument is correct that the mutinies ended not through external coercion but through an anguished affirmation of consent.[46]

Joseph Jolinon, a lawyer before the war, had defended mutineers from the 170th Infantry Division in 1917.[47] In 1920 he published an article on the mutinies at Coeuvres in the literary journal *Mercure de France* that did not identify itself as either fiction or nonfiction.[48] Later, Jolinon expanded his témoignage of the mutinies and their aftermath into two chapters of his novel *Le Valet de la gloire* (The Valet of Glory, 1929). He considered the mutineers a potential revolutionary vanguard. They sang the socialist anthem, the "Internationale," and gathered together in the woods, "organizing themselves as a republic on a war footing. Two men per company, designated by election, excluding even corporals, were called upon to gather together the provisions, so as to distribute them equally with efficiency. All questions were settled by vote."[49] The mutinies ended in the book under somewhat vague circumstances: "Provisions and resistance diminished together, and both were exhausted by the end of the third day."[50] Finally, so as not to identify any one of them as a leader, they designated a local woman to tell the colonel commanding the cavalry surrounding them that they were prepared to surrender.

Jolinon's surrogate, Claude Lunat, had listened at great length to the complaints of the men about to rebel, but mysteriously vanished from the plot line during the actual mutinies. He reemerged when he was designated defense counsel for the mutineers before the court martial. Lunat initially refused to participate in what he saw as impending judicial murder, but his

45. Access to case files (Série J) is granted only by special permission (*dérogation*), at the discretion of the Service Historique de l'Armée de Terre. I was given unrestricted access to the files for the Fifth Infantry Division, but the most recent study of the mutinies of 1917 appears to have been written without access to this series. See Denis Rolland, *La Grève des tranchées: les mutineries de 1917* (Paris: Imago, 2005).
46. See Smith, Audoin-Rouzeau, and Becker, *France and the Great War*, 117–31.
47. Biographical notice in Norton Cru, *Témoins*, 622.
48. Joseph Jolinon, "La Mutinerie de Coeuvres," *Mercure de France*, 15 August 1920.
49. Joseph Jolinon, *Le Valet de gloire* (Paris: Redier, 1923), 206.
50. Ibid., 208.

superior told him, "It is your duty to do it; I will have no use for you if you refuse. Would you let them be condemned in advance?"[51] Lunat did his duty, as he saw it, not to his commanders but to his persecuted comrades. In the proceedings, he pointed out the dubious criteria used to identify leaders. One of the accused pointed to his two brothers killed in the war, his wife in the hospital, and his seven children as mitigating circumstances. He received a cold response from the court: "When you have two brothers killed, you should have only one thought—how to avenge them." The men came to look like sacrificial victims even before their execution: "A stupor came over their hardened features, which rapidly aged them. Their eyes no longer dared look, their brains could hardly think."[52]

As Offenstadt has argued, the fusillé became a powerful symbol for the Left after the war because, by definition, he was the victim of arbitrary forces inseparable from those that drove the war itself. Capitalist hierarchy needed capricious military power to defend itself. To repress the authentic Republic imagined by the mutineers, the French army needed to demonstrate its mastery through the murder of selected victims. Of the thirty-five soldiers defended by Lunat, seventeen drew death sentences, the remainder fifteen years of hard labor. Appeals for leniency were refused, though only one of the condemned (not defended by Lunat) was actually executed. The selection of the fusillé had a simple explanation: "This man was no more guilty than one hundred others, but he had no family to weep for him."[53] The victim rendered himself a true hero to by refusing to accept a bandanna over his eyes when facing the firing squad. "I have never retreated before death," he said to his executioners, "Go ahead." Later, his comrades carried out their own act of resistance, carving "Died bravely" (*Mort en brave*) on the cross marking his grave.

Like Bernier and Naegelen, Werth and Jolinon sought closure in total rejection of the war. The fusillé became the victim of capricious military authority and of the social iniquities that legitimized that authority. But he also proved a conveniently coherent figure for the novelist. By definition, the fusillé lacked agency. He could thus die to pay for the nation's consent. But more important, the experience of the fusillé stopped forever at the moment of his death. His death absolved him of any implication in perpetuating the war. Moreover, he did not have to face the moral ambiguities of the postwar years—the bitter fragmentation of socialism and the weary trek through life after the armistice for Claude Lunat that Jolinon re-

51. Ibid., 211.
52. Ibid., 218.
53. Ibid., 224.

counted in great detail in three more books.[54] The fusillé could thus become the left-wing counterpart of right-wing heroes such as Charles Péguy and Henri Alain-Fournier, who never had to fight in the trenches because they had been killed in the first weeks of the war. Like them, death rendered the fusillé uncompromised and heroic, by cutting his time short.

But the main problem with rejection as a strategy of closure was its vagueness or outright silence about the future. At the end of *Clavel soldat,* the grieving mother said to him:

> For him not to be dead, I would give up France and Germany . . .
> The dead ones . . . thought Clavel, who will avenge them? And on whom will they be avenged?[55]

Werth, at least, understood that rejection had no self-evident aftermath. Barbusse, in clinging desperately to his apocalyptic conception of time, at least had a way of understanding the future. But where could rejection lead except to introverted bitterness?

If Bakhtin is correct that verbal discourse is always social, closure through rejection could function well enough in the public sphere in the 1920s. The French had their array of stresses, like the other peoples of postwar Europe. But the Third Republic, the economy, and French society all seemed to have stabilized somewhat by the late 1920s. Above all, there was no immediate threat from a resurgent Germany. Total rejection of war cost little in this context. In literary circles, it would prove a short step from novelists' rejection of the war in the 1920s to critics' rejection of war novels of that period. "The literature of war," Albert Thibaudet would sniff in 1936, "improvised by the combatants, and above all by others, provided disappointments. One quickly sought to get away from the war, as the philosophers say, in favor of transcendence."[56] Fourteen years later, Claude-Edmond Magny wrote of the Great War novel of the 1920s: "We know the expression of [Raymond] Radiguet defining the war of 14–18 as 'four years of extended vacation [*grandes vacances*].' This atmosphere remained in the Republic of Letters for the following ten years."[57] Even Daniel Mornet, a Great War témoin and postwar professor of French literature at the Sor-

54. Jolinon, *La Tête brûlée* (1924); *Le Joueur de balle* (1929), *Les Revenants dans la boutique* (1929).

55. Werth, *Clavel soldat,* 376.

56. Albert Thibaudet, *Histoire de la littérature française de 1789 à nos jours* (Paris: Stock, 1936), 522.

57. Claude-Edmonde Magny, *Histoire du roman français* (Paris: Stock, 1950), 22. Radiguet, born in 1903, had in fact written a searing novel about growing up during the war, *Le Diable au corps* (Paris: Grasset, 1923).

bonne, devoted little attention to war books in an extended 1927 study of contemporary French literature.[58]

At the end of the 1920s, the publication of Erich Marie Remarque's *All Quiet on the Western Front* carried rejection to its logical conclusion. Many of the details had been in the literary mix for years—the naïve hero-victim and most especially the gruesome images of death, mutilation, and putre-faction. But the book seemed uniquely able to "solve" the problem of ex-perience and identity at the front. Experience in the trenches ended in complete annihilation, physical and moral. While an international history of Remarque's novel as a cultural event remains to be written, clearly the book universalized the narration of experience to a degree unmatched by any other testimony of the Great War. With no fewer than thirty-two trans-lations and 3.5 million copies sold worldwide within fifteen months of its publication, it eclipsed even the most successful French works in popular appeal.[59] The moral of *All Quiet on the Western Front* was that the war had been a tragedy and the soldier its victim. Total war required total demobilization, if all Europe was not to suffer the fate of Paul Baümer. Such a moral became increasingly problematic in the 1930s, in France as elsewhere.

Trauma and the Disarticulation of Time

"Trauma," wrote Dominick LaCapra, "is a disruptive experience that disarticulates the self and creates holes in existence; it has belated effects that are controlled only with difficulty and perhaps never fully mas-tered."[60] Trauma marks the defeat of experience as narrative. It cuts off the development of the individual in time. The hidden or suppressed traumatic experience recurs perpetually in the present, blocking off the future. "Clo-sure," in effect, does not exist, rather a continual return to the beginning of the traumatic story. Most theorists of trauma believe that it can never be completely overcome.

While conceptions of trauma predated 1914 by some decades, historians have long agreed that the Great War and trauma helped construct each

58. See Daniel Mornet, *Histoire de la littérature et de la pensée françaises contemporaines: 1870–1927* (Paris: Larousse, 1927). Mornet had written a nonfiction account, *Tranchées de Verdun* (Paris: Berger Levrault, 1918).

59. See Brian A. Rowley, "Journalism into Fiction: *Im Westen nichts Neues*," in Klein, *First World War in Fiction*, 101–11. The French edition of *All Quiet* sold 441,400 copies between June and December 1929. Chartier and Martin, *Histoire de l'Édition française*, 230.

60. Dominick LaCapra, "Writing History, Writing Trauma," in *Writing History, Writing Trauma* (Baltimore: Johns Hopkins University Press, 2001), 41.

other. Freud himself made this connection in his work from 1918 to 1920 explaining an ego split between an instinct for self-preservation and an instinct for aggression. Shell shock, a clinical form of trauma in the Great War, emerged as a pathological strategy to reconcile the divided parts of the ego, which broke down because of the stresses of combat.[61] The victim of shell shock ceased to be able to live in time. The traumatic experience imposed itself through nervous tics, mutism, and above all through phantasms and nightmares. Long construed as the distillation of the stresses and injuries of modernity itself, trauma continues to fascinate scholars in history, literature, and cultural studies.[62] Yet shell shock in the Great War was a specific traumatic condition, whose actual incidence will always remain unknown. Whatever that incidence, wartime psychologists diagnosed it in only a small percentage of combatants. By the 1930s, however, trauma in the sense of disarticulated time had a cultural resonance far beyond the military psychiatric ward.

Something had to replace simple but total rejection as the moral of the story of experience in the trenches. The Great Depression, the rise of fascism, and Stalinism all seemed to make the bourgeois, liberal Third Republic look increasingly anachronistic. The nineteenth-century regime withered before twentieth-century problems. It became increasingly clear that the Treaty of Versailles had created not peace but a deferred settling of scores. Ongoing conflict in the overextended French empire meant that the nation was never entirely at peace between 1918 and 1939. Worst of all, the rise of Hitler and the breathtaking speed of German rearmament after March 1935 made clear the bankruptcy of the policy of ensuring French safety through German weakness. The renewed threat of a general European war affirmed trauma as the predominant principle of narrative explanation in the French Great War novel. War itself had become the past that would not become the past—and indeed the past which seemed increasingly likely to overwhelm the present and any foreseeable future.

The emplotment of experience in the Great War, then, came to revolve around responding to the specter of renewed war. For my purposes, the essence of trauma in the novel of the 1930s is the removal of agency and an inability to move forward in time.[63] Considered as a structuring princi-

---

61. Freud's major works on the subject are *Psycho-Analysis and the War Neuroses* (1919) and *Beyond the Pleasure Principle* (1920). On the development of his theory of trauma, see Ruth Leys, *Trauma: A Genealogy* (Chicago: University of Chicago Press, 2000), 18–40.

62. See, for example, Paul Lerner and Mark S. Micale, eds., *Traumatic Pasts: History, Psychiatry, and Trauma in the Modern Age, 1870–1930* (Cambridge: Cambridge University Press, 2001).

63. There seems nothing universal about the novel as a genre of trauma. Most important

ple of narrative, trauma could accommodate most any political point of view, from pacifist Left to fascist Right. In itself, trauma seemed apolitical. Narratives and narrators could also respond differently to disarticulated time, once identified. Some simply found closure in diagnosis, and a moral in despair. Others sought to intervene in the disarticulated narrative to restore the forward movement of time. The Great War novel of the 1930s took témoignage to trauma in many politically different versions of the same direction.

Testimony to trauma in the novel could emplot general and timeless human failings that had led to the war of 1914–18 and would lead to war in the future. In other words, the Great War had simply made clear the immutable laws of human nature. Gabriel Chevallier's *La Peur* (Fear, 1930) did not expound any particular political point of view, apart from a racist disdain for African Americans expressed only at the end of the book. The novel recounted the irresistible force of circumstance in war creating and recreating itself. In an introductory chapter, Chevallier avowed that he had never been much of a patriot, let alone a militarist. Even at the age of nineteen, he wrote, "I did not think that there had been much grandeur in plunging a bayonet into the chest of a man, so as to rejoice at his death." Yet he accepted the war when it came, like the vast majority of his compatriots.

> Because it had been difficult to do otherwise? That was not the real reason, and I must not make myself out as better than I was. I went to war contrary to my convictions, but of my own free will [*plein gré*], not to fight, but out of curiosity, to see.[64]

Naive curiosity led to assent. Assent led unavoidably to consent, which in effect removed individual agency. The title "Fear" summarized this loss of agency, which could render the soldier a coward one day and a cold-blooded murderer the next, depending on circumstances over which he had no control. Consent had proved a discursive trap from which there was no escape:

> For years, when they had exhausted our courage, and when not a single conviction motivated us anymore, they claimed to make heroes of us. But we saw too well that "hero" meant "victim." For years, they required of us this great

---

accounts of the Holocaust are nonfictional first-person narratives. Dominick LaCapra paid little attention to novels of the Holocaust in *History and Memory after Auschwitz* (Ithaca: Cornell University Press, 1998) and *Writing History, Writing Trauma*.

64. Gabriel Chevallier, *La Peur* (Paris: Stock, 1930), 12.

consent [*grand consentement*] which no moral force could enable us to renew continually, one time or ten times, with resolve, in order to make an end
of it. But each time we survived, after we had given the gift of our consent,
we were even more trapped than before.[65]

Consent had become wholly external to the self. Assent to war meant surrendering agency and submitting to a self-sustaining, totalizing logic. The
last autonomous act of the narrator had been submitting to his own curiosity at the outbreak of war.

The plot of *La Peur* ended in early 1919 with an ironic and bitter prog-
nosis for European civilization. In the last weeks of the war, the narrator's
division comprised two metropolitan French regiments and one regiment
of African Americans. A favorite French story involved the distribution of
coffee after a meal in the African-American regiment. When one soldier was
refused more coffee by his sergeant, he shot his superior on the spot. The
Americans of color, it seemed, always walked around with weapons loaded.
The other noncommissioned officers disarmed the perpetrator and immediately hanged him as the onlookers laughed.

The poilus loved this story. They judged that people who took the lives of
others so cheaply would make extraordinary soldiers. We are counting on
them to finish the war.[66]

Europeans had started this war and had given themselves totally to it. It
could be finished only by persons of African descent even more brutalized
than Europeans. The future belonged to them. An older friend, bearing the
not-coincidental name "Sergeant Nègre," assured the narrator that "human stupidity is incurable." Nègre smugly observed that he would be too
old to fight in the next war. From his position of safety, he would be able
to cry with selfish impunity: "Go on, boys, carry it to the finish!"[67]

A more sophisticated emplotment war as endemic to the human condi-
tion is Roger Vercel's 1934 novel *Capitaine Conan*, made into a film by
Bertrand Tavernier in 1996. Like *La Peur*, the novel did not expound any
particular partisan viewpoint, though it certainly could not be labeled paci-
fist. Vercel situated his story on the extreme edge of what most readers in
France would consider the "Great War." *Capitaine Conan* was set in the
Balkans, where the French invaded from Salonika when moving toward
Austria-Hungary in the closing weeks of the war. Most of the novel took

65. Ibid., 317.
66. Ibid., 297.
67. Ibid., 312–13.

place after the armistice on the Western Front. The French were not even fighting the Germans but rather Bulgarians about whom they appeared to know and care little. Later the French units were moved to Romania, to fight pro-Bolshevik forces in a battle adjacent to the civil war in the new-born Soviet Union. Brutality in the book was driven by human nature and circumstance rather than by the geopolitical or ideological issues that the Great War was supposed to have been about. War creates brutes and is created by them. The larger society would always be implicated in this brutality, in the ways it relied on the brutes created by war, only to try to rein them in and exclude them later.

The complex plot of Vercel's short book was based on a friendship between two alter egos, the title character and the narrator. Conan, who had been a haberdasher in civilian life, finished the war as head of a special unit of commandos. Unusually among characters in French Great War novels, he combined unapologetic brutality and self-awareness. Conan managed to master the experience of his first killing, which was integrated into a coherent, unproblematic narrative of his survival:

> In a bend in the trench, I ran into this big guy. I expected it more than he did. I fired first, but like this without really aiming. He fell. I said to myself: "Not possible, you're pretending! It's got to be more difficult than that to kill a man!" I kicked him in the butt, I put the barrel of my revolver to the back of his neck. He didn't budge. He was really there, dead! . . . What amazed me was that it was done so quickly! . . . Just like you breathed on him![68]

The narrator, Lieutenant Norbert, was originally an infantry commander who became a prosecutor for the division courts martial after the armistice. He was appalled, fascinated, and sometimes envious of Conan's straightforward brutality. Norbert greeted his appointment with some cynicism, given that, most often, courts martial resulted from the misfortune of perfectly understandable behavior in the wrong place at the wrong time. "During the war," he reported, "becoming 'yellow' was one of the risks, but as it was one of the smaller ones, you didn't think about it. Two months after the armistice, you got a little cold thinking about just how you escaped, more than once, those twelve bullets fired close together [from the firing squad]."[69]

Two cases loomed large in the book. Particularly troubling was the case of Private Jean Erlane, a twenty-year old conscript from a wealthy family who out of fright deserted to the enemy (a capital offense). Conan proved

---

68. Roger Vercel, *Capitaine Conan* (1934; repr., Paris: Albin Michel 1997), 27.
69. Ibid., 55.

paradoxically indulgent. Males who could not become warriors had no business being at the front in the first place. After Norbert explained the matter, his friend responded:

> In a case like that, you need to send him back to his wet nurse. I know it was just about taking fright, my friend! I've seen it. Those types who get scared stiff, then, to tell you the truth, they are no longer responsible.
>
> Try to fight with the likes of that? It would be like in a bullfight, but instead of a bull you release a fat ox. You understand? Blow his face off? Like crushing a toad. Useless and dirty.[70]

Norbert shared Conan's rather perverse pity but also felt a keen sense of duty to the law. Erlane was sentenced to death with military degradation, pending review of the case by superior authority.

Returning to his office after the conviction of Erlane, Norbert found the dossier for a new case. Conan himself stood accused of homicide. Following an argument in the villa where Conan had decided to billet himself, he had pushed its Bulgarian owner down the stairs. Conan showed no remorse or regret. He had been praised and promoted for slaughtering Bulgarians during the war, so he had no second thoughts about killing one more now that it was over. In perhaps the most dramatic scene of the novel, Conan explained that he understood his situation all too well:

> You think that because I shout, I don't understand? For a long time, I've understood that they are ashamed of us, that they no longer know where to hide us. [. . .] Killing somebody, anybody can do it, but to kill him in such a way as to lodge fear in the skulls of ten thousand others, that is our job! [. . .] For that, you've got to go to the knife, do you understand? It is the knife that won the war, not the canon. A poilu who could hold out against an armored column would run at just the thought of guys coming at him with knives. We were maybe three thousand, not more, on all the fronts. These three thousand were the victors, the real ones! The others needed only to clean up, from behind![71]

Yet what, from the point of view of the author, was at stake in such a position? Plainly, the war had not been won by three thousand knife-wielding brutes, but rather by millions of soldiers more like Norbert than like Conan, and firing industrially produced weaponry. To Vercel, the most important outcome of the war had not been defeat or victory, justice or injustice. The issues most associated with France and the Great War—the German invasion, Alsace and Lorraine, the more abstract issues of democ-

70. Ibid., 147.
71. Ibid., 189.

racy—were quite absent from the war in Bulgaria. Rather, war developed its own logic freed from ideology. Wars produced Conans; they always had and they always would. His was simply a distilled version of consent, from which the society around him tried hypocritically to distance itself once the shooting stopped. But his type would be needed again, because the cyclical nature of war was immutable. At the end of the book, and sometime in the 1920s, Norbert tracked down Conan. He had resumed his career as haberdasher and was dying from a disease of the liver. They had a brief, almost sterile conversation. In his farewell, Conan reminded Norbert of their conversation about the three thousand warriors who won the war.

> Those three thousand there, maybe you will find them again sometime, one or two of them, here or there, in some little village or other . . . Look at them well, my dear Norbert; they will be like me.[72]

For Vercel, the Great War and the brutes it called forth had not so much disarticulated time as revealed its true structure. Demobilization could never be more than a temporary condition.

Novels written from a more overtly political point of view had more to explain than those that attributed the return of war to general human weakness. Any political perspective had to fit experience in the Great War into a narrative structure that made some statement about the future. The Left by the 1930s had particular challenges. Socialists across Europe had sworn for years before 1914 to preclude a European war by refusing en masse to fight it. But in the event, workers not only assented to war by rallying by the millions to various national colors, but waged it until the day it ended through service at the front, factories, and fields. If consent had been a crime, many on the Left had been guilty. And after the war, the Left had become bitterly divided between Socialists and Communists, mostly over the proper relationship to the Soviet Union, the one country where revolution actually had ended the Great War, or at least transformed it. Barbusse had died an ideologically broken man in 1935. For many on the Left, time was no longer the friend of socialism. Doubt gnawed at the Hegelian-Marxist temporality of irresistible progress.

Henry Poulaille certainly saw himself as the keeper of Barbusse's flame, and evidently had been dubbed by the great man himself a "proletarian writer."[73] Unlike Barbusse, Poulaille had actual working-class origins. His father was a carpenter, his mother a caner of chairs. In four volumes total-

---

72. Ibid., 219.
73. Anonymous preface to Henri Poulaille, *Pain de soldat* (1937; repr., Paris: Grasset, 1995), n.p.

ing well over fifteen hundred printed pages, Poulaille chronicled the story of the Magneux, a family of working-class Parisians.[74] The dedications of the last two volumes made clear the moral of the story. Poulaille dedicated *Pain de soldat* (Bread of the Soldier, 1937) to, among others, "those who made war without having anything to defend and for nothing." Even more ominously, Poulaille dedicated *Les Rescapés* (The Rescued, 1938):

> To those who were the pseudo-victors of the "last of wars."
> To those who will be in the next one.
> May they know that war produces only the vanquished.

Louis Magneux, the young son of the family, was eighteen years old in 1914 and was mobilized two years later. He entered the front lines in time for the Chemin des Dames offensive in April 1917. Magneux was still willing to bring his rifle into battle, "but decided to forget to bring grenades. It didn't make sense to him to take part in the sort of filthy act in which he would need them."[75] Magneux concurred with Jolinon's view that the mutinies of 1917 had been essentially socialist. To Magneux (not himself a participant), they involved a desperate reappropriation of a socialist form of masculinity: "Whatever remained of the man in them liberated itself in these cries, in the couplets of the songs of insurrection."[76] Singing the "Internationale" in uniform was the true revolutionary act.

Poulaille expanded the role of the fusillé by making Magneux a guard for the proceedings of the courts martial following the mutinies. He thus became a perpetrator deprived of agency in judicial murder, able only to feel a shame that haunted him to the end of the novel. His involuntary participation in the war against the fusillés constituted his true traumatic experience, worse than anything he experienced under enemy fire. The circle of victims was thus extended to include the perpetrators. After the firing squad had done its work,

> Their footsteps on the dry ground make a heavy sound. They feel an immense sadness that nothing can lift. Not one of them can look at the poor guy that they just assassinated in the name of military law, the worst of laws.
> His tragic cries stay in their ears. For most of them, this is all they knew of a drama in which they appeared only in the epilogue. But these plaintive cries: "My wife, my little children," they are forever engraved upon them.[77]

74. Poulaille, *Le Pain quotidien* (1931); *Les Damnés de la terre* (1935); *Pain de Soldat* (1937); and *Les Rescapés* (1938).
75. Poulaille, *Pain de soldat*, 526.
76. Ibid., 316.
77. Ibid., 315.

Unlike the fusillé, Magneux survived the war, and was thus condemned to live in the murky moral universe that followed. The defeat of the Left's traditional apocalyptic view of time was forecast in his own defeat in the transition from war to postwar. Magneux had been wounded in the hand at the battle of Malmaison in late 1917, a tactical victory in the Chemin des Dames sector that supposedly affirmed the revived "morale" of the French army after the mutinies. But after his recovery, Magneux sought only personal escape from the war, though he stopped short of desertion. Momentary hopes for President Wilson and the liberal paradise envisaged by the Fourteen Points shortly gave way to his renewed disillusionment, caused by the triumph of nationalist politics, demobilization, and his own unemployment. A visit to a left-wing political meeting only deepened his alienation.

> "Class" . . . a term that for a long time, nearly five years, meant, in effect, something else. Thanks to the grinding effect of the Union sacrée, this term now had only its new, military meaning, the designation of conscripts by classes. One sought in vain to restore the old meaning of the word.[78]

He remarked in despair to his friend and comrade Weil:

> "What to believe in, if not the Revolution?"
> "Why believe?" declared Weil.[79]

As the war ended, Magneux faced a dilemma: faith in a failed collectivism versus the pursuit of a morally bankrupt bourgeois individualism.[80] He finally gained secure employment in the Paris suburbs and then sent for his love interest, Julia, who arrived in July 1919. "We will live like bourgeois," Magneux confessed to himself. "Really," he admitted, "deep down I had always hoped to lead a middle-class life. I played at being a revolutionary." He concluded unconvincingly: "We won the war. [. . .] [N]ow we have to win at life."[81] The couple celebrated on July 14, 1919, the day of the great victory parade in Paris. But Magneux had to excuse himself during the singing of a patriotic song. Gazing at himself in a mirror, "he

---

78. Poulaille, *Les Rescapés* (Paris: Éditions Grasset, 1938), 299. Magneux, for example, would have belonged to the "class" of 1916, the year he turned twenty. The character's views to the contrary, this was not at all a new meaning of "class."

79. Ibid., 310.

80. Poulaille had a successful career from 1925 until 1960 as director of the Press Service for Éditions Grasset, a pioneer in book marketing. See Chartier and Martin, *Histoire de l'Édition française*, 140–43.

81. Poulaille, *Les Rescapés,* 311.

could not take his eyes off that pale mask that looked back at him in the glass; this withered face, this face of a content idiot, it really was him."[82] In the end, he accepted his implication in the selfishness of postwar life, as he had previously accepted his implication in the war.

> It's about taking up life again. It's about taking up life again.
> Me! Me! Me! . . .
> To hell with this. to hell with everything.
> It's one way of being happy . . .
> It is a way for the rescued to be happy.[83]

The "rescued" Magneux proved anything but. His traumatic experience left him with little except a helpless awareness of his predicament. In pursuing a middle-class life with Julia, he had entered into collaboration with a socioeconomic discourse that eventually would only bring more war. The past that would not become the past would become the future. Magneux, ultimately, would live in the postwar world cursed by the knowledge he alluded to in the preface to *Les Rescapés,* that "war produces only the vanquished."

By the time *Les Rescapés* was published in 1938 the world had become too dangerous a place for readers to find much inspiration in a novel that concluded in the self-awareness of a tortured, helpless, and isolated survivor. An alternative on the Left involved accepting the inevitable return to the true traumatic event of the Great War—the acceptance of war in August 1914, which led inevitably to consent and political pathology. But the goal would be to intervene in the story and alter the ending, thereby heading off a new war certain to be even worse than the Great War.

The most able writer of the interwar Left, Jean Giono, wrote first a famous novel that posited a somewhat ambiguous temporality, then a famous essay that affirmed a conspicuously gloomy one. Critics rightly consider *Le Grand Troupeau* (The Great Herd, 1931) one of the few French Great War novels of durable literary merit, because of the power of its imagery and its nearly unique integration of life and death behind the lines and at the front. The book cuts constantly and seemingly effortlessly between the trenches and a family farm. Its plot is simple in outline, highly complex in detail, and secondary in importance to the broader interplay among death, mutilation, and regeneration. It has been common to read *Le Grand Troupeau* as a fable of war versus nature, and of war as something that perverted na-

82. Ibid., 320.
83. Ibid., 322.

ture and the relationship between humanity and nature.[84] But I would argue for a more troubling reading. Perhaps war was part of nature after all,
and nature itself operated according to a temporality of trauma.

In the hands of a less-skilled stylist, the title of the famous opening chapter, "Elle mangera vos béliers, vos brebis et vos moissons" (She [the war]
will eat your rams, your ewes, and your harvests) would seem heavy handed
or even silly. The day after the mobilized men from the village departed in
August 1914, the villagers turned out to see a massive herd of sheep de-
scend from the mountains. Behind Burle, the head shepherd, staggered the
head ram, black and bleeding horribly from his belly. Burle muttered repeatedly, "It's a waste of life."[85] The ram was diseased as well as wounded,
and died shortly:

> He raised in one movement his heavy branchy head, as though under orders.
> He looked at the sky as though between his two horns, a long interminable
> look. The neck stretched, he let out a small groan of a sheep. He spread out
> his thighs, stretched out his legs. He let out a packet of black blood and tripes
> with the sound of balloon that popped.[86]

That night, after the herd had passed, a young woman named Rose, whose
parents owned a butcher shop, heard a sound outside her house. It turned
out to be a lost lamb. When she picked up the lamb, it tried to nurse by
nestling its head toward her breasts. Her mother called to her to go back
to bed. Rose agreed, but asked her mother to "go open up the hallway.
Don't go by the store. It is full of meat and it smells of blood. He [the lamb]
would be afraid."[87] A ram would die ominously, but a lamb would be rescued and nurtured. Life, in other words, would renew itself irresistibly.

In a scene at the front much later in the book, Olivier, one of the four
main characters, encountered a farmhouse covered with wisteria. In the
doorway was the corpse of a young woman. Her head had been torn open
by a large piece of shrapnel. In the yard, a sow was digging in the earth and
tearing away at something:

> The sow raised its head. It was eating meat. She looked at Olivier with her
> tiny red eyes. She wrinkled her snout. She bared her big teeth like a mad dog.
> Olivier drew two steps closer. A mare tapped her feet in the grass.

84. See, for example, W. D. Redfern, "Against Nature: Jean Giono and *Le Grand Troupeau*," in Klein, *The First World War in Fiction*, 73–83; and Pierre Citron, *Giono, 1895–
1970* (Paris: Seuil, 1990), 158. Carine Trevisan considered this reading from a gender perspective in *Les Fables du deuil: la Grande Guerre, mort et écriture* (Paris: Presses Universitaires de France, 2001), 117–20.
85. Jean Giono, *Le Grand troupeau* (1931; repr., Gallimard, 2000), 17.
86. Ibid., 23.
87. Ibid., 25.

A dead and naked baby was under the feet of the sow. She had torn off a shoulder, and she was eating its chest. She leaned over the tiny stomach, still white. She bit into the stomach. She stuffed in a mouthful, in order to swallow the entrails of the infant.[88]

The horrified Olivier engaged the sow in personal combat with a large knife. Stabbing her repeatedly, "he was blinded by the blood, covered with blood, the growling and the death rattles, and he struck with all his might. His eyes were slimy with blood. He saw light hit the knife and he struck." Bitten in the shoulder by his enemy, Olivier won the fight by cutting her throat. A situation caused by the war had turned nature against man, and man against nature.

The novel concluded with a note of optimism, here in an affirmation of a highly gendered natural order. Delighted at the birth of a physically perfect son, in contrast to his crippled twin sister, Olivier invited a shepherd to say a blessing for the newborn male. A ram walked in to acknowledge the baby, as though it were a newborn lamb. The shepherd encouraged this, citing the presence of animals at a birth as a sign of good fortune. The shepherd acted as a priest, performing the reconciliation of nature and man through blessing the birth:

Child, said the shepherd, for all my life I have been the leader of beasts. You, my little one, by the graciousness of your father, I come to look for you at the edge of the herd, at the moment that you enter the great herd of men, to give you my best wishes.

[. . .] It will be given to you to have a great talent for bearing the burdens of others, to be at the roadside like a fountain.

And you will love the stars![89]

When the mother urged that the baby be covered up, fearing he might catch cold, the shepherd counseled that the infant needed to witness the whole scene: "We must make him see right away what hope is." The novel ended with the ram bellowing and the shepherd's star rising in the night sky. Nature would always renew itself.

The curious mix in *Le Grand Troupeau* of gloom and hope, violence and tenderness, makes it possible to ask whether the temporality of nature is actually compatible with the temporality of trauma. The state of nature is full of violence. Giono presented no hint that humans had injured the mutilated ram at the beginning of the book. Bleeding, and even disease and putrefaction, are likewise natural, biological processes. Living in accor-

88. Ibid., 238.
89. Ibid., 251–52.

dance with nature on the idealized farm revolved around ritualized violence. The peasants survived by exploiting their beloved sheep, and would
butcher and eat tomorrow the tiny lamb they cuddled today. Pigs are naturally omnivorous. They will eat babies or most anything else, given the
chance. Life would always win, in the sense that young children, lambs, and
pigs would always be born. But nature in the book had hierarchies. Men
ruled females, and men ruled animals. In his personal combat with the sow,
Olivier enforced both hierarchies quite literally at knifepoint. War had its
own rituals, many as well established as those of life on the farm. Perhaps
the moral of *Le Grand Troupeau* is that war is all *too* natural, an un-
breakable cycle of death and regeneration.

Giono wrote a famous 1934 essay titled "Je ne peux pas oublier" (I cannot forget) that seemed to explain and perhaps even alter the moral of his
1931 novel.[90] He focused on the fatal mistake of accepting war back in August 1914. Giono took great pains to establish himself as the least martial
of soldiers. He was certain he had never killed anyone, and he maintained
that he had gone into attacks either with his rifle intentionally disabled or
with no rifle at all. "All of the survivors of the war," he assured posterity,
"knew how easy it was with a little bit of dirt and urine to turn a Lebel rifle into a baton." He had never ordered anyone but himself to take part in
a dangerous action. He had never been wounded, except for a singeing of
his eyebrows during a gas attack, for which he still drew a pension of fifteen francs every three months. He had never been decorated, except by the
English for helping to look for blind victims in a burning hospital. Yet he
too had been the victim of trauma, of a past that would not become the
past:

> Twenty years have gone by. And for twenty years, despite life, pain, and hap-
> piness, I cannot wash the war off me. The horror of these four years is still
> in me. I carry the mark. All the survivors carry the mark. (377)

As a survivor, he saw it as his duty to testify, even though doing so reinscribed the traumatic experience itself: "The horrors, all fresh, made claim
over my lips. I made myself smell the odor of the dead. I made myself see
the caved-in stomachs, I filled up the chamber of my soul in which I spoke
of muddy ghosts with eyes eaten out by birds. I imagined putrefied friends,
my own and those of the men who were listening to me" (381).

The root causes of his trauma had been capitalism, and the Third Re-

---

90. Jean Giono, "Je ne peux pas oublier," *Europe* 16 (November 1934): 377–89. Hereafter cited by page number in the text

public as its instrument. "The capitalist state needs war," he wrote bluntly (385). But he did not critique capitalism in any detail or articulate its specific relationship to the regime. He had come to hate the Third Republic because of its ability to engineer first assent and then consent to war. He held responsible "the teachers, all the teachers that I had since my sixth year, the magistrates of the republic, the ministers, the president who signed the posters, finally all those who had whatever interest in making use of the blood of children (*enfants*) twenty years old." Of course, twenty-year-olds are no longer children. But Giono was not, he maintained, a fully responsible human being when war came. This absolved him of responsibility.

> I did not have the courage to desert. I have one, sole excuse. It is that I was young. I was not a coward. I was tricked by my youth. Those who knew I was young tricked me. (78–79)

If the capitalist state had needed war in August 1914, sooner or later it would need war again. Some day, the oppressed and the young would either be drawn into the vortex of war, or would refuse it. Giono saw what needed to be done: "There is only one remedy: our strength. There is only one means of making use of it: revolt" (387). But he showed little confidence in the ability of the masses to behave differently. He hinted at the dread implicit in *Le Grand Troupeau* that war may be so ferociously constructed into European civilization that it had become a function of "nature" itself:

> And every time I roam the paths of the earth, I meet little children with hair lit up by the sun and playing in the grass. And I know that they are but butcher's meat, and that there is nothing more to do but cry. (383)

The Left in *Le Feu* had not needed a sophisticated critique of capitalism, or even to reject the war of 1914–18. According to Barbusse's apocalyptic conception of time, history itself would produce a better world. Giono's solution to the continuing trauma of the Great War likewise required apocalypse. But he completely lacked the positivist faith that Barbusse had clung to so fiercely. Ideologically speaking, Giono had good reason to cry.

For the extreme Right, the problem of closure revolved around rewriting the "victory" of 1918 as defeat. "Defeat" lay in the apparent affirmation of the hated Third Republic in 1918, and the pernicious Enlightenment values it espoused. Rewriting victory as defeat became easier with time. The increasingly obvious weakness of France in the 1930s could be blamed on the regime. The extreme Right understood its enemy well. Some of the most able French writers of the interwar period, such as Louis-Ferdinand Céline and Pierre Drieu La Rochelle, carefully fashioned a particular concept of defeat as the inversion of consent. They constructed an antihero that mirrored its Other, the citizen-soldier. The outcome of an impending future war would offer at the very least vindication, at most an opportunity to reenact the prior war with a different ending.

Consent had been about the absolute implication of individual into the collectivity, all in the name of a republican France that joined the regime and the affective community of the nation. Defeat for the extreme Right was about selfishness, aimless desire, and loathing, for the self as well as the collectivity. Consent lent itself to a spare language of stoic resignation; defeat, to a rich, venomous slang. The antihero was proud to show himself a coward. Whereas consent radicalized reason, traumatic rejection radicalized desire. Consent required a utopian outcome of the war; defeat, a present and future dystopia. As for the Left, the individual soldier remained first and foremost the great loser of the Great War. But to the extreme Right, the sadder-but-wiser loser knew not just that he was a loser, but why. The act of luxuriating in the decadent self-awareness of the antihero, who saw defeat in the present and hoped for more of it in the future, provided its own way to master experience, and to create narrative and narrator.

Less than one quarter of Céline's *Voyage au bout de la nuit* (Journey to the End of the Night, 1932) actually took place during the war. But the experience of its antihero Ferdinand Badamaru at the front provided a structure for his experience in the novel as a whole. He simply wandered from one unresolved situation to the next, learning little about himself or the world around him that he did not already know. Events that might be considered pivotal happened outside the narrative proper. For example, Badamaru was wounded seriously enough to be hospitalized, though readers are told nothing about exactly what happened. Readers learn in passing and without explanation that Badamaru was awarded the Médaille Militaire, a decoration not given lightly. But what drove the story was the same need to testify that drove soldiers' writing since 1914. Céline still had to create a narrator and narrative, however miserable:

> The biggest defeat in every department of life is to forget, especially the things that have done you in, and to die without realizing how far people can go in the way of crumminess. When the grave lies open before us, let's not try to be witty, but on the other hand, let's not forget, but make it our business to record the worst of the human viciousness we've seen without changing one word. When that's done, we can curl up our toes and sink into the pit. That's enough work for a lifetime.[91]

91. Ferdinand Céline, *Journey to the End of the Night,* trans. Ralph Manheim (New York: New Directions, 1983), 18. Hereafter cited by page number in the text.

At a stroke, Céline created a stable narrative and narrator by seeking out the worst in the human condition. Such a subject could not easily be disappointed or challenged. Badamaru's passage into the army became a kind of trick he played on himself. Bantering during the mobilization with an acquaintance at a café at the Place Clichy in Paris, Badamaru responded to a fleeting reference of praise for the French as a race: "What you call a race is nothing but a collection of riffraff like me, bleary-eyed, flea-bitten, chilled to the bone" (3). Yet he found himself perversely drawn to the public enthusiasm for which he had such contempt. He proclaimed himself eager to join up. He wanted simply to confirm that his compatriots were as loathsome as he thought. Badamaru joined the marching crowd of men joining the colors, as cheering crowds bombarded them with flowers. As they marched on and on, the crowds thinned and the music stopped. Just as Badamaru pronounced his fun over, he realized that it was too late: "They'd quietly shut the gate behind us civilians. We were caught like rats" (6).

Yet Badamaru wandered through the war much as he had wandered into the army. As a scout during the chaotic fighting of the fall of 1914, he spent most of his time avoiding danger rather than gathering intelligence. But like so many before him, he claimed to have been transformed by experience at the front: "You can be a virgin in horror the same as in sex. How, when I left the Place Clichy, could I have imagined such horror? Who could have suspected, before getting really into the war, all the ingredients that go to make up the rotten, heroic, good-for-nothing soul of man?" (9). But soon the war looked like a familiar kind of woman: "I was suddenly on the most intimate terms with war. I'd lost my virginity. You've got to be pretty much alone with her as I was then to get a good look at her, the slut, full face and profile" (10).

So fully formed a character proved largely impervious to the horrors of the front. When a shell explosion killed his colonel, toward whom he admitted no ill will, he observed succinctly: "The colonel's belly was wide open, and he was making a nasty face about it. It must have hurt when it happened. Tough shit for him!" (3). He had no more pity for a group of future fusillés paraded by him, "some due to be shot the next day, and no downer in the mouth than the others. It didn't spoil their appetites either, they ate their ration of that tuna fish that's so indigestible (they wouldn't have time to digest it) whole, waiting by the side of the road for the convoy to shove off—and they ate their last chunk of bread, too, with a civilian chained to them, who was said to be a spy but he didn't know it" (26). Badamaru learned only one thing in his transition from defeated civilian to defeated soldier: "The one thing that's really indecent is bravery. You expect physical bravery? Then ask a worm to be brave, he's pink and soft like us" (39).

Once recuperating behind the lines, Badamaru's one goal was never to return to the front. He managed to get himself transferred to a mental hospital, and there he took up with Lola, an oh-so-sincere American volunteer. He enjoyed her body, but he was annoyed that "she kept bothering me with the soul, she was always going on about it. The soul is the body's vanity and pleasure as long as the body's in good health, but it's also the urge to escape from the body as soon as the body is sick or things are going badly" (43). He became particularly annoyed when she interrogated him on his mental illness, self-diagnosed simply as fear. Lola, herself the citizen of a republic, was appalled. She parroted the received wisdom of consent. "But it's not possible to reject the war, Ferdinand!" she scolded. "Only crazy people and cowards reject the war when their country is in danger" (54). She left the hospital without kissing him.

Later, Badamaru unburdened himself to a fellow patient, explaining exactly what he loathed so much about the war and the regime waging it. Badamaru hated the Third Republic precisely *because* it could so effectively engineer consent. He longed for the ancien régime, when the sovereign "didn't give a hoot in hell about his beloved people." Quite the reverse, "he smeared his asshole with them" (56–58). The Enlightenment philosophes, nefariously, began to replace religious superstition with far more dangerous notions. In no time, each male individual became implicated in the whole, as citizens of a republic:

> First teach everybody to read the papers! That's the way to salvation. Hurry hurry! No more illiterates! We don't need them anymore! Nothing but citizen-soldiers! Who vote! Who read! And who fight! And who march! And who send kisses from the front! In no time the people were good and ripe!

The regime, to Badamaru, had engineered the means of pointless obedience and sacrifice that kings could scarcely have dreamt of.

The diseased republic would one day achieve the peace it deserved. Badamaru reported that peace, "a hysterical bitch," had begun to unveil herself even before the armistice at the Olympia dance hall, dancing to oddly named "Negro-Judeo-Saxon" music (59). He left the army as mysteriously as he had entered it. "The army finally dropped me," he confided. "I'd saved my guts, but my brains had been scrambled for good" (94). Yet he exited from the war simply a slightly more self-aware version of the figure that marched into it. He would seek more of the same as a civilian, by packing himself off to the French colonies in Africa—a land of unlimited desire, savagery, selfishness. There, European man could truly become himself: "In the European cold, under gray, puritanical northern skies, we seldom get to see our brothers' festering cruelty except in times of carnage, but when roused by the foul fevers of the tropics, their rottenness rises to the surface" (95). And so continued the meanderings of Badamaru, which later took him to New York, Detroit, and ultimately back to France. All repeated essentially the same story, the defeat of the self-aware, self- and other-hating victim. This figure nevertheless achieved a form of mastery, through his ironic detachment from his defeat and a certain luxuriating in his own decadence. For Badamaru, any temporality *except* that of trauma scarcely seemed conceivable, because he had so thoroughly mastered it. Future national defeat could only vindicate his particular version of narrative and experience.

In *Gilles* (1939 and 1942) Pierre Drieu la Rochelle saw through defeat the possibility of reclaiming a fascist version of apocalyptic time. As we saw in chapter 2, Drieu employed rites of passage in *La Comédie de Charleroi* (1934) to produce a self-pitying and self-loathing narrator perpetually in search of transformation. More explicitly than Céline, Drieu saw 1918 as the traumatic episode, when the French had shown themselves unfit to capitalize on defeating the Germans. He concluded as early as 1922 that "the French left this war diseased, fever-stricken, and full of faults and the fatal manias of the sick."[92] The hated Third Republic had abused France through its all-too-effective ability to create republican citizens, the antithesis of Drieu's idealized fascist man. While the republic lived, its citizens would wander through reenacted dramas of failed transformation. Of course, the so-called victory in 1918, even if rewritten as defeat, would soon or later lead to new war. This future war, Drieu argued, would provide the chance to change the outcome of the story by destroying the Third Republic, and should be welcomed on that basis.

Gilles is a lengthy, self-indulgent, even tedious work—whose monotonous structure was at least part of the point. The Great War was simultaneously marginal and omnipresent. None of the action in the novel took place at the front. On leave in Paris in the grim autumn of 1917, the penniless Gilles Gambier literally laid himself at the doorstep of the Falkenbergs, a wealthy, assimilated Jewish family originally from Alsace. The son of the family had belonged to Gilles's regiment and had been killed at the front. "Monsieur Falkenberg," the narrator recounted, "had made his children Catholic at the time of the Dreyfus affair. This did not prevent him from becoming a Dreyfusard. But all of that was long ago. His sons had been killed. France took him at his word."[93] The anti-Semitic Gilles, who

92. Pierre Drieu la Rochelle, *Mesure de la France* (Paris: Grasset, 1922), 72.
93. Drieu la Rochelle, *Gilles* (Paris: Gallimard, 1939) 107. Hereafter referred to as *Gilles* (1939).

disdained capitalism because of its obsessive materialism, married Falkenberg's daughter Myriam for her money. He never pretended to be faithful to her in body or soul. He tried his hand, with little success, at playing the functionary for the Foreign Ministry, and later the writer for a literary journal appropriately entitled *L'Apocalypse*. His misadventures in romance and pretend battle droned on. Gilles confided rather melodramatically of a breakup with one mistress: "It was a new Verdun, the moment in which the overwhelmed human being can no longer support the vault of heaven, and lets it collapse in an imbecilic chaos."[94]

Only in a lengthy epilogue, from which Gilles himself was mostly absent, did Drieu emplot the possibility that renewed war could lead to apocalyptic transformation. The scene was Spain during its civil war, around 1937. A motley international crew of duplicitous, insincere, and selfish characters meddled in and got swept up in events on the pro-Franco side. They comprised a Dutchman, a Belgian, a Spaniard, an Irishman, a Pole—but no Frenchman, Englishman, or German. The characters imagined the fascist new world to come, in a setting conspicuously resembling the one concluding Barbusse's *Le Feu*. Their international fascist *patrie*, like Barbusse's international socialist *patrie*, had a somewhat diffuse character. A central pillar would be Catholicism, a subject largely absent earlier in the book. The comrades agreed that "we are for the virile Catholicism of the Middle Ages,"[95] though what this meant became clearer only at the very end of the book. Fascism, ultimately, appeared to be more about form than about content. Or otherwise stated, the form would provide the content, as indicated by the visionary of the group, the Belgian: "Fascism is not a doctrine, it is a method, the direction of the century. It is up to us to bring together in it three dispersed forces—socialism, religion, and virile spirit."[96]

Their experience in the Spanish civil war, they imagined, would make it possible to rewrite experience in the Great War. They had rediscovered consent, minus hated republican citizenship:

> We savor in common the sacrifice to something that, in the prolonged danger, proves itself more and more engraved into the hearts of each one, each one being responsive to all. It is the miracle of finally being able to love one's self in others, and to love others in one's self.[97]

Once projected on to a European stage through a new war, fascism would forge a new collectivity and a new identity that would transcend nations

94. Ibid., 413.
95. Ibid., 474
96. Ibid., 476.
97. Ibid., 472.

themselves as affective communities: "'Nationalism is out of date,' replied O'Connor after a moment of reflection. 'What the democratic powers could not succeed in doing at Geneva the fascist powers will. They will make European unity.'"

Drieu became so attached to this outcome that he emplotted it two different ways, under very different external circumstances, in the 1939 and 1942 editions of *Gilles*. In 1939, his work had to pass the censors of the Third Republic, unknowingly in the last year of its existence. This version advocated a ferocious prosecution of a new war in order to remake the world, a conclusion parallel to that of Barbusse back in 1916. He predicted that the struggle against German and Italian fascism would annihilate democracy in the heart of Europe: "England and France will become fascist in making war on fascist Germany and Italy; likewise Russia, which is already practically fascist."[98] Semifascist Russia and the United States, inevitably, would become drawn into the new Great War. Caught between the two invading behemoths, "there will be born a European patriotism of all who have become fascists." At last seeing the true danger—Soviet and American domination—Germany and Italy would abandon their outmoded dreams of hegemony. Europe and Europeans would unite and become their true and redeemed selves by fighting Bolshevism.

By 1942 Drieu had become the collaborationist editor of the *Nouvelle Revue Française*. In the second edition of *Gilles*, gone were references to France and Britain becoming fascist through defeating Germany and Italy. In predicting the outcome of the next war (though actually writing after the fall of France), Drieu could not resist a swipe at the moribund Third Republic:

> At the last minute, France will abandon its universal task, it will return again to fighting and, sooner or later, it will retire to the front lines, burned by the communist revolvers, at the instigation of a few Jews. France will not know how to save itself, and a new victory would not be worth any more than a defeat. But there are ideas born of the patries that will detach themselves from them, and will find other, more vast forms in which to incarnate themselves.[99]

The 1942 edition labeled a prospective American victory as much a defeat for Europe as a Soviet one. The key to reliving and correcting 1918 in the 1942 edition lay in the awakening of "European" fascist patriotism in Germany and Italy. But as he cautioned the victor of 1940:

---

98. Ibid., 476.
99. *Gilles* (1942; repr., Paris: Gallimard, 1973), 678.

> This [fascist] spirit will only be born if Germany gives in advance a full,
> moral, guarantee of the patries, of all the patries of Europe. Then alone
> will it be able to fulfill efficiently the role devolved to it by the tradition of
> the Holy Roman–Germanic empire, to lead Europe in the direction of the
> future.[100]

Drieu had become a diplomat as well as a collaborator, by appealing a bit
obliquely to Vichy's unrealistic desire for sovereignty over all of France,
while simultaneously deferring to the inevitable German leadership of the
New Europe.

Gilles himself suffered the same fate in both editions. He had become a
journalist, and at Christmas 1937 found himself in a bullfighting plaza in
Burgos, where he had persuaded pro-Franco forces to show him the front.
An overwhelming Republican force suddenly attacked the plaza. As enemy
mortars began to fall around him, Gilles was told by his minders to depart.
He declined and instead picked up a rifle in search, it seemed, of certain
death and the yearned-for transcendence. Gilles had himself become what
Drieu had preached—a fascist, "Christian" warrior. Crucially, the restless
sexual desire that had driven him throughout the book had at last burned
itself out: "Women, he no longer desired them. He was horrified, henceforth, to hear someone speak to him of a woman."[101] Now purified, he
could confidently reenact 1914, sure that 1918 would play itself out differently. He imagined his impending death: "It is necessary to die ceaselessly
in order to be reborn ceaselessly."[102] Trauma as a narrative would be re-
versed. Instead of repeated failed transcendence, experience would become
repeated rebirth. But Gilles was dead, an obscure martyr known only to
himself. Drieu's need to eliminate him precisely at the moment of his transformative enlightenment did not suggest unlimited confidence in the fascist
future.

Indeed, for varying reasons, none of the emplotments of trauma in the
novels considered in this section provided a particularly compelling moral
message even at the time these were published. In the case of Chevalier, no
one would take much edification in barbarized African Americans winning
either the last war or the next one. Vercel's brutalized Captain Conan
would not be much more inspiring, and not much of a guardian for a Western civilization menaced by fascism. Leftist versions relied on revisiting the
traumatic experience of 1914 and altering the outcome. But novelists such
as Poulaille and Giono seemed themselves to have had precious little con-

100. Ibid., 675.
101. *Gilles* (1939), 484.
102. Ibid.

fidence in such a scenario should war return to Europe. In the event, the working classes of Europe would not resist war in 1940 any more than they had in 1914, with even more calamitous results. Fascist explanations offered either wallowing in defeat or deluded transcendence in the event of renewed war. Fascism in France would remain a marginal political movement under Vichy, as it had under the Third Republic. It hardly provided an acceptable voice through which to understand experience in the Great War after 1945. In order to document experience effectively over the long run, trauma would require emplotment in a less partisan and more introspective and complex psychological kind of novel.

Témoin to Tragedy

If narrative time requires resolution of the crisis that drove the narrative in the first place, two of the most famous French Great War novels of the 1930s testified to the defeat of narrative time itself. Both novels were parts of massive multivolume works: Jules Romains's twenty-seven-volume *Les Hommes de bonne volonté* (Men of Good Will, 1932–46) and Roger Martin du Gard's eight-volume *Les Thibaults* (The Thibault Family, 1922–40). Both authors had international reputations—Romains became a member of the Académie française after 1945, and Martin du Gard won the 1937 Nobel Prize for literature. Both had served in the military during the Great War, but neither as a combatant. Indeed, the fact that neither Romains nor Martin du Gard wrote about his own experience proved to some extent the point. Experience had now become a matter for the author in the foucauldian sense of the term, the figure through whom society marked the fear of the proliferation of meaning. By the end of the 1930s, one had to be an author to narrate experience in the Great War, but not necessarily a combatant.

Yet Romains and Martin du Gard should also be considered témoins, who helped change the meaning of testimony in the Great War. Both followed in the tradition of Balzac and Zola, in that they provided complex and exhaustively detailed narratives meant to serve as historical documents in their own right. Literature would serve history, and vice versa. By the time Romains and Martin du Gard completed their protracted narratives, the cultural "work" had already been done, in the establishment of a metanarrative of the Great War and its meaning. The two authors testified to the "truth" of this metanarrative and helped put the finishing touches on it. By the end of the 1930s, the war of 1914–18 had become understood definitively as tragedy, and the soldier who had fought it as a victim. This metanarrative both shaped and was shaped by the set of cultural practices known collectively as "memory," and would continue to do so for many decades to come.

Like no other French Great War novelist, Romains explicitly connected trauma, tragedy, and consent. The two most famous volumes, *Prélude à Verdun* and *Verdun* (both 1938), pointed to the epic battle of 1916 as the traumatic episode, when means and ends in the Great War became definitively disarticulated. Human consciousness would never be able to keep up with events, and thus people would not consciously be able to intervene in them. Tragedy would thus document trauma, as the characters become swept up by circumstances they understood only too late. The novelist began *Prélude à Verdun* as a historian, with a masterful emplotment of the war up to 1916. Romains assumed two racially distinct but morally equivalent sets of protagonists. Hubris consumed both, as each punished the other. First diplomats and then generals failed to deliver a decisive victory.

> No one man had a will sufficiently strong to make its weight felt upon the whole complexity of war, no man was clear-seeing enough, to envisage in a single glance the total magnitude of events and the life of the soldier in the trenches.[103]

No one saw less than the soldiers themselves. Indeed, had they ever actually understood their plight, they have might put a stop to it, on their own.

> The men, French and German in collaboration, might make some very awkward discoveries; might, in so many words, say to one another: "what are we doing here? Shouldn't we all be better off if we just went home?" (27)

The psychological portrait of Jerphanion, the central character of these two volumes, personalized the convergence of consent, trauma, and tragedy. Like Romains, Jerphanion had been a schoolteacher before the war, and he understood well how the Third Republic had engineered citizens and soldiers through education. Unlike Romains, Jerphanion served in the front lines, as a lieutenant in the infantry. Jerphanion understood events through extended reflections after the fact, when he had been relieved from duty in the trenches or was on leave in Paris. As a witness, he was haunted by the frailties of testimony, the impossibility of seeing things clearly and completely at the same time. This time lag made it impossible for consciousness to keep up with events. Experience "as it happens" proved again at odds with narration:

---

103. Jules Romains, *Verdun*, trans. Gerard Hopkins (New York: Alfred A. Knopf, 1939), 37. Originally published as *Prélude à Verdun* and *Verdun* in 1938. This translation combined both books in a single volume. Hereafter cited by page number in the text.

> The most one can do is throw one's line at a venture in the hope of hooking some fragment of experience that may serve as evidence, or, rather, as one scrap of evidence among others. (144)

Yet, Jerphanion was witness to a larger narrative whose meaning was both true and self-evident. "His" war and "the" war had become two versions of the same story. The Third Republic produced consent, the pathologies of which slowly became clear during the war itself. The sacrifices required by consent would prove unredeemable. The soldier would emerge from the Great War permanently damaged, whether he suffered physical injury or not. The temporality of his life had been overturned forever, in that the crisis of experience in the trenches could never be convincingly resolved.

"I cannot now begin to conceive," Jerphanion wrote to his friend Jallez even before the epic battle began, "how this war can possibly turn out 'well,' meaning by 'well' something that our idealism could accept." At best, the tsar would come to rule in Constantinople, and the British empire would consolidate its dominance over vast swaths of the world. As for France, "I know perfectly well that my country will be far too exhausted to impose its will on Europe, even assuming that will to be good" (145). No plausible outcome could justify the sacrifices the war had required. Jerphanion had become aware of this even during his last leave, when he already felt the veteran's dissatisfaction with the postwar world. His apartment had seemed small, his study devoid of warmth, his beloved wife nearly an annoyance. He confessed to Jallez: "Is it worthwhile going through all I'm going through if this is what I've got to come back to?" (157). He was haunted by "a vision of life as it used to be when it was real and lovely," such as the Grands Boulevards in June or in long, reflective walks with Jallez. "I don't think it can ever be like that again," he lamented. "I wear its picture on my heart as I might the portrait of some dear dead woman of the past" (158).

Only in *Verdun,* specifically during a leave after fighting in the battle itself, did Jerphanion understand that consent lay at the heart of the defeat of narrative time. The war traumatized him precisely because he considered himself totally and individually implicated in it. The French held Verdun because of a horizontally structured authority: "Even when one takes it [commitment to the war] into account one disguises it in borrowed plumage that gives it an air more flattering to self-pride: one calls it duty, patriotism, and so forth. . . . Its true name is something much cruder: nothing more or less than the pressure of society" (446). "Society," as he explained further, was plainly the society engineered by teachers such as himself in the schools of the Third Republic.

Specifically, the republic had taught Rousseau's synthesis of discipline and freedom that lay at the heart of consent and its pathologies. Too late, Jerphanion had become able to see the illusion of freedom created by this synthesis:

> A man's got to stay where he is. He's caught like a rat in a trap, in a tangle of intersecting threads—the fear of a firing squad, a sense of shame, or dishonour, the moral impossibility of doing otherwise, a sort of mystical terror—on all sides he is hemmed in. (451)

A given individual might genuinely believe he served out of a positive choice made by a genuinely free will. Yet the now self-aware Jerphanion confessed, "if we were intent on splitting hairs, we could prove easily enough that even this free and sincere will to sacrifice was something that he would never have come by unaided, that it was the product of that silly nonsense called education, or, in other words, of society's most cunning trick to mould a man to its design" (451). Consent, in the end, had turned the citizen against himself: "But once he [the citizen] has realized that, whatever happens, he has got to do what he is told, he likes nothing so much as to believe that the initial order came from himself" (452).

This was not mere self-absorbed whining, nor was Jerphanion a victim in the mold of the zombielike Paul Baümer, psychologically and morally dead whether he survived in body or not. Through eleven volumes covering the postwar period (the last published just after World War II), Jerphanion retained a reflective intellect, actively engaged in putting his life back together. Nor did Jerphanion ever become the enemy of democracy. In today's language of psychology, we might describe his postwar trajectory as "working through" his trauma.[104] But both the fictional character and, through him, the novelist wanted to witness to a specific kind of tragedy. The Third Republic had produced consent, and consent had so radicalized the war that that it could end only in trauma. Jerphanion's belated awareness of his predicament served simply to add pathos to his personal story, and detail to the metanarrative of which it was a part.

Martin du Gard placed the emplotment of tragedy at center stage.[105] *L'Été 1914* (*Summer 1914*) and *Épilogue* concluded his massive narrative of a prosperous bourgeois family facing the new century, *Les Thibaults*. The Great War proved a vortex for the family, destroying one brother who actively resisted it and another who tried to operate at its margins. Neither

104. See Dominick LaCapra, "Interview for Yad Vashem, June 9, 1998," in *Writing History, Writing Trauma,* 143–44,

105. See Maurice Rieneau, "Guerre et Révolution dans le Roman Français: 1919–1939" (doctoral diss., Université de Paris IV, 1972), 465–504.

was a combatant, yet both died because of what happened to them at the front. The war broke not just the Thibault family but time itself. In a sophisticated if somewhat manipulative way, Martin du Gard left it to the reader's knowledge of current events to complete the construction of the tragedy, which would repeat itself as a new war. Martin du Gard deprived his characters not only of agency (as did Romains) but also of much awareness of their predicament. Consciousness became the exclusive domain of the author, who mercilessly led the reader through the characters' frantic embrace of ideals whose failure had become all too clear by the time the concluding volumes of *Les Thibaults* were published.

Certainly, Martin du Gard had more overt left-wing political sympathies that Romains. The very title *L'Été 1914*, and its extraordinary level of detail in the emplotment of the mobilization, reflected the Left's traditional focus on the outbreak of war as a crucial episode opening the way to trauma.[106] Yet Martin du Gard almost mocked the naiveté of the Left and its concept of apocalyptic historical time, particularly in the way he narrated the disastrous demise of Jacques Thibault, a headstrong revolutionary disdainful of his bourgeois origins.

The assassination of Archduke Franz Ferdinand found Jacques in Switzerland, conspiring with a cosmopolitan band of like-minded activists. During the exhaustively chronicled weeks that followed, they interpreted the coming conflict as a military competition for markets between two capitalist blocs. "It all hangs together," concluded an Austrian. "In the background, dominating the situation, always we find the same two groups of capitalist powers up against each other."[107] For Jacques, the response of the working class, carefully guided by men such as himself, ought to have been obvious: "The strike, of course! A general, simultaneous strike! That's our trump card."[108] Upon his return to Paris, he preached to a deceptively friendly crowd: "We must rally round the leaders of the International, and bid them spare no pains to organize the general strike, the mass attack of the forces of the proletariat, on which hangs the fate of France, the destiny of Europe."[109] He ignored signs of rising French nationalism all around him.

106. For opposing views on the historical accuracy of the book, see David L. Shalk, *Roger Martin du Gard: The Novelist and History* (Ithaca: Cornell University Press, 1967); and Jean-Jacques Becker, "Les Origines de la première guerre mondiale dans *l'Été 1914* de Roger Martin du Gard," *Relations internationales* 14 (1978): 143–58.

107. Roger Martin du Gard, *Summer 1914*, trans. Stuart Gilbert (New York: Viking Press, 1941), 83. Originally published as *L'Été 1914* in 1936 and *Épilogue* in 1940. This translation combined both books in a single volume.

108. Ibid., 92.

109. Ibid., 493.

Jacques and his companion Jenny happened to be present at the assassination of Jean Jaurès on July 31, 1914. Only the murder of the great Socialist internationalist began to convince Jacques that the masses of Europe would not behave as his preconceived narrative required. As Martin du Gard chided him, "His attitude had been, not that of the visionary expecting a miracle, but that of the scientist awaiting the results of an infallible experiment."[110] Deeply upset and disillusioned, Jacques and Jenny initially retreated from the whole matter by consummating their long-simmering relationship. The issue of this single encounter would be Paul, the last of the Thibaults, but who would not bear the name because he had been born out of wedlock.

As Paris embraced war, Jacques returned to Switzerland to plan his next move. One French resident of Switzerland, Romain Rolland, chose to remain there "above the fray," content with preaching the evils of the war in print.[111] Another resident alien, V. I. Lenin, bided his time plotting revolution. But Jacques, the virile antiwar warrior, planned a grand gesture rooted in an apocalyptic conception of time. He stubbornly held to his belief that the masses simply did not yet know the truth. With the help of Meynestrel, the leader of a revolutionary band and a trained pilot, Jacques planned to distribute antiwar tracts to soldiers on both sides of the ferocious fighting in Alsace. He believed with apparent sincerity that, once enlightened, soldiers on both sides would suspend combat in mid-battle and force a transformative peace. The message, Jacques insisted, conveyed sufficient truth in itself to make Europe free. This made it possible for him to scold prospective readers of the tract: "Your mistake lay in failing to forestall the conflagration while there was still time."[112] Now it was almost too late:

> Now, everywhere, an iron discipline has gagged the voice of individual protest. Everywhere you have been reduced to the blind subservience of animals in blinkers. Never before has humanity been brought so low, intelligence so completely stifled. Never before have governments forced men's minds into so total an abdication of their rights; so brutally repressed the aspirations of the masses.[113]

At some level, Jacques knew his project to be doomed. At best, they would be court-martialed and doubtless would become fusillés of one side

---

110. Ibid., 576.
111. Rolland wrote eight articles in the *Journal de Genève* between August and December 1914, published as *Au-dessus de la mêlée* (Paris: Ollendorf, 1915).
112. Martin du Gard, *Summer 1914*, 694.
113. Ibid., 694–95.

or the other. Yet he tried to assure himself as a desperate grasp at agency, "every act of heroism is absurd, and criminal."[114] The virile warrior against war had proved himself a man with Jenny before leaving France. He would do the same on the battlefield by dying the hero's death. Jacques calmed himself by reaffirming his deluded conception of what he was about to do:

> He saw the war cut short perhaps; mutinies and fraternization followed by an armistice. "And even," he murmured, "if my effort fails, what an example! Whatever happens, my death's an *act,* an act that will bring honour back again."[115]

Jacques survived just long enough to witness the true futility of his act. The plane had mechanical trouble and crashed over the French front lines, incinerating the tracts and killing Meynestrel immediately. Jacques had been gravely wounded, with no feeling in his shattered legs and piercing pain from burns and fractures elsewhere. Yet he remained more or less aware of everything that happened around him until the moment of his death. He was first taken prisoner by the retreating French, then shot as an encumbrance. His killer was a perfectly typical common soldier named Marjoulat—who previously had never even killed an animal and who was of the very sort that was supposed to see the truth proclaimed in the now-incinerated tracts.

As Northrop Frye put it, "tragedy seems to lead up to an epiphany of law, of that which is and must be."[116] The "must be" here is the explanation of the Great War as a tragedy that destroyed all it touched, including the would-be heroic warrior who tried to make war upon it. So predictable was the annihilation of Jacques that the reader could come to imagine the effacement of the author himself. It was not Martin du Gard who humiliated, mutilated, and killed Jacques but the war. All the author needed to do was provide content for the preexisting form. The war, in its seemingly obvious emplotment by 1936 as tragedy, could accomplish the rest.

Yet tragic heroes like Jacques by definition would be exceptional characters. In Frye's words, "they are so much the highest points in the human landscape that they seem the inevitable conductors of power about them; great trees are more likely to be struck by lightning than a clump of grass."[117] Jacques's brother Antoine, the central character of *Épilogue,* was

114. Ibid., 711.
115. Ibid., 711; italics in original.
116. Northrop Frye, *The Anatomy of Criticism* (1957; repr., Princeton: Princeton University Press, 1990), 208.
117. Ibid., 207.

one such clump of grass. Although devoted to his brother, Antoine was the opposite of the flamboyant Jacques. The ultra-respectable and ambitious research physician "had no dependents, no costly vices. Only one passion: work."[118] In August 1914 he dutifully accepted mobilization as a medical officer. Yet the war would destroy him both physically and ideologically, as it had destroyed Jacques.

Simple misfortune first damaged Antoine's health, then ultimately took his life. He had suffered a punctured lung from a bullet wound in 1916 and then inhaled a small amount of mustard gas in the fall of 1917. The earlier wound, together with bronchial lesions caused by the 1917 gassing, had made him susceptible to chronic and ultimately fatal pulmonary infections. But he did not actually die until one week after the armistice of November 11, 1918. Ever the dedicated physician, this accidental battlefield casualty sought to leave a testimonial medical record of his death—the insomnia, the aphonia, the coughing fits that literally brought up parts of his pulmonary tract. Like Jacques, he also sought belatedly to recover some agency through determining the specific circumstances of his death. He carried out a plan to inject himself with a fatal dose of morphine as his last conscious act. His struggle was to emplot his physical decline and his intellectual and moral advancement as a testimony of experience to pass on to the future.

In the last section of the book, Martin du Gard altered the form in order to emphasize the content. It emplotted with the authenticity of "real time" a very specific period (May 18 to November 18, 1918), from the day Antoine realized the fatal nature of his illness to the day of his death. But rather than the standard prose narrative of a novel, *Épilogue* concluded with a compilation of "original" documents—various letters to and from Antoine, and his personal journal. Martin du Gard as author took a step back in order to let the documents "speak for themselves." The massive multivolume novel of the Thibaults would conclude with the immediacy of a personal journal.

Against the backdrop of his impending death, Antoine recorded his satisfaction at the ascendancy of Woodrow Wilson. Antoine might die, but progress would live on. "What Wilson's aiming at," he wrote on July 7, "is so clear, so sensible, so well in keeping with man's truest instincts, with the trend of human progress" (925). The masses, he believed as fervently as his brother, were intrinsically peaceful. If asked, the peoples of the world would embrace a League of Nations powerful enough to keep the states of

---

118. Martin du Gard, *Summer 1914*, 111. Hereafter cited by page number in the text. All italics are in the original.

Europe at peace. On September 3 he wrote: "Am very hopeful, and pretty well convinced that after the year 1920 there will be a republican, patriarchal, industrious, peace-loving Germany—one of the most solid guarantees of a United Europe" (975).

Most specifically, Antoine hoped for a better world for his nephew Paul, for whom Antoine wanted his journal to provide a set of valedictory lessons based on his own experience. "I am thinking of Paul," he wrote on October 16. "Of you, my dear Paul. With infinite relief. A new world is coming to birth. You will witness its consolidation and play a part in it. Steel your resolve, to play a *worthy* part" (998). Antoine wrote at length about Jacques, and tried to portray his deceased brother's virtues and shortcomings fairly. He admired the "innermost, authentic self" that governed Jacques, as well as his energy and high ideals (948). But Jacques had been consumed by the same sort of ideological fervor that led to the deaths so many young and idealistic men in the summer of 1914:

> Their imagination enables them to conjure up mentally a host of sensations with which, so far, they have had no direct personal contacts. But this they fail to realize; they mistake *knowing* for *experiencing*. They believe that they personally experience cravings and emotions for which they merely *know that others feel*. (950)

So what had experience taught Antoine as he sought closure in the written record of his own life? "Incidentally," he wrote on August 14–15, "I find that I no longer believe in responsibility." "Could I have another lease of life," he admitted, "I'd like to live it under the sign of Doubt" (957). Ultimately, he confessed that in terms of moral coherence, he had not achieved much beyond his brother: "I shall leave this world without having been unable to overcome my utter incapacity for abstract thought" (963). This all-too-human Antoine did not seem like much of a champion for Wilsonian idealism, which he hoped against hope would shape the world Paul would inherit.

Martin du Gard left it to the reader to realize just how profoundly Antoine had failed to understand how the postwar world would unfold. Any reader would know too well by the time *Épilogue* was published that the high ideals of 1918 had failed to prevent a new war. Although the book was completed by March 1939,[119] its publication was delayed by the outbreak of war until January 1940. This was during the *drôle de guerre,* or "phony war" between the declaration of war in September 1939 and the German invasion of May 1940. Simple arithmetic would reveal Paul's im-

---

119. Shalk, *Roger Martin du Gard,* 157.

plication in the new war. Conceived at the end of August 1914, Paul would have been born sometime in the spring of 1915. Not yet four years old when his uncle died in November 1918, Paul already had his future mapped out for him. He would have been twenty-four years old and no doubt in uniform at the time *Épilogue* was published. The new war would take over his life, repeating the traumatic and tragic experience. It scarcely mattered whether Paul was a "real" person or not. Martin du Gard, novelist and witness to a metanarrative of tragedy, had testified to the underlying truth of his story.

I have argued in this chapter that as testimony, the novel recounted a search for closure, for a proper temporal framework for understanding experience in the Great War. The emplotment of demobilization in the 1920s produced termination more than closure, typically simple revulsion and rejection of the war. But the multiple crises of the 1930s—depression, fascism, the threat of renewed war—made it necessary to place rejection in some sort of temporal context that made a statement about the future. Trauma as a narrative principle did this by showing that time had broken in some way, the result being an apparently inevitable return to war. "Closure" then revolved around non-closure through reporting the defeat of narrative time. Alternatively, authors could posit improbable or impossible means of intervening in the story of trauma and changing its outcome—whether reenacting August 1914 with a working-class refusal to wage war, or using a new war to replace the republican citizen with the fascist man. But neither pacifist nor fascist attempts to restore an apocalyptic conception of time seemed very convincing as the interwar period came to an end. The prophecy of trauma as an instrument of narrative seemed fulfilled when war recommenced in 1939. Events themselves seemed to have proved that experience in the Great War needed little explanation beyond tragedy and victimization.

Conclusion

It remains to situate the témoignage of French soldiers of the Great War into larger issues of testimony, such as the authority of the witness and the claims of experience. Témoignage, I have argued, results from the creation of narrator and narrative through the linguistic construction of experience. Broadly speaking, testimony can be thought of as having two components. The first is the succession of events or "nows" being emplotted in the narrative. Generally speaking, these events are subject to empirical investigation and being proven or disproven. A "river of blood" and a "mountain of corpses" either existed or it did not. Jean Norton Cru saw his task as evaluating testimony according to the empirical, in order to dispel current myths and to assist future historians. In this sense he saw his task as that of Leopold von Ranke and scientific history. The empirical speaks to what Renaud Dulong has called a "judicial model" of eyewitness testimony, subject to objective determinations of truth or falsehood. The second component of testimony is the moral or ethical, the indication of what difference the testimony seeks to make. Proper narrative requires a direction, an explanation of why the testimony was set down in the first place and why the experience narrated therein deserves the engagement of others through reading. Typically, this explanation directs the narrative toward some form of closure. The moral or ethical component need not entail a complex formula or a specific prescription. For example, a testimony can be driven by an idea as broad and straightforward as "War is wrong and corrupts all who touch it."

This book has accepted Paul Ricoeur's contention that experience "as it happens" and narrative are basically incompatible. Because of this incompatibility there exists a tension between the empirical and the moral—or between what Roland Dorgelès called *"my* war" and *"the* war." There are many ways of dealing with this tension. Norton Cru could dispute, in withering detail, the empirical plausibility of many events portrayed in *Les Croix de bois*.[1] But it was quite another matter for him to dispute Dorgelès's grief at the end of the book, to question that author's reflections on the brutality of going on with life through forgetting, or to critique his identification of war as the cause of immeasurable human suffering. Norton Cru pointedly avoided the moral component of Dorgelès's story, the component that mattered most to its author. For Dorgelès, as for Norton Cru, moral imperatives shaped standards of inclusion and exclusion. Dorgelès certainly included his sorrow in *Les Croix de bois*. He also certainly excluded (at least until his 1929 reflections) his eagerness to go to war in 1914.

The moral became predominant in témoignage because experience kept overwhelming the capacity of the narrative tools at hand to contain it in language. Rites of passage posed the problem of the unstable identity of the poilu being reincorporated into the surrounding war culture, itself in constant transformation. The attempt to master experiences such as death, mutilation, and killing produced a mosaic of conclusions that seemed at odds with narrative coherence itself. Consent became a means of conferring ideological meaning upon unmastered experience. Yet as consent deepened and radicalized, total and individual implication in the collective cause seemed to become an end in itself. "Victory" became an open-ended category, called upon to satisfy all claims and to heal all wounds. Consent, the provisional moral of the story of experience, was supposed to be so compelling and all encompassing that it could itself structure the otherwise inchoate fragments of experience.

The interwar novel resolved the tension between the empirical and the moral in favor of the latter. Only with trauma, a conception of permanently broken personal and historical time, did the story of experience in the trenches finally make sense. Disarticulated time made it possible to see the war as a self-evident tragedy and the soldier as a self-evident victim. Tragedy provided both form and content. Hubristic nationalism led populations to war, only to witness their own decimation and mutilation by the manmade horrors of industrial warfare. Trauma explained crisis without resolution as war again loomed in Europe by the late 1930s. Too late, it seemed, the tragic heroes recognized their own implication in the devasta-

---

1. Jean Norton Cru, *Témoins: essai d'analyse et de critique des souvenirs de combattants édités en français de 1915 à 1928* (1929; repr., Nancy: Presses Universitaires de Nancy, 1993), 587–93.

tion of war. Fiction further loosened the grip of the empirically deter-
minable on testimony. The moral of the story became an imperative to testify to trauma as the outcome of the Great War as tragedy. By the time of
Jules Romains and Roger Martin du Gard, the author no longer needed to
be a combatant to testify to this underlying truth.

So self-evident did the truths of tragedy and victimization become that
they have persisted to our own day in fiction about the Great War, in works
such as Bertrand Tavernier's film *La Vie et rien d'autre* (Life and Nothing
But, 1989), Sébastien Japrisot's novel *Un long dimanche de fiançailles* (*A
Very Long Engagement*, 1991, made into a film in 2004), and Jean Rouaud's novel *Les Champs d'honneur* (*Fields of Honor*, 1990). As Daniel
Sherman has noted, the first two works morphed into love stories, with
somewhat contrived endings that posited some kind of reborn hope for the
future: "If love does not conquer all, it empowers the characters and frees
them from obsessions with the past."[2] But even this kind of hope suggested
that trauma and tragedy had to be amputated or abandoned, because
they could not be resolved. *Les Champs d'honneur*, as Sherman argued, offered not hope but rather the consolation of investigating the past as
a therapeutic end in itself. According to my argument, all of these late
twentieth-century works can nevertheless be considered testimonies, even
so long after the fact. In this respect they are not dissimilar to those of Romains and Martin du Gard in the ways they have reinscribed an existing
metanarrative.

This tension in témoignage between the empirical and the moral seems
a modern preoccupation. As Carolyn Walker Bynum has shown, medieval
mystics could testify to the experience of any number of phenomena quite
impossible under natural law because they had a different concept of "what
happened." The "reality" of stories of miraculous lactation and bodily
transformation lay in the intense encounter between the individual mystic
and the sacred.[3] Whether these marvelous events "actually" occurred according to the standards of the empiricism of Ranke, in fact, is not knowable to historians. Whether they did or not "happen" in a modern sense is
in any event somewhat beside the point, if historical realism means trying
to reconstruct the past as contemporaries understood it.

Modern testimony gives rise to controversy in part because of a modern
preoccupation with the empirical, and in part because of what Joan Scott
called the "evidence of experience." In the Great War, the témoin derived

---

2. Daniel J. Sherman, *The Construction of Memory in Interwar France* (Chicago: University of Chicago Press, 1999), 329.

3. See Carolyn Walker Bynum, *Holy Feast and Holy Fast: The Religious Significance of
Food to Medieval Women* (Berkeley: University of California Press, 1987).

his authority from a specific status based in his experience. He had gone through an initiation to combat that his civilian readers and posterity had not; he had survived long enough to put his experience into writing; and he had imposed some kind of meaning on that experience. His authority, that of the narrator as the term has been used throughout this book, shaped readers' understanding of the empirical. We have come to understand the horrors of the trenches of the Great War in a certain way because of the moral authority of those who were there. Subsequent narrations of the Great War as tragedy rested on the borrowed or inherited authority of combatants themselves. Yet this authority would seem to rest on a circular logic. The authority of witnesses derived its legitimacy from forms of experience of which they themselves were the creators and arbiters. This self-contained system for producing meaning illustrated precisely what had led Joan Scott to interrogate the evidence of experience in the first place. And what is a historian to do when témoins who speak with the same authority say utterly contradictory things?

A conundrum seems to exist in the use of modern testimony. This book suggests that there are real limits to which the empirical is knowable. For example, who is to say that the dead did not somehow rise in the "Debout les morts!" story? Natural law tells us that physical bodies do not rise, but the story as told would seem to provide for other kinds of bodies and for much more ancient conceptions of "what happened." Testing the empirical can be easier said than done, as the many inconsistencies and peculiarities in Norton Cru's work certainly indicate. Most historians, in any event, gave up some time ago the notion that unvarnished truth was there for the researching in the documentary text. If it were, there would be little need for historians, only archivists and publishers. In French soldiers' testimonies of the Great War, the line between fiction and nonfiction has remained stubbornly unclear. It has been difficult for historians of the Great War to live with témoignage, but impossible to live without it.

Of course, this conundrum between the empirical and the moral is not unique to testimony from the war of 1914–18. Annette Wieviorka has argued that for more than sixty years the balance between the empirical and the moral in testimony of the Holocaust has been shaped by the changing requirements of history, memory, and politics.[4] In the ghettos and camps themselves, those who could often wrote furiously, from the historian Em-

---

4. Annette Wieviorka, *L'Ère du témoin* (Paris: Plon, 1998). A concise English summary appears as "From Survivor to Witness: Voices of the Shoah," in *War and Remembrance in the Twentieth Century,* ed. Jay Winter and Emmanuel Sivan (Cambridge: Cambridge University Press, 1999), 125–41. Wieviorka's book has been recently translated in its entirety as *The Era of the Witness,* trans. Jared Stark (Ithaca: Cornell University Press, 2006).

manuel Ringelblum to Adam Czerniakow, head of the Judenrat (Jewish Council) of the Warsaw Ghetto. Yet, Wieviorka argued, testimony did not find great resonance in the public sphere until the trial of Adolph Eichmann in Israel in 1961. Unlike the postwar trials at Nuremberg, which had relied primarily on documentary evidence, the prosecutors of Eichmann brought the survivors to center stage. The point was not to gather evidence in itself, for there was more than enough documentation to convict Eichmann. Rather, the prosecutors sought to teach the world a moral lesson from first-hand witnesses about an unprecedented human crime and how to prevent a recurrence of that crime in the future. "With the Eichmann trial we enter a new period," she writes, "one in which the memory of genocide became a fundamental part of Jewish identity, and in which that identity demanded public recognition."[5] One such form of recognition involved supporting the state of Israel. Likewise, as Lisa Yoneyama has argued, the form and content of the testimony of *hibakusha* (atomic bomb survivors) in postwar Japan has been heavily mediated by the requirements of postwar nationalism and international geopolitics.[6] Witnesses had a unique, moral, and political role to play in keeping the past alive in the present.

The Eichmann trial inaugurated what Wieviorka calls "the era of the witness" (*l'ère du témoin*). Testimony became a precious and perishable commodity, to be gathered as fully as possible, and as quickly as audiovisual technology could capture it. Exemplary of this development has been the collection of 3,600 interviews (totaling over ten thousand hours) in the Fortunoff Video Archives for Holocaust Testimonies at Yale University, as well as the work of the Survivors of the Shoah Visual History Foundation established by film director Steven Spielberg. The latter project has as its goal nothing less than interviewing on videotape (and later making available on the Internet) the testimony of every living Holocaust survivor (estimated at around three hundred thousand in 1997).[7] Wieviorka was more than a little skeptical of what she called this "industrial dimension" to the gathering of testimony, though she never condemned it outright. But as was the case with Great War testimony edited and published after the death of the author, the interviewer and the director of the video can become coauthors, steering the witness, as might a lawyer during a trial.[8] Eventually, scholars

5. Wieviorka, "From Survivor to Witness," 133.

6. Lisa Yoneyama, *Hiroshima Traces: Time, Space, and the Dialectics of Memory* (Berkeley: University of California Press, 1999).

7. Wieviorka, *L'Ère du témoin*, 140–50.

8. On audiovisual testimony, see Dominick LaCapra, "Holocaust Testimonies: Attending to the Victim's Voice," in *Writing History, Writing Trauma* (Baltimore: Johns Hopkins University Press, 2001), 86–113.

will pose the same questions of the mass-produced testimony of victims of the Holocaust and *hibakusha* that I posed of Blaise Cendrars at the beginning of this book. Where is the "real" witness in these stories, and which stories convey their "real" experience?

Perhaps the fact that Great War testimony does not have the present-day political resonance of Holocaust testimony or *hibakusha* testimony has made it possible to consider with more dispassion just how *témoignage* should be used by historians. Jay Winter has tried to resolve the conundrum between the empirical and the moral in testimony of the Great War through applying Avishai Margalit's category of the "moral witness." As Margalit defined them, moral witnesses emerge from situations of genocide (such as the Holocaust) or extreme mass persecution (such as the worst years of Stalinism). They are a specific variety of righteous people who have suffered in some direct way from the evil to which they bear witness. To Margalit, the importance of such testimony becomes clear only after the fact. Moral witnesses testify in the hope "that in another place or another time there exists, or will exist, a moral community that will listen to their testimony."[9] Suffering, survival, and a willingness to speak do not in themselves make people eligible for the status of moral witness. They must be able not just to tell the story of their encounter with evil "as it was" but to discern and convey its proper meaning. Their ability to do so invests them with "a special kind of charisma," which "comes from having a special kind of experience which is elevated to some sort of high spirituality that makes the witness a moral force."[10] In short, moral witnesses are narrators in the sense used throughout this book: figures who can tell the story of experience correctly, ascertain its meaning, and convey that meaning to the public sphere. The moral status of the witnesses places their stories, or at least the moral of their stories, in some sense beyond interrogation.

Winter reasserted the primacy of the moral and to some extent subordinated the empirical to it. As he wrote in the introduction to a new translation of Henri Barbusse's *Le Feu:* "The book offered a moral condemnation of war as radical evil, a conclusion which only people who had earned the right to say it—the soldiers—could affirm in wartime."[11] This truth of war as radical evil, Winter argued, had been obscured by "falsifications mobilized in the service of a cause that went beyond the events reported."[12] The

9. Avishai Margalit, *The Ethics of Memory* (Cambridge: Harvard University Press, 2002), 155.

10. Ibid., 178.

11. Jay Winter, "Introduction: Henri Barbusse and the Birth of the Moral Witness," in *Under Fire,* by Henri Barbusse (New York: Penguin Books, 2003), xi.

12. Jay Winter, "Le Témoin moral et les deux guerres mondiales," *Histoire et sociétés: revue européenne d'histoire sociale,* no. 8 (2003): 102.

moral authority of the soldier-witness came from his encounter with the absolute evil of war. His testimony was intrinsically oppositional, in that it set itself against "'counter-truths' and truths taken hostage for a variety of purposes he opposed."[13] Thus Jean Norton Cru, obsessed with the empirically knowable, and Henri Barbusse, who wrote "realist" fiction that Norton Cru castigated as empirically impossible,[14] simply represented two sides of the same coin. To Winter, both were authentic moral witnesses because their morals were in the right place.

There are several specific points on which I might take issue with this reading of Barbusse and Norton Cru. As we have seen, witnesses to the war of the trenches were eager to condemn war in the abstract, but often remarkably protective of the specific war that they made and that had made them. Norton Cru, at least in writing, never rejected or lamented his own participation in the war of 1914–18. *Le Feu* was not about rejecting the Great War but about recasting its ideological foundations and winning it, with full recognition of the cost of doing so. But my main point is that the category of "moral witness" as applied here solves the conundrum between the empirical and the moral in the same way it was solved back in the 1930s. The problem with such a solution is not so much that it is wrong as that it requires us to accept the *conclusion* of the story of experience as the *entire* story. Trauma, tragedy, and victimization were where testimony of the Great War ended, not where it was from the beginning. Witnesses could indeed embrace absolute moral positions—from absolute consent during the war to absolute rejection of it afterward. But these positions proved subject to considerable reconfiguration.

There are, of course, a variety of ways in which historians can make use of testimony. Only a cold or hypocritical sort of Rankean would try to banish morality from historical analysis altogether. Carolyn Bynum sought to evoke a moral admiration at the creativity of women mystics operating in a highly constrained world. Jay Winter, likewise, wanted readers to admire the ability of witnesses such as Barbusse and Norton Cru to conserve a moral compass in extreme circumstances. Christopher Browning laid out two broad ways historians have used Holocaust testimony. One emphasizes the survivors, "how they have remembered and narrated, struggled, and coped with those effects [of what happened to them] rather than the events themselves."[15] The other uses testimony critically but juridically, as imperfect but indispensable evidence to ascertain more empirically "what happened" at sites such as the at the Starachowice slave labor camp, the

---

13. Ibid.
14. Norton Cru, *Témoins*, 555–65.
15. Christopher Browning, *Collected Memories: Holocaust History and Postwar Testimonies* (Madison: University of Wisconsin Press, 2003), 38.

subject of Browning's present research. Such an approach has an ethical component in seeking the empirical truth as an end in itself, in the tradition of Norton Cru.

This book has tried to clarify not so much events and circumstances as how combatants became witnesses and how stories of French soldiers of the Great War came to take on the combinations of form and content that they did. Taken as a whole, these stories do not speak with one moral voice any more than they do with one empirical voice. The challenge has been to think about them coherently as a body of documentation nonetheless. This book has acknowledged its own implication in narrative practice, as it has told its own story of how tragedy and victimization emerged as the predominant means of representing experience in the Great War. It has also set about interrogating the metanarrative that constructed, and was constructed through, the representation of experience. Historians should not, I would argue, seek to replace a metanarrative of tragedy with another metanarrative. I have thought it necessary to begin by recognizing the contrivance, however necessary, of narrative itself. One lesson I take from this book is an old one: the imperative of humility before the evidence, and forbearance whenever we try to understand the past as people of the past did. But no confrontation of the historical evidence, perhaps, should seek to answer more questions than it raises.

Bibliography

Témoignage

Alain. "Mars ou la guerre jugée." *Nouvelle Revue Française* 16 (1921): 527–52.

Barbusse, Henri. *Clarté.* Paris: Flammarion, 1919.

———. *Les Echaînements.* 2 vols. Paris: Flammarion, 1925.

———. *Paroles d'un combattant: articles et discours (1917–1920).* Paris: Flammarion, 1920.

———. *Under Fire.* Translated by Robin Buss. Introduction by Jay Winter. New York: Penguin Books, 2003. Originally published in French as *Le Feu* in 1916. Barrès, Maurice. *Le Suffrage des morts.* Paris: Émile-Paul Frères, 1919.

Barrès, Philippe. *La Guerre à vingt ans.* Paris: Plon, 1924.

Bélinay, Frédéric de. *Sur le sentier de la guerre.* Paris: Gabriel Beauchesne, 1920.

Benjamin, René. *Les Soldats de la guerre: Gaspard.* Paris: Arthème Fayard, 1915.

Bernier, Jean. *La Percée.* Paris: Albin Michel, 1920.

Bessières, Abbé Albert. *Le Chemin des Dames.* Paris: Bloud et Gay, 1919.

Bloch, Marc. *Écrits de guerre, 1914–1918.* Edited by Étienne Bloch. Paris: Armand Colin, 1997.

———. *Memoirs of War, 1914–15.* Edited and translated by Carole Fink. Ithaca: Cornell University Press, 1980.

Bonnet, Georges. *L'Âme du soldat.* Paris: Payot, 1917.

Brunel de Pérard, Jacques. *Carnet de route (4 août–25 septembre 1914).* Paris: Georges Crès, 1915.

Céline, Louis-Ferdinand. *Journey to the End of the Night.* Translated by Ralph Manheim. New York: New Directions, 1983. Originally published as *Voyage au bout de la nuit* in 1932.

Cendrars, Blaise. *The Astonished Man.* Translated by Nina Rootes. London: Peter Owen, 1970. Originally published in French as *L'Homme foudroyé* in 1945.

———. *Oeuvres complètes de Blaise Cendrars.* 6 vols. Paris: Denöel, 1960–61.

———. *J'ai tué.* Paris: Éditions Georges Crès, 1919.

———. *La Main coupée.* 1946. Reprint, Paris: Denöel, 1991.

Chevallier, Gabriel. *La Peur.* Paris: Stock, 1930.

Cross, Tim, ed. *The Lost Voices of World War I*. Translated by Ann Green and Julian Green. Iowa City: University of Iowa Press, 1988.

Derville, Etienne. *Correspondances et notes (août 1914–juin 1918)*. Edited by Abbé Eugène Evrard. Tourcoing: J. Duvivier, 1921.

Dorgelès, Roland. *Les Croix de bois*. Paris: Albin Michel, 1919.

——. *Souvenirs sur les Croix de bois*. Paris: À la Cité des livres, 1929.

Drieu la Rochelle, Pierre. *La Comédie de Charleroi*. Paris: Gallimard, 1934.

——. *Mesure de la France*. Paris: Grasset, 1922.

——. *Gilles*. Paris: Gallimard, 1939.

——. *Gilles*. 1942. Reprint, Paris: Gallimard, 1973.

Dubrulle, Paul. *Mon régiment dans la fournaise de Verdun et dans la bataille de la Somme: impressions de guerre d'un prêtre-soldat*. Paris: Plon, 1917.

Duhamel, Georges. *Les Sept Dernières Plaies*. Paris: Mercure de France, 1928.

Dupont, Marcel. *En campagne (1914–1915): impressions d'un officier de légère*. Paris: Plon, 1916.

Freud, Sigmund. *Civilization, War and Death*. Edited by John Rickman. Translated by E. Colburn Mayne. London: Hogarth, 1939.

Galtier-Boissière, Jean. *En rase campagne, 1914: un hiver à Souchez, 1915–1916*. Paris: Berger-Levrault, 1917.

Genevoix, Maurice. *Ceux de 14*. 1950. Reprint, Paris: Flammarion, 1983.

——. *Jeux de glaces*. Paris: Wesmael-Charlier, 1961.

——. *Sous Verdun*. Paris: Hachette, 1916.

Giono, Jean. *Le Grand Troupeau*. 1931. Reprint, Paris: Gallimard, 2000.

——. "Je ne peux pas oublier." *Europe* 16 (1934): 377–89.

Hallé, Guy. *Là-bas avec ceux qui souffrent*. Paris: Librairie Garnier Frères, 1917.

Henches, Jules Émile. *À l'école de guerre: lettres d'un artilleur*. Paris: Hachette, 1918.

Jolinon. Joseph. "La Mutinerie de Coeuvres." *Mercure de France,* no. 15 (August 1920): 70–96.

——. *La Tête brûlée*. Paris: Redier, 1924.

——. *Le Valet de gloire*. 1923. Reprint, Paris: Redier, 1929.

Klein, Abbé Félix. *La Guerre vu d'une ambulance*. Paris: Armand Colin, 1915. Laby, Lucien. *Les Carnets de l'aspirant Laby, médicin dans les tranchées: 28 juillet 1914–14 juillet 1919*. Edited by Sophie Delaporte. Paris: Bayard, 2001.

La Mazière, Pierre. *L'H.C.F.: l'hôpital chirurgical flottant*. Paris: Albin Michel, 1919.

Léger, Fernand. *Une correspondance de guerre à Louis Poughon, 1914–1918*. Paris: Les Cahiers du Musée National d'Art Moderne, Hors Série/Archives, 1990.

Lemercier, Eugène Emmanuel. *Lettres d'un soldat*. Paris: Librairie Chapelot, 1916.

Libermann, Henri. *Ce qu'a vu un officier de chasseurs à pied*. Paris: Plon, 1916.

Lintier, Paul. *Avec une batterie de 75, Le Tube 1233, souvenirs d'un chef de pièce, 1915–1916*. 1917. Reprint, Paris: L'Oiseau de Minerve, 1998.

——. *Avec une batterie de 75, Ma Pièce: souvenirs d'un cannonnier, 1914*. Paris: Plon-Nourrie, 1916.

Maillet, André. *Sous le fouet du destin: histoire d'une âme aux jours héroïques, 1915–1916*. Paris: Perrin, 1920.

Mairet, Louis. *Carnet d'un combattant (11 février 1915–16 avril 1917)*. Paris: Georges Crès, 1919.

Mallet, Christian. *Étapes et combats: souvenirs d'un cavalier devenu fantassin, 1914–1915*. Paris: Plon, 1916.

Marot, Jean. *Ceux qui vivent . . .* Paris: Payot, 1919.

Martin du Gard, Roger. *Summer 1914.* Translated by Stuart Gilbert. New York: Viking Press, 1941. Originally published as *L'Été 1914* (1936) and *Épilogue* (1940).

Mazenod, Pierre de. *Dans les Champs de Meuse: souvenirs d'un commandant de batterie (1914).* Paris: Plon, 1921.

Meyer, Jacques. *La Biffe.* Paris: Albin Michel, 1928.

Naegelen, René. *Les Suppliciés: histoire vecue.* Paris: Éditions Baudinière, 1929.

Norton Cru, Jean. "Courage and Fear in Battle: According to Tradition and in the Great War." Lecture delivered 14 February 1922 at Williams College in the series of Weekly Public Lectures by the Faculty, Fonds Norton Cru, Bibliothèque universitaire, Aix-en-Provence, Cote Ms. 75.

——. *Du témoignage.* Paris: Gallimard, 1930.

——. *Témoins: essai d'analyse et de critique des souvenirs de combattants édités en français de 1915 à 1928.* 1929. Reprint, Nancy: Presses Universitaires de Nancy, 1993.

O'Brien, Tim. *The Things They Carried.* New York: Broadway Books, 1990.

Pawlowski, Gaston de. *Dans les rides du front.* Paris: La Renaissance du Livre, 1917.

Péricard, Jacques. *Face à face: souvenirs et impressions d'un soldat de la grande guerre.* Paris: Payot, 1917.

Pézard, André. *Nous autres à Vauquois, 1915–1916.* Paris: La Renaissance du Livre, 1918.

Planhol, René de. *Étapes et batailles d'un hussard, août–septembre 1914.* Paris: Attinger Frères, 1915.

Poulaille, Henri. *Pain de soldat, 1917–1917.* 1937. Reprint, Paris: Grasset, 1995.

——. *Les Rescapés.* Paris: Éditions Grasset, 1938.

81ème Poil . . . et Plume (trench newspaper), May 1916.

Rolland, Romain. *Au-dessus de la mêlée.* Paris: Ollendorf, 1915.

Romains, Jules. *Verdun.* Translated by Gerard Hopkins. New York: Alfred A. Knopf, 1939. Originally published as *Prélude à Verdun* and *Verdun* (1938).

Sartre, Jean-Paul. *Les Mots.* 1964. Reprint, Paris: Gallimard, 2004.

Teilhard de Chardin, Pierre. *Écrits du temps de la guerre, 1916–1919.* Paris: Éditions du Seuil, 1965.

Thierry, Albert. *Les Conditions de la paix: méditations d'un combattant.* Paris: Ollendorff, 1918.

Tuffrau, Paul. *1914–1918, quatre années sur le front: carnet d'un combattant.* Paris: Imago, 1998.

Vercel, Roger. *Capitaine Conan.* 1934. Reprint, Paris: Albin Michel 1997.

Vial, Francisque. *Territoriaux de France.* Paris: Berger-Levrault, 1918.

Werth, Léon. *Clavel chez les majors.* Paris: Albin Michel 1919.

——. *Clavel soldat.* 1919. Reprint, Paris: Éditions Viviane Hamy, 1993.

Secondary Sources

Anderson, Benedict. *Imagined Communities: Reflections on the Origin and Spread of Nationalism.* Rev. ed. London: Verso, 1991.

Appleby, Joyce, Margaret Jacobs, and Lynn Hunt. *Telling the Truth about History.* New York: W. W. Norton, 1994.

Audoin-Rouzeau, Stéphane. *À travers leurs journaux: 14–18: les combattants des tranchées.* Paris: Armand Colin, 1986.

Audoin-Rouzeau, Stéphane, and Annette Becker. *14–18: Understanding the Great War.* Translated by Catherine Temerson. New York: Hill and Wang, 2002; originally published in 2000.

Beaupré, Nicolas. *Écrire en guerre, écrire la guerre: France, Allemagne, 1914–1930.* Paris: CNRS Éditions, 2006.

———. "Les Écrivains combatants français et allemands de la grande guerre (1914–1920): essai d'histoire comparée." Doctoral diss., Université de Paris X-Nanterre, 2003.

Becker, Annette. *La Guerre et la foi: de la mort à la mémoire, 1914–1930.* Paris: Armand Colin, 1994.

———. *Oubliés de la grande guerre, humanitaire et culture de guerre: populations occupées, déportés civils, prisonniers de guerre.* Paris: Noêsis, 1998.

Becker, Jean-Jacques. *1914: comment les français sont entrés dans la guerre.* Paris: Presses de la fondation nationale des sciences politiques, 1977.

———, ed. *Histoire culturelle de la grande guerre.* Paris: Armand Colin, 2005.

———. "Les Origines de la première guerre mondiale dans *L'Été 1914* de Roger Martin du Gard." *Relations internationales,* no. 14 (1978): 143–58.

Becker, Jean-Jacques, et al., eds. *Guerre et cultures, 1914–1918.* Paris: Armand Colin, 1994.

Beidelman, T. O. *The Cool Knife: Imagery of Gender, Sexuality, and Moral Education in Kaguru Initiation Ritual.* Washington, D.C.: Smithsonian Institution Press, 1997.

Bernardini, Jean Marc. *Le Darwinisme social en France (1859–1918): fascination et rejet d'une idéologie.* Paris: CNRS Histoire, 1997.

Bochner, Jay. *Blaise Cendrars: Discovery and Re-creation.* Toronto: University of Toronto Press, 1978.

Bonnell, Victoria E., and Lynn Hunt, eds. *Beyond the Cultural Turn.* Berkeley: University of California Press, 1999.

Bourke, Joanna. *An Intimate History of Killing: Face-to-Face Killing in Twentieth-Century Warfare.* New York: Basic Books, 1999.

Boutefeu, Roger. *Les Camarades: soldats français et allemands au combat 1914–1918.* Paris: Fayard, 1966.

Bozon, Michel. *Les Conscrits.* Paris: Berger Levrault, 1981.

Browning, Christopher. *Collected Memories: Holocaust History and Postwar Testimonies.* Madison: University of Wisconsin Press, 2003.

Bynum, Carolyn Walker. *Fragmentation and Redemption: Essays on Gender and the Human Body in Medieval Religion.* New York: Zone Books, 1992.

———. *Holy Feast and Holy Fast: The Religious Significance of Food to Medieval Women.* Berkeley: University of California Press, 1987.

———. *The Resurrection of the Body in Western Christianity 1200–1336.* New York: Columbia University Press, 1995.

Cazals, Rémy, and Frédéric Rousseau. *14–18: le cri d'une generation.* Toulouse: Éditions Privat, 2001.

Cendrars, Miriam. *Blaise Cendrars.* Paris: Éditions Ballard, 1993.

Challener, Richard D. *The French Theory of the Nation in Arms, 1866–1939.* New York: Columbia University Press, 1955.

Chartier, Roger, and Henri-Jean Martin, eds. *Histoire de l'édition française: le livre concurrencé, 1900–1950.* 1986. Reprint, Paris: Fayard, 1991.

Coomaraswamy, Ananda K. *The Dance of Shiva: Fourteen Indian Essays.* New York: Noonday, 1957.

Darrow, Margaret. *French Women and the First World War: War Stories of the Home Front.* Oxford: Berg, 2000.

Delaporte, Sophie. *Les Gueules cassées: les blessés de la face de la grande guerre*. Paris: Noêsis, 1996.

Dulong, Renaud. *Le Témoin oculaire: les conditions sociales de l'attestation personnelle*. Paris: Éditions de l'École des Hautes Etudes en Sciences sociales, 1998.

Ehrenreich, Barbara. *Blood Rites: Origins and History of the Passions of War*. New York: Henry Holt, 1997.

Elshtain, Jean Bethke. *Women and War*. New York: Basic Books, 1987.

Feher, Michael, Ramona Naddaff, and Nadia Tazi, eds. *Fragments for a History of the Human Body*. 3 vols. New York: Zone, 1989.

Ferguson, Niall. *The Pity of War: Explaining World War I*. New York: Basic Books, 1999.

Foucault, Michel. *Discipline and Punish: The Birth of the Prison*. Translated by Alan Sheridan. New York: Vintage Books, 1979. Originally published in French in 1976.

Frye, Northrop. *The Anatomy of Criticism*. 1957. Reprint, Princeton: Princeton University Press, 1990.

Fussell, Paul. *The Great War and Modern Memory*. New York: Oxford University Press, 1975.

Gennep, Arnold van. *The Rites of Passage*. Translated by Monika B. Vizedom and Gabrielle L. Caffee. 1908. Reprint, Chicago: University of Chicago Press, 1960.

Girard, René. *Violence and the Sacred*. Translated by Patrick Gregory. Baltimore: Johns Hopkins University Press, 1977. Originally published in French in 1972.

Grimes, Ronald L. *Deeply into the Bone: Re-inventing Rites of Passage*. Berkeley: University of California Press, 2000.

Holmes, Richard. *Acts of War: The Behavior of Men in Battle*. New York: The Free Press, 1986.

Horne, John, ed. *State, Society, and Mobilization during the First World War*. Cambridge University Press, 1997.

Horne, John, and Alan Kramer. *German Atrocities, 1914: A History of Denial*. London: Yale University Press, 2001.

Huss, Hu Marie-Monique. *Histoires de famille: cartes postales et culture de guerre*. Paris: Noêsis, 2000.

Jay, Martin. *Songs of Experience: Modern American and European Variations on a Universal Theme*. Berkeley: University of California Press, 2005.

Kantorowicz, Ernst. *The King's Two Bodies: A Study in Medieval Political Theology*. Princeton: Princeton University Press, 1957.

Katz, Corrine A. *Affecting Performance: Meaning, Movement, and Experience in Okiek Women's Initiation*. Washington, D.C.: Smithsonian Institution Press, 1994.

Keegan, John. "An Army downs tools, mutiny in the First World War: theory and the poor bloody infantry." *Times Literary Supplement,* 13 May 1994.

Kermode, Frank. *The Sense of an Ending: Studies in the Theory of Fiction*. London: Oxford University Press, 1966.

Klein, Holger, ed. *The First World War in Fiction: A Collection of Critical Essays*. London, Macmillan, 1978.

Kriegel, Annie. "Naissance du mouvement Clarté." *Le Mouvement Social,* 1963, 117–35.

Kselman, Thomas. *Death and the Afterlife in Modern France*. Princeton: Princeton University Press, 1993.

LaCapra, Dominick. *History and Memory after Auschwitz*. Ithaca: Cornell University Press, 1998.

———. *History in Transit: Experience, Identity, Critical Theory*. Ithaca: Cornell University Press, 2004.

———. *Writing History, Writing Trauma.* Baltimore: Johns Hopkins University Press, 2001.

Leed, Eric. *No Man's Land: Combat and Identity in World War I.* Cambridge: Cambridge University Press, 1979.

Lerner, Paul, and Mark Micale, eds. *Traumatic Pasts: History, Psychiatry, and Trauma in the Modern Age, 1870–1930.* Cambridge: Cambridge University Press, 2001.

Leys, Ruth. *Trauma: A Genealogy.* Chicago: University of Chicago Press, 2000.

Magny, Claude-Edmonde. *Histoire du roman français.* Paris: Stock, 1950.

Margalit, Avishai. *The Ethics of Memory.* Cambridge, Mass.: Harvard University Press, 2002.

McKeon, Michael, ed. *Theory of the Novel: A Historical Approach.* Baltimore: Johns Hopkins University Press, 2000.

Mornet, Daniel. *Histoire de la littérature et de la pensée françaises contemporaines: 1870–1927.* Paris: Larousse, 1927.

Mosse, George. *Fallen Soldiers: Reshaping the Memory of the World Wars.* New York: Oxford University Press, 1990.

———. *Nationalism and Sexuality: Middle-Class Morality and Sexual Norms in Modern Europe.* New York: Oxford University Press, 1985.

Offenstadt, Nicolas. *Les Fusillés de la grande guerre et la mémoire collective (1914– 1999).* Paris: Odile Jacob, 1999.

Outram, Dorinda. *The Body and the French Revolution.* New Haven: Yale University Press, 1989.

Page, Melvin E., ed. *Africa and the First World War.* London: Macmillan, 1987.

Prochasson, Christophe, and Anne Rasmussen. *Au nom de la patrie: les intellectuels et la première guerre mondiale.* Paris: Découverte, 1996.

———, eds. *Vrai et Faux dans la Grande Guerre.* Paris: La Decouverte, 2004.

Prost, Antoine. *Les Anciens Combattants et la société française.* 3 vols. Paris: Presses de la Fondation Nationale des Sciences Politiques, 1977.

———. "Les Limites de la brutalization: tuer sur le front occidental, 1914–1918." *Vingtième Siècle: Revue d'histoire* 81 (2004): 5–20.

Prost, Antoine, and Jay Winter. *Penser la Grande Guerre: un essai d'historiographie.* Paris: Seuil, 2005.

Rabinow, Paul, ed. *The Foucault Reader.* New York: Pantheon Books, 1984.

Racine, Nicole. "The Clarté Movement in France, 1919–1921." *Journal of Contemporary History* 2 (1967): 195–208.

Ricoeur, Paul. "La Fonction narrative et l'expérience humaine du temps." *Archivio de filosofia* 80 (1980): 343–66.

———. "Narrative Time." In *The Narrative Reader,* ed. Martin McQuillin, pp. 255–61. London: Routledge, 2000.

Rieuneau, Maurice. *Guerre et révolution dans le roman français: 1919–1939.* Paris: Klinksieck, 1974.

Rémond, René. *La République souveraine: la vie politique en France, 1879–1939.* Paris: Fayard, 2002.

Roberts, Mary Louise. *Civilization without Sexes: Reconstructing Gender in Postwar France, 1917–1927.* Chicago: University of Chicago Press, 1994.

Rolland, Denis. *La Grève des tranchées: les mutineries de 1917.* Paris: Imago, 2005.

Rousseau, Frédéric. *L'Affaire Norton Cru.* Paris: Seuil, 2003.

———. *La Guerre censurée: une histoire des combattants européens de 14–18.* Paris: Seuil, 1999.

Rousseau, Jean-Jacques. *The Social Contract.* Translated by Donald A. Cress. Indianapolis: Hackett, 1983.

Roynette, Odile. *"Bons pour le service": l'expérience de la caserne en France à la fin du XIXe siècle.* Paris: Belin, 2000.

Scarry, Elaine. *The Body in Pain: The Making and Unmaking of the World.* New York: Oxford University Press, 1985.

Scott, Joan W. "The Evidence of Experience." *Critical Inquiry* 17 (1991): 773–97.

———. *Only Paradoxes to Offer: French Feminists and the Rights of Man.* Cambridge, Mass.: Harvard University Press, 1996.

Shalk, David. *Roger Martin du Gard: The Novelist and History.* Ithaca: Cornell University Press, 1967.

Sherman, Daniel J. *The Construction of Memory in Interwar France.* Chicago: University of Chicago Press, 1999.

Shevin-Coetzee, Marilyn, and Frans Coetzee, eds. *Authority, Identity, and the Social History of the Great War.* Oxford: Berghan Publishers, 1995.

Smith, Leonard V. *Between Mutiny and Obedience: The Case of the French Fifth Infantry Division during World War I.* Princeton: Princeton University Press, 1994.

———. "Le Corps et la survie d'une identité dans les écrits de guerre français," *Annales: HSS* 55 (2000): 111–33.

———. "The Disciplinary Dilemma of French Military Justice: September 1914–April 1917: The Case of the 5e Division d'Infanterie." *Journal of Military History* 55 (January 1991): 47–68.

———. "Jean Norton Cru, lecteur des livres de guerre." *Annales du Midi,* no. 232 (2000): 517–28.

———. "Paul Fussell's *The Great War and Modern Memory:* Twenty-five Years Later." *History and Theory* 40 (2001): 241–60.

Smith, Leonard V., Stéphane Audoin-Rouzeau, and Annette Becker. *France and the Great War: 1914–1918.* Cambridge: Cambridge University Press, 2003.

Strachan, Hew. *The First World War.* New York: Viking, 2004.

———. "Training, Morale, and Modern War." *Journal of Contemporary History* 41 (2006): 211–27.

Thibaudet, Albert. *Histoire de la littérature française de 1789 à nos jours.* Paris: Stock, 1936.

Trevisan, Carine. *Les Fables du deuil: la Grande Guerre, mort et écriture.* Paris: Presses Universitaires de France, 2001.

Turner, Victor. *The Forest of Symbols: Aspects of Ndembu Ritual.* Ithaca: Cornell University Press, 1967.

Verhey, Jeffrey. *The Spirit of 1914: Militarism, Myth and Mobilization in Germany.* Cambridge: Cambridge University Press, 2000.

Watson, Janet. *Fighting Different Wars: Experience, Memory, and the First World War in Britain.* Cambridge: Cambridge University Press, 2004.

White, Hayden. *The Content of the Form: Narrative Discourse and Historical Representation.* Baltimore: Johns Hopkins University Press, 1987.

Wieviorka, Annette. *The Era of the Witness.* Translated by Jared Stark. Ithaca: Cornell University Press, 2006. Originally published as *L'Ère du témoin* in 1998.

Winter, Jay. *Sites of Memory, Sites of Mourning: The Great War in European Cultural History.* Cambridge: Cambridge University Press, 1996.

———. "Le Témoin moral et les deux guerres mondiales." *Histoire et sociétés: revue européenne d'histoire sociale,* no. 8 (2003): 99–115.

Winter, Jay, Geoffrey Parker, and Mary Habeck, eds. *The Great War and the Twentieth Century.* New Haven: Yale University Press, 2000.

Winter, Jay, and Emmanuel Sivan, eds. *War and Remembrance in the Twentieth Century.* Cambridge: Cambridge University Press, 1999.

Wojciehowski, Delora A. *Old Masters, New Subjects: Early Modern and Poststructuralist Theories of Will.* Stanford: Stanford University Press, 1995.

Yoneyama, Lisa. *Hiroshima Traces: Time, Space, and the Dialectics of Memory.* Berkeley: University of California Press, 1999.

Index

medical services, 37, 41–42, 57, 83–87
memory, 13, 16–17, 45–46, 67, 73, 97,
148–49, 153–54, 185–86, 201–2. *See
also* time
metanarrative, 8–10, 19, 44–45, 185, 194,
202
Meyer, Jacques, 102–4
moral (of a story), 6, 13–14, 19, 33, 37, 43,
46–47, 55, 79–80, 87, 90, 110, 138,
166, 195
moral witness. *See* Margilit, Avishai; Winter, Jay
Mornet, Daniel, 163–64
Mosse, George, 82
mutinies of 1917, 11, 161–62, 172

Naegelen, René, 77–78, 158–59, 162
nation, nationalism, 10, 29–30, 68–69,
118, 124–25, 129–30, 135, 142–46,
154, 156, 178, 183, 189, 196
No Man's Land, 4, 44
Norton Cru, Jean, ix–x, 8, 13–14, 18, 35,
80–81, 91, 93, 142, 195–96, 198, 201–2

O'Brien, Tim, 3, 14
Offenstadt, Nicolas, 159, 162
Owen, Wilfred, 87

Pacifism, 141, 159, 176–77, 189–90
patrie. See nation
Pawlowski, Gaston de, 126–27
Pechmalbec, Daniel, 93–95, 98, 104
Péguy, Charles, 50–51, 140, 142, 146, 163
Péricard, Jacques, 72–75
perpetrators, 2, 90–91, 124
Pézard, André, 78, 115–19, 121, 138
pity, 84–87, 159–60, 169, 179
Planhol, René de, 47
plot, 17–18. *See also* time
Poulaille, Henry, 170–73, 184–85
propaganda. *See Bourrage de crâne*
Prost, Antoine, 93
publication of *témoignages*, 33–34, 43, 56,
85, 109n11, 122, 127, 149, 164
public sphere, 1, 18, 54, 72, 88
putrefaction, 71, 75–76, 78, 86, 105, 122,
175–76

Radiguet, Raymond, 163
Ranke, Leopold von, 195, 197, 201

rationality, 11, 113–14, 137, 142
relativism, x, 14
Remarque, Erich Marie, 9–10, 108, 149, 164
Rémond, René, 156
Renaissance individualism, 60–61. *See also*
individuality
republican ideology, 19, 23, 67–68, 94,
108–11, 180, 187–88
resurrection, 63, 65
Ricoeur, Paul, 17, 195
Rieuneau, Maurice, 18
Rivière, Jacques, 63
Robert, Marthe, 150
Rolland, Romain, 190
Romains, Jules, 185–88, 197
Rouaud, Jean, 197
Rousseau, Frédéric, 107
Rousseau, Jean-Jacques, 23, 110, 187. *See
also* republican ideology

Sartre, Jean-Paul, 14–16
Scarry, Elaine, 111
Scott, Joan, 12, 197–98
Seigel, Jerrold, 7
sex, 9, 52–53, 81–82, 84, 120–21, 179–
80, 184
shell shock, 75, 88, 165
Sherman, Daniel, 197
socialism, 28–29, 53, 69–72, 145, 151,
156, 159, 161–63, 170–77, 184–85,
189–90
Somme, Battle of the (1916), 62, 65, 79,
100–102, 134–36
Stendhal, paradox attributed to, 35–36, 39

Tavernier, Bertrand, 167, 197
Teilhard du Chardin, Pierre, 64
Thibaudet, Albert, 163
Thierry, Albert, 142–46
Third Republic, 66–67, 108–9, 111, 121,
124–25, 141, 165, 176–77, 180–81,
183, 185, 187–88. *See also* republican
ideology
time, 13, 17–18, 20, 32–34, 47, 54, 81, 85,
99, 136, 148, 150–51, 154–55, 157,
164–66, 170, 173–74, 177, 181–82,
186–87, 189, 192–94, 196
tragedy, 1, 8, 18–19, 44–45, 185–86, 191,
196, 201–2. *See also* metanarrative; victim
trauma, 12, 19, 44, 164–65, 174, 176, 181,
184, 194, 196, 201

CPSIA information can be obtained
at www.ICGtesting.com
Printed in the USA
LVHW011555311221
707636LV00007B/275